WHO BOMBED THE HILTON?

RACHEL LANDERS is a filmmaker with a PhD in history.

Rachel Landers' *Who Bombed the Hilton* is a terrifying tale written with sparkling good humour and panache. Landers takes the 'tatty, fractured saga' of a horrific terrorist attack in the heart of Sydney, and, backed by remarkable research, she brings it to life. She makes of it a testament to the victims and the investigators, as well as a warning to us in our own age of terror. As we struggle with terrorism, and with the danger of damaging our democracy by our measures to counter it, we do well to remember this story of 'the one who got away'.
— *Anna Funder, author of* Stasiland *and* All That I Am

WHO BOMBED THE HILTON?

RACHEL LANDERS

NEWSOUTH

A NewSouth book

Published by
NewSouth Publishing
University of New South Wales Press Ltd
University of New South Wales
Sydney NSW 2052
AUSTRALIA
newsouthpublishing.com

© Rachel Landers 2016
First published 2016

10 9 8 7 6 5 4 3 2 1

This book is copyright. Apart from any fair dealing for the purpose of private study, research, criticism or review, as permitted under the *Copyright Act*, no part of this book may be reproduced by any process without written permission. Inquiries should be addressed to the publisher.

National Library of Australia
Cataloguing-in-Publication entry

Author: Landers, Rachel, author.
Title: Who bombed the Hilton? / Rachel Landers.
ISBN: 9781742233512 (paperback)
 9781742241470 (ebook)
 9781742246413 (ePDF)
Subjects: Ananda Marga (Organisation) – History.
 Australian Security Intelligence Organisation – History.
 Trials (Conspiracy) – New South Wales.
 Judicial error – New South Wales.
 Terrorism investigation – Australia.
 Australia – Politics and government – 1976–1990.
Dewey Number: 345.94407

Design Josephine Pajor-Markus
Cover design Blue Cork
Cover image The Sydney Hilton on 13 February 1978. *The Sydney Morning Herald*/Fairfax Syndication.

All reasonable efforts were taken to obtain permission to use copyright material reproduced in this book, but in some cases copyright could not be traced. The author welcomes information in this regard.

Contents

The Hilton and me *1*

The story we tell *9*

The bomb and the bin *19*

Sunday 12 February 1978 *29*

Monday 13 February 1978 *40*

Tuesday 14 February 1978 *50*

Wednesday 15 February 1978 *56*

Enter the Ananda Marga *63*

An Australian campaign of terror *71*

Abhiik Kumar *78*

It all goes quiet *97*

'The blast that shook Australia' *110*

Thursday 16 February 1978 *117*

Did the Hare Krishnas do it? *123*

The Bangkok Three *130*

From Scotland Yard to Newtown *145*

February to March 1978 *151*

Another bomb *169*

Shadowlands *178*

28 March 1978 *181*

A new wave of terror *190*

'A full-scale terrorist war' *209*

June 1978 *222*

The madness of the day *230*

Yagoona *243*

'Have you ever seen what this stuff can do?' *258*

July 1978 *268*

A hardline policy *283*

The immolation of Lynette Phillips *288*

'Campaigns of violence and intimidation' *297*

A new phenomenon *307*

1979 *316*

The locker and the gelignite *327*

The inquest, 1982 *335*

May 1983   *343*

1989 and after   *355*

Epilogue: 'My heart has been broken'   *367*

Note on sources   *373*

Notes   *375*

Acknowledgments   *401*

For D and D

I arrived outside the Hilton only about two minutes after the explosion. Already the air was thick with the noise of sirens and cries from the injured and the peculiar, pungent odour of human blood.

About 15 metres from the rear of the mangled garbage truck where the bomb had exploded I saw what appeared to be the torso of a man covered in a few bloody rags.

Another man was getting up from beside a taxi clutching his face, which had been cut by flying glass from one of the many wrecked shop windows. A young girl was lying behind a car sobbing as the first ambulance screamed to a halt.

Some of the younger State policemen appeared dazed by the shattering event. A more senior Commonwealth officer took control and started moving some youths who had rushed to the scene back down George Street towards the Town Hall.

Ambulancemen and police threw black plastic covers over the human debris.

A team of paramedics began working frantically on one of the police officers who had been caught in the blast. It was hard to recognise him as a policeman. The only distinguishing form was the blue 'NSW Police' insignia on his shoulder. Ambulancemen worked feverishly patching a wound at his side and setting up a saline drip.

> It was now about 15 minutes since the bomb went off. The area was teeming with uniformed and Special Branch officers, firemen and ambulancemen. A crowd of onlookers was growing rapidly about 100 metres away near the Town Hall. Police also began to move away the handful of journalists who had arrived at the scene.
>
> The first ambulances left for the hospital and the search for clues to the blast was underway.

Peter Logue, AAP, 'Witness Reminded of Northern Ireland', *Sydney Morning Herald*, 14 February 1978.

The Hilton and me

I'm sitting in the Tea Room in Sydney's Queen Victoria Building across from a man whose name I can't tell you. Let's call him Fred. Fred's a dapper, grey-haired former senior detective in his late sixties who was lionised for his skill in running a series of spectacular covert operations in the 1990s. It has been said that he could wire up an operative and send him into the fray — a drug operation, a dirty cop shop — and they could strip the agent naked if need be and never locate the recording device. Fred is also known for his excessive operational caution. Contact between us was made by a third party and only then were my details forwarded to him. He has asked the waiter to move us to an isolated table and only accepts the third one offered — near an exit, good visibility, away from other diners.

He sits eating his grilled fish with his back to the wall. If I wish to continue contact with him I am to buy him a SIM card and forward it through the third party. While he is, shall we say, assisting me with my inquiries, all this would be a lot more gripping if I was confident he actually had inside information about the bombing of the Hilton Hotel in Sydney at 12.40 am on 13 February 1978 that left three dead and nine wounded. Often described as the first (and, for almost four decades, the only) act of terrorist murder on Australian soil, it is a crime which — despite decades of convoluted trials, inquiries, counter inquiries, commissions, parliamentary declarations and more plot twists than an airport potboiler — remains unsolved.

As Fred and I nibble away at the set lunch menu, he is questioning (head swivelling to check for other diners' straining ears) why aspects of the security surrounding the inaugural Commonwealth Heads of Government Regional Meeting were so lax. Why were snipers positioned on top of the QVB (he gestures furtively to the right of where we are sitting), yet none of the police stationed across the road, outside the Hilton, were ordered to check garbage bins? The Hilton conspiracy theorists have long pointed to this aberration in what was purportedly standard police protocol as proof positive of the involvement of Australia's secret service (ASIO) and/or Australian military intelligence and/or New South Wales Special Branch in planting the bomb in the bin themselves. A theory, I find after some robust research, as fanciful and delicate as a Fabergé egg. Is Fred telling me because he believes it has substance? Or is he testing my agenda? Finding out where my allegiances lie? Does he know something? Or is he just another person tugging at the edges of this tatty, fractured saga? Sad to say, despite my heightened expectations, the latter turns out to be true.

Why is this one crime so absolutely maddening? Australians by nature are not known for their excessive discretion, yet Fred is simply one in a long line of people circling the investigation who are wedded to communicating in opaque coded sentences. Half a dozen leading investigative journalists have sworn only to speak to me off the record, then proceeded to point me towards the same prime suspect — a man who was never questioned by the police. Then they warn me to go no further and recount horror tales of being targeted and harassed. Federal government ministers deny that they authored top secret reports now made public in the National Library under the 30-year rule, despite these reports bearing their names. Malcolm Fraser, the prime minister at the time, told me a few years back that it was a stupid topic to research and instead of wasting my time trying to winnow out the truth of the bombing I should be focusing on the contemporary plight of refugees. Even those individuals suspected of the crime, then allegedly verballed, charged, accused of another crime altogether, jailed then freed, seem committed to joining the chorus of obfuscators. I approach one who says he doesn't want to talk but sends me his own highly ambiguous autobiography. I contact another who is equally wary but then enthuses about how eager he is to see the finished film.

This is what I am supposed to be doing — researching a treatment for a documentary film. A film in which the story is fast metastasising beyond the tidy narrative trajectories beloved by commissioners at our two public broadcasters. I know — I've made a dozen tidy tales for them over the last 10 years. The kind of history documentaries currently in vogue omit the murky and the puzzling or indeed multiple and possibly contradictory versions of what was. One of these commissioners keeps telling me what he wants is a hero's journey! As if he's hoping that some manly, handsome secret policeman now in his dotage (perhaps like my lunch partner, Fred) will step forth from the shadows and simplify the whole thing for us and iron out the wrinkles. But this is what history is — it's a mess. Bits of one event flop into others, things don't end properly. Witnesses misremember, they evade. They say the car was red when it was blue, the man was dead, the man limped away, the man was a woman.

I retreat into the archives. The truth of this story

lies not with the living but with the dead. In bits of papers such as this:

> Medical Report upon the examination of the dead body of: Name: UKNOWN MALE believed to be William Favell 36 ...
>
> The body was in bits and pieces brought in plastic bags ...There was singed hair at certain areas showing it was the head and brief[s] noted that it was a groin. The parts were badly shattered with hardly any bone left intact. Embedded in the body were large amounts of foreign matter such as cigarette butts, labels etc. There was also shrapnel, glass splinters and paint. Cause of Death: Multiple Injuries. Antecedent Causes: EXPLOSION.[1]

Favell, a garbage collector, was collected from the asphalt on George Street in plastic bags. He had a seven-year-old daughter.

When I first enter the New South Wales State Records building, it's strangely intoxicating to come across stark reminders of what actually occurred. The Hilton bombing records are unique in Australia. In 1995, in order to placate various politicians on the left and the right who were making fervent calls[2] for a joint state–federal inquiry into the Hilton bombing along with the conspiracy claims (fuelled in part by a 1995 ABC documentary called *Conspiracy*, which you can catch on YouTube), New South Wales Premier Bob Carr and Prime Minister Paul Keating agreed to open the files relating to the Hilton bombing to the public. They have sat in the New South Wales State Records ever since.

Housed in a paddock on the fringe of the city, the archives building looks like a set from a sci-fi movie. It's hard to get a sense of the physical dimensions of the holdings as only one folder is released at a time, and the catalogue descriptions give a poor indication of what is going to emerge from the Tardis-like vault behind the reception counter. A request for a promising item may only result in a slim manila folder containing time sheets. Another innocuous-sounding listing emerges as a large box stuffed full of revelations. By my estimate the Hilton archive is larger than a walk-in wardrobe and smaller than a two-bedroom house.

This book is the story of my journey through that archive, supplemented by research in many other primary archival sources in Australia and overseas, to find answers.

What I found surprised me.

I was a schoolgirl in Sydney when the bomb went off and I remember exactly where I was when I learnt what had happened. Our teacher, Mrs K, an overly dramatic, skinny woman with a penchant for stiletto heels, recounted the ghastly news and made us bow our heads in a minute's silence. Things seemed very serious and a girl in my class burst into noisy tears, sputtering that her uncle had known one of the deceased. Despite the clarity of that memory, I, like most people who remember the actual bombing, couldn't really explain what had happened in the years that followed or, indeed, who did or didn't do it. It strikes me as odd that such a key moment in Australia's history is so unexplored. If you're too young to have any recollection of the bombing it must be intriguing why such a colossal crime remains unsolved and so saturated in conspiracy theories.

After trekking through the evidence available, it is clear that most of the answers lie in the first 12 months after the bombing. After that, the narrative becomes hijacked by a miscarriage of justice story — a story taken up by activists and an emerging new generation of journalists and papers like *Nation Review* and the *National Times*. This is the story people remember, but it tends to obscure the truth. It's a story that was very much of its time — a sort of impassioned tale of the late 1970s, following in the wake of the anti-Vietnam War sentiment early in the decade and the rage around the dismissal of the Whitlam Government in 1975. It's a story that lives in the public domain as the goodies — counter-culturists, the free press, anti-authoritarian citizens — versus the baddies — the police, the secret services, politicians, institutions. It's also a narrative arc that Australians adore, that of the underdog fighting for truth and justice and triumphing. The thing is, this story tells you nothing about who might have planted a bomb outside the Hilton Hotel that February night.

The story
we tell

The public story goes like this:

13 February 1978. There is a gathering of regional Commonwealth heads of state (CHOGRM) at the Hilton Hotel. This includes leaders from Tonga, Nauru, Singapore and India. Early in the morning, before the summit opens, a bomb goes off when a bin outside the George Street entrance is emptied into a garbage truck. Two garbagemen, Alec Carter and William Favell, are killed, and a policeman, Paul Burmistriw, is badly injured. He will die nine days later. Inside there is pandemonium. Prime Minister Fraser calls out the Army to protect the foreign leaders.

By morning a task force of over 100 is assembled to catch the bomber. In this team are 58 detectives, 15 of whom are experienced homicide investigators.[1]

The Premier and the Prime Minister offer a reward of $100 000. Suspects start to be brought in for questioning, including the feminists and anarchists who had been protesting during the arrival of various leaders the day before. Members of the religious sect the Ananda Marga are also questioned — they are alleged to have been behind attacks on Indian nationals in Australia over the previous six months in protest at India's imprisonment of their leader, Baba. It is thought that India's Prime Minister Desai, who was staying at the Hilton, could have been a target. The Ananda Marga public relations secretary, Tim Anderson, immediately refutes these suspicions in a press conference, stating that the sect is shocked by the bombing and extending the sect members' sympathy to the families of the dead and injured.

The Australian wing of the Indian-based Ananda Marga is made up of a few hundred followers. They practise yoga, meditation, run their own schools and soup kitchens and raise money for disaster relief.

Within days the investigation appears to have ground to a halt. There are repeated newspaper articles reporting a lack of leads, dead ends and appeals for information from the public. Simultaneously, various individuals make claims about it being an elaborate plot hatched by ASIO, military intelligence and New South Wales Police Special Branch (the police charged with looking after VIPs) in order to scuttle any ongoing investigations critical to their practices and justify their respective futures.

Months crawl by — the papers keep up their rat-tat-tat of gloom — no new leads and no evidence.

15 June 1978. Three young members of the Ananda Marga sect are arrested: Tim Anderson, 26; Ross Dunn, 24; and Paul Alister, 22. The police say they have caught Dunn and Alister with explosives in a car at Yagoona in south-western Sydney as they were attempting to blow up Robert Cameron, the leader of the Nazi National Alliance. According to the police, Anderson was caught with incriminating evidence at the sect's headquarters in Newtown. All three confess that night to conspiracy to murder Cameron. One of the arresting officers is Roger Rogerson.

July 1978. A few weeks after the arrests it transpires that a man named Richard Seary was with Dunn and Alister the night they were arrested. Seary had been posing as a sect member but was in fact working as an informant for New South Wales Special Branch and had tipped off the cops about the Cameron conspiracy. Seary then thickens the plot by adding (two weeks after the event) that, en route to Yagoona, Dunn and Alister admitted they had committed the Hilton bombing.

Anderson, Dunn and Alister say that the police have planted the evidence — explosives and incriminating letters — and have physically assaulted them

The story we tell

and fabricated the confessions. They say Richard Seary is a liar and a fantasist.

February 1979. Anderson, Alister and Dunn (who will become known as the Yagoona Three) stand trial for conspiracy to murder Cameron. The Hilton bombing accusations are not pursued for insufficient evidence. The jury cannot agree on a verdict and a new trial is ordered.

August 1979. A second jury finds the three young men guilty of a conspiracy to blow up Robert Cameron and they are sentenced to 16 years' imprisonment.

Throughout the trials there is growing public support for the Yagoona Three. Their conviction is increasingly reported as a flagrant miscarriage of justice, as a standout example of police corruption involving police 'verballing' suspects, i.e. writing their confessions for them. There is also growing suspicion about the credibility of Richard Seary and his role as a police informant. A vigorous movement to free Anderson, Alister and Dunn is mounted.

September–October 1982. Everything comes to a head at the coronial inquest into the Hilton bombing. It's a kind of zoo of competing interests. The Yagoona Three use it to discredit Richard Seary and thus highlight the illegitimacy of their convictions. A policeman injured at the Hilton, Terry Griffiths, embroiled in a highly litigious compensation battle with the state government, uses it to promote evidence that points to the culpability of ASIO and Special Branch. Richard Seary uses it to reiterate his 1978 claims about Alister and Dunn confessing to the bombing.

The inquest is halted and a prima facie case is put forward for Dunn and Alister to stand trial for triple murder. Again, the most sensational case of terrorist triple murder in Australia is not pursued for lack of evidence. The three young men remain in jail for the Cameron murder conspiracy.

By the early 1980s, the movement promoting the Yagoona Three case as a miscarriage of justice grows exponentially. Evidence emerges suggesting that both Richard Seary and the police were far from reliable and eventually, in response to public and press agitation, the state government agrees to hold an inquiry into the matter. On 20 June 1984, pursuant to the provisions of Section 475 of the *Crimes Act 1900* (NSW), an investigation is launched into the convictions of Anderson, Alister and Dunn for conspiracy to murder Robert Cameron.

1984–1985. The 475 inquiry. This inquiry, headed by Justice James Wood, is exhaustive and detailed. Seary's role is found to be seriously flawed and there are problems in the police chain of evidence that would indicate reasonable doubt.

1985. The three men are released, pardoned, and compensated for their seven years in jail.

1989. A convicted armed robber (and prison

escapee), Raymond Denning, attempts to reduce his sentence by telling police that Tim Anderson, a former cell-mate and former friend, had confessed to being the Hilton bomber. Despite the accusation seeming so self-serving on Denning's part, Anderson is arrested. However, with such flimsy evidence, it seems unlikely that the charges will stick.

Then, out of the blue, a former Margii, Evan Pederick, having heard about Anderson's arrest, walks into a local Queensland police station and confesses to being the Hilton bomber. He adds that he had placed the bomb in the bin at the behest of Tim Anderson.

Pederick is tried for murder (he only pleads guilty to the lesser charge of conspiracy to murder) but the jury finds him guilty of murder nonetheless and he is sentenced to concurrent sentences of 20 years for each murder and 18 for conspiracy.[2] He's given a non-parole period of 13 and a half years.[3]

October 1990. Anderson is put on trial and, despite dozens of serious problems in the prosecution case, he is convicted.

He then appeals his case and wins. Anderson is released. Pederick then appeals his own conviction, on the basis that if Anderson has successfully appealed his case by totally discrediting Pederick's original confession, then his own conviction must be unsound. He fails in this appeal but nonetheless has his sentence truncated and is released after eight years.

While this effectively leaves the crime unsolved, this narrative line does seem to indicate an overzealous police investigation — one that refused to let lack of evidence get in the way of a good suspect. Dodgy cops, dodgy informants, innocent young men denied justice. The Yagoona Three become our Guildford Four.

There is no question that police around the world did and do fabricate evidence and confessions which lead to the imprisonment of the innocent. While the various Alister, Anderson and Dunn trials are proceeding, Lindy Chamberlain is facing her own multiple trials brought by prosecutors convinced she is guilty of murdering her two-month-old daughter, Azaria. A large part of Australian society at this time has concerns about corruption within the state and federal police forces. The conduct of the prosecutions against Anderson, Alister and Dunn seems to prove that their suspicions are well-founded.

Somehow all these events — from the arrests in Yagoona the night of 15 June 1978 all the way through to the 1989–90 Anderson murder trial and appeal, and including the opening of the Hilton case files to the public in 1995 — act like squid ink. They obscure and distract. Things are not what they seem.

One of the complexities of negotiating the Hilton archive is that much of it has been ordered to fit the events above, and original documents do not appear in the order in which they occurred or were collected.

For example, many of the original witness statements taken in the first few days after the bombing appear in the file box item 9/8112.1 (formerly HB67.1) and are collated specifically for the prosecution case for triple murder against Anderson in 1989–90 and thus are selected for how they support Pederick's 1989 confession, and not how the files appeared in the original 1978 police investigation. This happens time and time again where fundamental groundwork in the case is stretched and scattered, re-ordered over the long years to serve the agendas of the various trials for both the defence and the prosecution.

This is not a case one can work backward through time. You have to start again. You have to forget things you think you know. Indeed I begin to suspect that some of the spectacular cock-ups on the part of the police and prosecution teams in Pederick and Anderson's trials a decade after the bombing are explicitly caused by the fact they didn't do this.

One of the most obvious examples is to do with Evan Pederick's original 1989 confession about attempting to blow up Prime Minister Desai as he arrives at the George Street entrance to the Hilton. Pederick gives a very detailed description of the Indian leader greeting Fraser around 2 or 3 pm on Sunday 12 February as he steps onto the red carpet while Pederick fiddles desperately with his malfunctioning remote control that would (if it was working) have blown up 200 or 300 people. A lengthy investigation and two murder trials (Pederick's and Anderson's) are set in motion on the basis that this is fact. However, even the most perfunctory glance at the original police statements and briefings on the day (or indeed the daily newspaper reports) reveal that this is simply untrue. Desai arrived at the *Pitt Street* entrance at 4.20 pm.

As soon as this is discovered the police decide that Pederick simply mistook the nut-brown dhoti-wearing Sri Lankan president, Junius Jayewardene, for the similarly coloured and clothed Desai. They run with this until someone checks the arrival times of the esteemed guests and discovers that actually Jayewardene arrived early Sunday morning, so it can't be him Pederick saw, and they have to shift the facts again. They decide Pederick must have tried to blow up Desai and Fraser and the whole shebang as they were *leaving* the hotel on George Street at 5.20 pm. The problem here is that by that time, according to Pederick's confession, he had already fled the scene and was well on his way to Brisbane. These sorts of mistakes in the prosecution case are but a few examples of many. Mistakes that lead to Anderson's release. The thing is, in neither of these two trials was there even a cursory glance at the evidentiary material discovered back in 1978. Rather than return to the original statements, these later investigating teams relied on the police statements that had been collated for the 1982 inquest — basically material that was relevant to the assumptions about the crime at the time — and everything else was left out.

So I begin to unpick the embroidery. A few things the police of the late 1970s can be relied upon to do is to have dodgy spelling and to poorly black out headings on secret documents. The coarse grain of police issue stationery versus the deep imprint of type from heavy police fingers thudding down on typewriter keys means that holding up the paper against the fluorescent lights in the archives makes it clear whether the document came from ASIO or Interpol or the CIA.

I unpick and put in chronological order thousands of pieces of paper — lay out the facts as they arrived the first time, unadorned, uninterpreted, flying in from dozens of sources and every corner of the world.

What really went on? Were the police corrupt? Why did they target the Ananda Marga? Did the conspiracy theorists believe what they wanted to believe? Who *did* bomb the Hilton?

The bomb and the bin

I obsess about where to start — two days before the blast? Ten minutes? Six months? Four years? Who? What? When? Where? I need to lash myself to someone. I need a name. I need that manly hero the helpful TV commissioning editor suggested.

Norm Sheather.

Of all the myriad personalities I have encountered in the Byzantine Hilton bombing archive, it is Detective Inspector Norman Sheather of whom I have grown most fond. He arrives pristine in the archives on 13 February 1978, six hours after the bombing — competent, controlled, steady-eyed, a man without agenda or prejudice. It is so easy to think of Australian police from this era as being thick, thuggish and corrupt that it is inspiring to encounter someone who is so transparently good at his job. Norm is still alive — perhaps retired in some hamlet growing roses or ensconced in an inner-city high-rise taking philosophy classes and learning Mandarin — but he too has resisted my entreaties. Never mind. Norm breathes in every line of Item 9/8112.1 and its companion 9/8112.2 containing the original witness statements, the analysis of the bombing, and the ASIO appraisals. He speaks from the volumes that contain his detectives' running sheets, which lay out his incisive investigative path as he starts to steer the newly minted Hilton task force into the open sea.

Somewhere just before dawn on Monday 13 February 1978, as the light begins to penetrate George Street to reveal its attendant horrors, Norm Sheather gets a call. He is told about the bombing at the Hilton. There are two dead garbagemen, a number of injured, some badly, particularly a young policeman. There is grave concern for the safety of the assembly of international prime ministers and presidents staying at the hotel. Over 500 soldiers are about to be deployed to protect them. Sheather is to head the Hilton bombing investigation with a team of over 100 personnel.[1] This number includes 58 detectives — 15 of whom are experienced homicide investigators. This is the largest police task force assembled in Australia.[2]

Fifty-eight detectives, only primitive computers. Suspected terrorist murder. The first in Australia. No clear target. A warning call. Imagine Sheather, conscious of the enormity of all this. Where do you start?

Prime Minister Fraser's dream of Australia hosting a secure international political event is poleaxed. The New South Wales Premier Neville Wran summed it up when he said 'for the first time in our history terrorism against innocent and uninvolved people, has become a fact in our country'.[3] Compared to our twenty-first-century age of routine surveillance, CCTV and counter-terrorism laws, those in charge of security at CHOGRM look hopelessly naïve. Shouldering the blame and fielding accusations of incompetence is Superintendent Reginald Douglas, Deputy Chief Superintendent of the Metropolitan Area, the man responsible for VIPs in all parts of New South Wales (except for VIP living quarters, which are the provenance of the Commonwealth Police). It was Reg and Reg alone who decided that it was not necessary to search the garbage bins surrounding the hotel. Within hours DCS Douglas is facing hostile questioning from the press.

'Why had the bins not been searched?'

'I did not think it was necessary.'

'Do you accept responsibility for what happened?'

'I am in charge of the operation and I must take responsibility.'[4]

Sheather needs to be all-seeing and all-knowing. He must simultaneously look backward to recreate every moment leading up to the bomb blast, and forward to chart a focussed way to gather and decipher evidence. Too broad a focus will drown the investigation in detail, as happened during the vast Yorkshire Ripper investigation running at the same time in the UK.[5] Too narrow a target, and the temptation will be to fit the facts to the suspect.

He starts with what he knows to be irrefutable. At 12.42 am on Monday 13 February 1978, William Favell up-ended a garbage bin into the back of a garbage truck outside the Hilton Hotel. Whatever was in the bin exploded on impact. What was in the bin was a bomb. Someone put it there.

Within hours Sheather sends one part of his team to collect hundreds of witness statements to bring the days leading up to the blast into focus. Another part he gears for the hunt. This pack sniff for suspects.

This is what they find as they conjure the past.

The first witness statements come from those who know that garbage bin intimately. Council workers, garbage collectors, street sweepers, truck drivers. Invisible yet constant worker bees managing the tide of city detritus. They have lost two of their own. They have no reason to be anything other than precise and tidy in their accounts to the police. They give Sheather the first key.

Phillip Morris of the Sydney City Council supplies the detailed schedule of the 'cleansing service' route over the days leading up to the bombing.[6] At 11.30 on Friday night, 10 February, 48 hours before the bombing, the garbage shift commences. The bins outside the Hilton are emptied at approximately 12.30 am on Saturday by William O'Conner.[7]

Sometime between 12.30 am Saturday and 12.42 am Monday, a person or persons place explosive material inside the bin directly outside the George Street entrance to the Hilton Hotel.

The bin is not emptied again until the blast.[8]

This, according to the conspiracists, is evidence of the ASIO/Special Branch plot. That garbagemen were deliberately and consistently stopped from emptying the bin over the next two days by 'officials — including police'. Regular checking of garbage bins for explosives by police was standard protocol for events such as this — as was using bomb sniffer dogs. What ASIO and Special Branch (completely separate organisations) had done was make and plant their own bomb in the bin (with the assistance of military intelligence) and then made sure that for anything up to 48 hours no one would go anywhere near it. The idea was that they would place a warning call and 'discover' the explosives themselves. This would justify the existence of their respective organisations and counter any threats (such as criticism or external investigations) to diminish their resources.[9]

I am here to tell you this is absolutely untrue. For an object the conspiracists argue is deliberately kept from being emptied (implying its contents are somehow protected), an enormous number of people are free to shove any number of objects (including an enormous placard) into the bin, lean on it or use it as a convenient seat over a very long period of time. For the conspiracists to be correct, the following have to be lying in their statements: seven garbagemen (including a street sweeper), an accountant, two hippies, a signwriter, a father of two out for the day with his kids, an anarchist and the Hilton commissionaire. They also have to be colluding with each other, the police who have been told to wave away garbage trucks and, one assumes, ASIO and their mates at Special Branch.

Saturday, 11 am, 11 February. The next garbage shift commences. Neville Alexander Porter, 'a married man [residing] in Sydney with his wife and family', a man who has worked for the Sydney City Council for 26 years and as a driver for 25, tells Sheather's detectives:

'This shift included working in the vicinity of George Street, where the hotel is.' Neville is working with crewman Terry Sweeney. When they arrive at the Hilton at 1.45 pm, Neville states unequivocally, 'I could see police and civilians standing near the entrance to the hotel … there were cars parked at the kerb also cars standing abreast forming a second line. I didn't stop to clear the middle bin, outside the entrance to the Hilton, because I would have had to stop and form a third line of traffic, although I could see that rubbish was sticking out the top of the bin. For the same reason I didn't clear the bin at the southern end of the hotel.'[10]

At 1.45 pm, Saturday 11 February 1978 — 35 hours before the blast — the bin is full.

When Porter (not the police) rather civilly decides not to halt all traffic on a busy Saturday on George Street, operations are in full swing at Sydney's Hilton Hotel as staff and security prepare to receive the first guests of the inaugural Commonwealth Heads of Government Regional Meeting. This is the 'biggest diplomatic summit in Australia's history' and most expensive political conference Australia has ever hosted.[11] The guests include 11 prime ministers and presidents from the Asia–Pacific region who are due to fly in and spend a week discussing issues vital to the region. They represent over 737 million people. It is a big deal, not just because of the size or the cost, but because it marks Australia beginning to think about its identity geographically, as part of the Asia–Pacific. It's an opportunity for the country to assert its independence rather than always following the lead of its traditional Western allies. For Fraser the event is a potent step in projecting himself as an international statesman. However, it's a delicate balancing act — with the exception of the notorious New Zealand Prime Minister, Robert 'Piggy' Muldoon, none of the other leaders are white. Memories of the White Australia Policy are still fresh and Fraser is at pains not to present the country as the white big brother to other nations of the region.[12]

The summit is the inspiration of Malcolm Fraser — who has embraced Australia's biggest wave of non-Anglo immigration, including the Vietnamese 'boat people' — and has taken years to come to fruition. Two days before the official opening the papers have headlines screaming 'Security Like Fort Knox on Sydney Summit'. The man of most concern to security is the Indian Prime Minister, Mr Desai, who is placed under huge guard. It is alleged that the Indian sect Ananda Marga has been targeting Indian organisations around the world in protest over the imprisonment of their leader, Baba. There is excited reporting in the papers about federal and state police combing lobbies, about police stationed on rooftops, about the special anti-terrorist unit based at the airport.[13]

The Commonwealth Police, New South Wales Special Branch, ASIO and the New South Wales police have been preparing for the event for months. The security threats for each leader have been assessed and complex plans have been made for their protection. While the choice of the Hilton Hotel at the centre of Sydney's CBD as the venue has been roundly condemned as a security nightmare owing to its dual entrances on two of Sydney's busiest streets, Pitt and George, it is, at this stage, Australia's most glamorous hotel. Within the hotel is one of the world's first X-ray security scanners and explosive-detecting machines imported from the UK. All who enter the hotel are required to go through it. All the VIPs are on the very top floors.[14]

Throughout the Asia–Pacific region, the leaders of India, Sri Lanka, Fiji, Singapore, Papua New Guinea, Tonga, Nauru, Bangladesh, Western Samoa, Guyana, Malaysia and New Zealand begin to board international flights.

ASIO has supplied the threat assessments, and New South Wales Special Branch officers are assigned to the VIPs along with Commonwealth Police and New South Wales police, in addition to the leaders' own security staffs. The overall operation is coordinated by Superintendent Reg Douglas, the man responsible for the CHOGRM security.

The security protocol for the conference, 'Policing the Hilton Hotel', runs to dozens of pages. Potential threats include direct attacks on persons, assault, stabbing and objects being thrown. Thus each leader is surrounded by security personnel. The second-tier potential threats exist within the hotel itself. The security checks start at the entrance and become progressively tighter as one ascends — the top seven floors where the leaders will stay are virtually impregnable.

There is nothing in this document that refers to checking exterior garbage bins for explosives.

Douglas has an enormous task. Approximately 400 personnel are associated with the conference. The 11 leaders are arriving with their entourages throughout Saturday and Sunday, along with 180 accredited Australian and international journalists. The Hilton also has another 400 to 600 paying guests who must be free to come and go. Security staff constantly search the hotel's stairwells and lifts and keep a watch over the rooftops of the surrounding buildings. The Hilton is also surrounded by businesses that have a brisk Saturday trade and the public need access to the streets and to be able to move through the CBD.

Cracks in the system start showing immediately. There are security breaches on Saturday when a young man on the way home from his gun club manages to carry his rifle all the way through the lobby of the Hilton. Orders get misdirected and people turn up at the wrong place.[15]

On Saturday five Commonwealth prime ministers arrive and are greeted by Malcolm Fraser at the George Street entrance on a red carpet that leads into the Hilton. All walk past the garbage bin.

The garbage bin is not emptied that night. Morris states, 'There was no refuse collection on Saturday evening. This is normal council procedure, as they did not provide this service on <u>ANY</u> Saturday evening.'[16]

Sunday 12 February 1978

Dawn, 5.27 am. It's going to be a blistering day, 33 degrees Celsius. A Sydney beach day. As first light breaks, yellow crowd-control barriers are stacked ready for use, and the red carpet is rolled out. Police stand in serried ranks outside the George Street entrance of the Hilton Hotel, and police motorbikes roar up and down between the airport and the hotel as the first international flights touch down. Demonstrations have been threatened against the prime ministers of Singapore, Malaysia, India and New Zealand, and the press is due in force.

At 6 am Leonard John Stevens arrives on the street, broom in hand. 'I have been employed by the Sydney City Council for the past 21 years as a street sweeper. I have performed that duty in the George Street area for the past 10 years and have worked on Sunday mornings for the past three years.'[1] Leonard not only knows the area intimately, he describes his work with a pride and a kind of forensic detail that is almost cinematic in its breadth. Imagine as I do now that there is a bomb in the bottom of the garbage bin directly outside the Hilton.

Leonard approaches it sweeping from a southerly direction. He sees cars parked on the kerb which 'go right down to beyond a shop called Harolds which is a ladies wear shop at the northern end of the Hilton Hotel …', then:

> When I got to the bin which is outside the Hilton entrance and opposite the door to the Angus and Coote shop, I looked into the bin and saw it was half full. The metal insert [this sits inside the fixed concrete exterior] incidentally is about three feet long and is about 18 inches in diameter. I thought to myself that the bin hadn't been emptied, so I pushed it down to complact [sic] the rubbish with my hand, but it didn't budge. There was a Sun newspaper on top and whatever was underneath, it didn't move at all. It was very firm.
>
> I then went out onto the roadway and picked up a big heap of streamers and put them into a gfound [sic] on the roadway, because if I had put

them into the concrete bin, it would have filled it up too much. Further down the street, I saw what appeared to be chicken bones in the gutter between two cars, so I went back to the bin immediately outside the Hilton and put my hand in and pulled out the newspaper and took a couple of sheets off it. When I took the paper out there appeared to be other rubbish in the bin. I dropped the paper back in the bin and then I went down and picked up the bones and dropped them in the ground bin. I kept sweeping down the footpath and got to the bin near Harold's [sic] and I put my hand in and compressed the rubbish with my hand. This was much softer than the rubbish in the previous bin … It would have been 6.12 am …

Leonard's description of the bin outside the entrance to the Hilton being half full and Neville's statement that 18 hours earlier it had rubbish sticking out the top makes me believe that the bomb was placed during that period. This is pure speculation but I still think it was there — that firm, uncompressible object snug under a copy of *The Sun*.

Leonard also notices as he crosses over to sweep the other side of the street around 6.45 am that 'it looked to me as if there was a demonstration outside the Hilton Hotel and they were standing all over the footpath and naturally in the vicinity of the bin'.

Sunday 12 February 1978

As Leonard is busy sweeping, Jacques Stoupel, the Hilton commissionaire, emerges out the front at precisely 6.30 am. One can feel confident about this as his statement reads like a man who has been preparing for this — the biggest day of his professional life — for months. Much of his statement exudes professional excellence, except when he veers towards contempt for two things he clearly loathes: litter and unpalatable (presumably long-haired and unwashed) demonstrators.[2] So there he is, Jacques, at 6.30 waiting for Prime Minister Fraser. Jacques is immediately informed that Fraser is running late. The first upset to a well-planned day that will lead to catastrophe.

The PM's late arrival starts to jam things up a little. Jacques has heads of state and their entourages arriving throughout the day. It's his job to keep things running smoothly along with the police, the hotel security and the hotel staff. Finally Fraser arrives at 7.15 and enters the hotel. Then at 8 am Sri Lanka's Prime Minister Jayewardene disembarks from a limousine. Everyone is smiling and shaking hands. Fraser emerges from the hotel entrance to greet him. They walk in together up the red carpet.

All is going well. Jacques doesn't mention if he spies a group of demonstrators starting to saunter towards the entrance. His focus is on the imminent arrival of Prime Minister Lee Kuan Yew of Singapore, whose flight SQ85A landed at Kingsford Smith airport at 7.50 am.³ At Sydney airport the federal–state Special Anti-terrorist Unit is on alert.

A person who does note seeing the demonstrators is Keith Snashall, who is driving the garbage truck up George Street for the next scheduled refuse collection at 8.15 am. He also sees a dozen police, pedestrians and hotel staff and observes that the eastern kerb is 'completely parked out' with cars, taxis and buses. Making this journey more precarious are the pedestrians weaving between these vehicles to cross to the other side of the street. As he draws parallel to the bin he notes, 'I could see about one dozen demonstrators walking up and down outside the hotel.' He (unlike Porter the day before) decides to stop to clear the bins with the knowledge that in doing so 'he will completely block the traffic flow in a southerly direction along George Street ... halting the traffic for about three minutes'. However ...

'Just as my crew was about to leave the unit to empty the bins I noticed a young uniformed policeman standing outside the hotel on the footpath and he was indicating to me by using his hand that I should move my truck and keep moving.'⁴

The Prime Minister of Singapore, whom some demonstrators are expected to harass, is about to arrive. A garbage truck pulls up at the red carpet about to block traffic, a young policeman waves it on.

According to Superintendent Reginald Douglas's

Sunday 12 February 1978

notes entitled 'Policing of the Hilton Hotel', issued on 5 February 1978 to all serving officers, this particular officer would have been in 'A District', designating the police stationed at the George Street entrance. Their principal job, according to page nine of the notes, is to report any 'untoward incident'. They would be informed of imminent arrivals of VIPs and if any demonstrations are to be expected. Any eventuality not specifically mentioned was to be 'dealt with as it occurs with commonsense'.[5]

Waving away a garbage truck to avoid the potential awkwardness of the Prime Minister of Singapore sitting behind its stinking rear while the Australian Prime Minister watches Snashall and his crew empty the bins on a Sunday morning seems like commonsense to me. This is the only instance of a garbage truck being waved on by police.

The bin, however, is kept busy all day. Jacques Stoupel is vigilant about litter — he finds himself picking up refuse all morning in between assisting the reception of the prime ministers of Malaysia, Sri Lanka and Nauru. Just before lunch he picked up a 'cardboard milkshake container' and popped it in the bin 'without any difficulty' — noting that while 'the refuse in the bin was fairly high … there was sufficient room for me to place the container inside'.

While he has the rubbish under control, he becomes increasingly tetchy about the gathering demonstrators. He has to shoo away a couple who think it's a good idea to sit down on the footpath blocking the entrance. One of them, Stoupel observes, has hair of a 'dirty appearance'.

The most prominent demonstrators are anarchists, New Zealand expatriates and feminists protesting against New Zealand Prime Minister Muldoon's abortion laws and his locking up of 'political prisoners'. Other protesters include members of the Campaign for the Abolition of Political Police and a few members of the Indian sect Ananda Marga, who are protesting against the imprisonment of their leader, Baba. The bulk of the Margiis, however, are stationed at the airport awaiting the arrival of India's Prime Minister Desai. Photographs from the day reveal the demonstrators at the Hilton to be a rather relaxed bunch. They sit and stand in clusters in straw hats, summer dresses or T-shirts and flares, clutching hand-written signs and smiling at the police who hover around them.

As Reg Douglas's meticulous (but ultimately flawed) security plans indicate, the demonstrators are expected and, somewhat more surprisingly, are to be treated with civility, though no demonstrators are to be tolerated within the Hilton itself. If any are detected they are to be escorted outside and released.

Sunday 12 February 1978

> Arrests are to be carried out only where no alternative is to be found … It is essential that we prevent any unseemly behaviour such as Police fighting with demonstrators etc. within sight of the Heads of State — every means must be taken to peacefully avoid such an occurrence.[6]

Despite the growing irritation of Jacques Stoupel, the atmosphere between police and protesters seems fairly convivial throughout the day. Jacques's annoyance stems from a number of banner-wielding bearded types blocking the entrance and one flag-waving joker who shoves his placard into one of the upright cylinders through which the rope bordering the red carpet is looped. The police then move the barriers further back from the roped entrance, pushing the demonstrators further away.

Jacques keeps cleaning up, noting the bin is full by afternoon.

The bin continues its star turn — Stoupel observes a female protester resting her bum on it, holding a cup above her head. Around 11.30 am, Kevin O'Meara Gleeson, who has taken his kids to town for the day, also sits on the bin to watch the passing dignitaries. He also notices that it's full.[7] Just after midday, Edward Patching, the Foreign Affairs liaison officer to the Western Samoan delegation, comes out to watch the arrival of the prime ministers. He immediately observes that the two bins outside the Hilton 'near the kerb and between the red carpet and the police barriers, were full of rubbish'. Patching is appalled: 'I thought that this was unsightly and not in the good interests of the government to have garbage protruding through these cowls, in view of the heads of state'. Taking immediate action, Patching heads over to the middle bin at the side of the red carpet and forces 'the garbage in through the cowl'. However, owing to the 'compactness' of the garbage within, it springs back 'to just below the lip of the cowl'. He does the same thing to the bin next to it. In this endeavour he is more successful as this one is not 'as compacted as the other'.[8]

Anthony Cuthbertson, a signwriter and amateur photographer, observes that around 2.30 pm the middle bin starts to overflow. He also sees the demonstrators and their placards: 'Free all political prisoners in NZ' and 'Piggy Muldoon'. At one point the protester Carl Maltby stands a sign up in the bin: *Politicians are the pus of a suppurating society.* Cuthbertson adds that he believes that after the barriers were put up 'a number of the demonstrators used the garbage tin as an excuse to enter the restricted area'. He then adds, 'I made particular note of the garbage tin during the afternoon, thinking to myself that the overflowing garbage was an eyesore with visiting dignitaries due to arrive.'[9]

Anthony need not have worried unduly. In order to avoid the demonstrators there is a last-minute decision to take New Zealand's Prime Minister Muldoon (who arrives at approximately 2 pm) and India's Prime Minister Desai (who arrives around 4.20 pm) in through the Pitt Street entrance. It's only when Jacques rolls up the red carpet and starts to pack up that the demonstrators realise they have been duped and have missed their targets.

At Sydney airport, members of the Ananda Marga present Desai with a petition protesting the imprisonment of their leader, Baba. We know this from the grainy surveillance photographs taken before and during the event. In them, one figure is strikingly distinct — a tall willowy man with a thick black beard and a turban. He looms above the other Margiis at the airport.[10] His name is Abhiik Kumar. He is the spiritual leader of the Ananda Marga throughout Australasia. In the archive photographs someone has drawn a circle around his head. He is a man Detective Inspector Norm Sheather will come to know very well in the coming months.

By 5 pm all the leaders (including Desai and Fraser) depart via the George Street entrance for a cocktail party and after that a harbour cruise. The crowds, demonstrators and press depart.

At 10.30 pm the leaders return to the hotel via the George Street entrance. The conference proper is to begin the next morning.

It's a few hours before the bomb will explode. In

the days and years to come each minute will be sifted through minutely and contentiously.

Sunday, 11 pm. Police officers Burmistriw, Griffiths, Hawtin and Withers start their shifts outside George Street.

Between 11.30 pm and 12.30 am Monday morning the street remains moderately busy; people leaving a rock concert hosted by the radio station 2SM at the Opera House head up George Street, and Hilton guests and staff come and go. All pass by the bin.

Sunday 12 February 1978

Monday 13 February 1978

At 12.30 am Bill Ebb drives the Sydney City Council garbage truck north up George Street. Alec Carter is on the back, working the compactor; Bill Favell and John Watson fetch bins and deposit their contents in the back of the truck. Ebb sees that the bins outside the Hilton on the other side of the road are overflowing. He drives on looking for a safe place to perform a U-turn.[1]

12.35 am. A caller to the *Sydney Morning Herald* asks to speak to an editor. Journalist Tim Vaughan takes the call. A man with a European accent says, 'You'll be interested in what the police are going to be doing down at the Hilton soon.'[2]

12.35 am to 12.40 am. Criminal Investigation

Branch (CIB) switchboard operator Suzanne Jones receives a phone call on the 20966 line, Sydney's main police line. A man with a European accent asks to be put through to Special Branch. She rings the line and there is no answer. Jones tells the man, 'They don't seem to be there.'[3] All the Special Branch officers on duty are on the seventh floor of the Hilton — the restaurant and bar level.[4]

Ebb turns the truck around. It heads towards the Hilton. Carter and Favell clear the bins. To do so they have to remove the circular metal top and then empty the bin into the truck. The compactor is not on. The truck approaches the Hilton. Police, staff and pedestrians mill about.

Jones puts the caller through to the CIB duty officer Cec Streatfield. 'Listen carefully,' says the caller. 'There is a bomb in a rubbish bin outside the Hilton Hotel in George Street.'[5]

John Watson picks up the bin just before the one at the Hilton. He tosses its contents into the maw of the compactor. Alec Carter compacts it, operating the levers as he stands on the tray. Ebb has his foot on the brake.

A policeman walks towards the bin directly out the front of the Hilton and pushes a large McDonald's bag into the full bin. Two Chinese men who work in Chinatown ascend the escalator, heading for the Hilton coffee shop.

Monday 13 February 1978

Ebb moves the truck forward. The compactor is finished. Favell reaches for the bin directly outside the Hilton. It is overflowing.

Rosamund Dallow pulls up in a cab and heads to the Hilton entrance to start her security shift.

She passes Bill Favell carrying the bin. John Watson then passes him and runs for the one next to it. Favell carries the bin to the back of the truck.

The Hilton night receptionist Manfred Von Gries starts to descend the escalator.

Colin Wayne Nicholls, also a Hilton employee, a waiter on a break, sits outside the staff entrance, to the left of the escalators, as Rosamund enters the hotel.[6]

12.42 am. Cec Streatfield calls the police stationed at Central station (two blocks away from the Hilton). Sergeant Turner answers the phone.

The bin is emptied into the truck. There is a huge and violent explosion.

The back of the truck is blasted open on both sides. The street lights are blown out and windows shatter up to 16 storeys on both sides of the street.

Carter's right leg is blown off at the pelvis and his stomach split open. Shrapnel lacerates his liver and penetrates his spleen. He is dead.

Favell's torso is blown 40 metres back down George Street.

On the footpath, 15 metres from the truck, is a 'portion of spinal column and scalp'. There is also 'spine attached to portion of pelvis and remnants of thighs'. For a further 90 metres north of the truck more human remains are scattered. 'The largest part identified [is] a right leg found in the front window of the Fletcher Jones store'.[7]

Manfred Von Gries sees 'a policeman go up in the air'.[8]

Constable Burmistriw is hit in the head with shrapnel and swallows his tongue. Sergeant Hawkins clears his airway.

Constable Terry Griffiths has part of his foot blown off and his abdomen perforated by fragments from the blast.

Colin Nicholls's right leg is split from knee to pelvis.

Seven others are injured.

The marble hotel lobby is littered with debris and splashed with blood.

12.44 am. The sirens start. People are wailing, sobbing, screaming. Young coppers are dazed. There are people rushing towards the Hilton to look. A senior Commonwealth policeman takes charge and shoos people away. The first ambulance arrives and they begin frantically working on Burmistriw. The area starts to fill up with uniformed and Special Branch officers, firemen and ambulancemen.

Upstairs, Malcolm Fraser, woken by the explosion, is joined by his press secretary David Barnett

Monday 13 February 1978

and Foreign Affairs Minister Andrew Peacock. Fraser goes straight down to the main floor of the Hilton in his pyjamas and red dressing gown. He walks down to the scene of the blast. Security will not let him out onto the street, fearing another bomb. He is in a unique position. Upstairs are the leaders of 10 countries (the President of Bangladesh has not yet arrived) and a bomb has just exploded on their doorstep. He is responsible for their safety.

Around 1 am, Fraser calls a meeting of all involved in security from Special Branch, Commonwealth Police, New South Wales police and Hilton security — all are in intense shock.[9]

The immediate task is to ensure that the Hilton itself is safe. The police search the hotel for further explosives. All remaining garbage bins are checked. The air conditioning is turned off and the ducts searched.

The next thing is to review the security for CHOGRM, due to commence in seven hours. The 12 leaders are expected to travel by train to Bowral, a few hours from Sydney, on the second day of the conference.

1.30 am. Suzanne Jones on the CIB switchboard receives another call from the man with the foreign accent. Again he says, 'Put me through to Special Branch.' She does but the caller hangs up when the phone is not answered.[10]

1.45 to 2 am. A new bomb scare. An object

wrapped in hessian is located on the fire escape. It's a wrapped brick used to prop open the door.

Superintendent Reginald Douglas briefs the press in the media centre. He accepts responsibility for not telling police to search the rubbish bins.

3 am. The hotel is sealed. No one is allowed to enter. The police bomb squad continues searching for further explosives.

3.30 am. Before Fraser retires for the remainder of the night, he asks for a full written report on the security assessment of the Hilton and the Bowral visit.

Outside, the Scientific Branch detectives and Army experts begin to examine the wreckage. A team of up to 12 Scientific Branch detectives work through the night.[11]

In a few hours Norm Sheather will read the following eloquent précis of the crime scene compiled by Detective Sergeant RD Millington. This report will take him through that long, warm night and bring him to the moment he forms the Hilton bombing task force.

> The government Medical Officer has been contacted and all human remains will be x-rayed in an effort to locate any foreign metal substances that would assist in this inquiry.
>
> Numerous Police attended under the control of Supt. Douglas of Police Headquarters and Det.

Monday 13 February 1978

Inspector Toohey of 'A' District. Det. Sgt Forbes of Scientific attended and is making the necessary inquiries. Sgt Gibson of Police Ballistics attended and made arrangements for members of the Army Bomb Disposal squad to attend and subsequently army personnel under Lieut. Stephenson attended the scene and they with the aid of trained Alsatian dogs, at this time are making a thorough search of all garbage receptacles in George and Pitt Street ... within a 400-yard radius of the Hilton Hotel with the purpose of locating any further explosive devices. The garbage truck is under guard and being kept in George St., outside the Hilton Hotel where all the garbage therein will be examined together with an area of 200 yards radius of the George Street entrance to the Hilton Hotel, in an effort to ascertain the device that caused the explosion ...

Detective Inspector Perrin of Special Branch also attended and he is supplying a list of possible suspects whom it is thought could be responsible for this explosion as it is thought that the fact of the numerous Prime Ministers being residents of this Hotel that this action could be Politically motivated.[12]

The day unfolds ... The man completing the review of securing CHOGRM after the bombing is Alan Flemming, the 65-year-old head of the Protective

Security Coordination Centre and chairman of the inter-departmental committee advising the government on VIP security. A World War II veteran and intelligence officer, he had been brought out of retirement to head a new unit. Six months earlier his unit of 20 had been given sharply increased powers in preparation for CHOGRM and given the job of counter-terrorist planning. He has clearly failed in that and has until 8 am to come up with a new plan.

Also wearing failure is Superintendent Reg Douglas, who was in charge of all CHOGRM security. He admits to Flemming that he no longer believes that he can guarantee the security of the Sydney–Bowral train line with the 300 police at his disposal.

8 am. Flemming and his team complete the new security report. He flags calling in the Army.

8 am. The President of Bangladesh arrives at the Hilton straight from the airport — God only knows what he thinks.

10 am. CHOGRM starts inside the Hilton. The mood is bleak.

Norm gathers witness statements. He makes no assumptions. He continues to corral the information that pours in throughout the day and begins the hunt. Everyone who was present at the demonstrations the day before will be tracked down and questioned — the feminists, the anarchists, the Ananda Marga. Leads are pursued from eyewitness accounts around the time of the blast. Three men are seen driving a Mr Whippy van away from the explosion (reported by Trevor James Thomson, Station Assistant). A suspicious 'Arabic-looking' man is seen hanging around the escalator (reported by Hilton employee Manfred Von Gries). Other leads include someone seeing a Rolls Royce weaving up the street and information about an escapee from a Western Australian prison.

Yet Norm is not content to simply receive information that may or may not be tinged with agendas. Given that he has 12 world leaders in close proximity to that explosion, who can say who the target was? Even the press is speculating:

> … was the bomber a lone eccentric with a general hatred for politicians and other great ones or was there a specific target for their protest? The guessing game [goes] on all day. Was it Tonga, Nauru, Western Samoa or Fiji? Surely not. Mr Michael Somare has his enemies, but seems high on the list of improbabilities … Mr Desai, Mr Lee Kuan Yew, [Mr] Datul Onn of Malaysia, Mr Jayawardene of Sri Lanka and General Ziaur Rabmen of Bangladesh. All have troubles at home. Each could be [the] target. So could, if it comes to that, Mr Malcolm Fraser. Whoever the bomb was intended for, it is providing police with a major headache for the next three days.[13]

Thus Norm sends a telex out to the world. Titled 'Regarding a Fatal Bomb Explosion outside the Hilton Hotel', he sends it first to the respective countries of the visiting Commonwealth heads of state, next to the secretary-general of the International Criminal Police Organization (Interpol) in Paris, and then to every member country of Interpol. He asks simply for a 'list of persons belonging to international organised gangs and who are known to be responsible for various types of violent crimes (bombings, assassination attempts, hostage taking etc.)'.[14]

In 1978 the telex is at its pinnacle and it connects the most remote places on the planet to each other. Yet despite the information being conveyed in real time, it cannot be responded to instantly. Without sophisticated computers and email to flit across the globe, hard-copy files need to be searched, experts consulted, responses compiled. It may be a slow form of evidence-gathering (some of the responses will take up to two or three weeks to arrive), but when answers do come, they are considered and disturbing.

By the end of the day Norm Sheather sends Detective Superintendent Jim Black to face the press. He reports the accomplishment of lots of groundwork, the compilation of lots of statements, of messages sent to interstate police and to Interpol, but 'No positive leads.'[15]

Monday 13 February 1978

Tuesday 14 February 1978

Norm Sheather and the rest of Australia awake to the news that the Australian Army has been mobilised to take over the security for CHOGRM. Over 500 armed soldiers line the train route from Sydney for the world leaders' planned jaunt to the country town of Bowral. Not content with this security measure, the train is sent off empty while the leaders are stuffed into Iroquois helicopters and whisked to their destination. The press are incredulous and compare the scene to — Belfast! Beirut![1] — and report breathlessly that it is 'the most elaborate security operation in Australia's history'. One reporter can't help but add the barb that 'Operation Ghost Train was carried out with a sophistication that contrasted sharply with the position on

Sunday when a bomber was able to plant an explosive device in a street rubbish bin under the eyes of police guarding the conference venue'.²

The task force begins to focus. Those on it need to swiftly and effectively order the material that is streaming in. Sheather has three principal sources of information to contend with. The first from the public, the second from the task force's own investigations, and the third from ASIO and Special Branch. As the first and second are now in motion, he sets his mind to the third, and prepares for a briefing from ASIO.

These two organisations, ASIO and New South Wales Special Branch, have been regarded as conjoined twins in the minds of many, but they have different structures, agendas, duties and, importantly, different personnel. While they do occasionally work on the same cases, this does not necessarily mean they work together. Nor do they always share information.

At the time of the bombing, ASIO is headed by Sir Edward Woodward, and the organisation is fresh from the Hope Royal Commission on Intelligence and Security, which reported the year before. The royal commission is the catalyst for ASIO becoming more professional and less politically partisan, with officers who are better educated and better trained. ASIO's mandate is to collect intelligence from multiple sources by clandestine surveillance — technical and human sources (agents they recruit) — for the purpose

Tuesday 14 February 1978

of identifying security threats to Australia in the form of politically motivated violence. Its first obligation is to report directly to the federal government, and it is under no obligation to pass on its intelligence to the Commonwealth or state police or to New South Wales Special Branch.[3]

New South Wales Special Branch, on the other hand, in early 1978 is operating under pretty much the same system it has had since its inception in 1948 — that is, demonstrating 'little evidence ... of formal operating or reporting procedures'.[4] The ranks of Special Branch are drawn from the police — officers who had left school early and worked their way up through the system. Officially its purpose is to 'be aware' of subversive or extremist activity in New South Wales[5] and to report this information to the police commissioner. It is charged with gathering information on various factions within 'ethnic communities',[6] both to prevent internecine violence and to give protection to consular representatives. In addition it is to provide security escorts to VIPs, both local and international visitors. If, in the course of any of these functions, information arises that would be of importance from a national point of view, it is to be passed on to ASIO through the commissioner of police.

Unofficially, Special Branch is known to be a place of nepotism, corruption, ineptitude, 'dirt' files and good times. Apparently most afternoons a bar opens in the Special Branch office following a long lunch. One senior policeman told me they were very good at mixing martinis. Little wonder they were not in the office at 12.40 am when the phone call warning about the bomb came in.

So ASIO is a national organisation in the throes of professionalising its staff, and Special Branch is a New South Wales–based outfit packed with working-class mates who enjoy a boozy, cruisy, working environment … hardly joined at the hip. Both, however, are deeply shocked by the bombing. Special Branch feel the sting of knowing they were ensconced in the bar at the Hilton when Suzanne Jones was trying to get hold of them to transfer the warning call. ASIO is even more disturbed — they had been assiduously monitoring 'organisations of interest'[7] by multiple means and had reason to feel confident that they would have had some forewarning of an attack of this nature.

Sir Edward instructs ASIO to provide all assistance to Sheather, and on the afternoon of 14 February a senior ASIO officer provides him with a three-hour briefing.

The officer brings Sheather up to date on the list of subversive groups identified as of potential concern to security at CHOGRM. This list had been provided to the Commonwealth and New South Wales police, including Special Branch, in the days leading up to the conference. The officer hints strongly that ASIO has

Tuesday 14 February 1978

operatives working undercover within these groups.

The groups identified were:

A. Demonstrators condemning Singapore's detention of political prisoners, targeting President Lee Kuan Yew of Singapore and Malaysia's Prime Minister Dato' Onn. 'Organisations which might act, although we have no evidence so far of interest, are the Overseas Student Service of the Australian Union of Students and a small group of anti–Lee Kuan Yew ex-Singaporeans resident in Sydney, which Singapore authorities have described as a branch of the Malayan People's Liberation League (MPLL).'

B. Militant trade union protests against the Fijian Prime Minister instigated by 'Apisai Vuniyayaw Tora', a militant Fijian trade unionist jailed in that country for illegal industrial activity. That said, 'So far subversive organisations having influence in trade unions have shown no interest.'

C. A number of members of the New South Wales Ananda Marga have 'recently discussed the possibility of forming a delegation to speak to the Indian PM Mr Desai during CHOGRM in order that they may present pleas for the release of their spiritual leader PR Sarkar [Baba]'. If refused, ASIO anticipates them holding a demonstration at an as yet undetermined site. 'We expect that final planning for the demonstration will not proceed until the return to Australia of the AM spiritual director Jason Holman Alexander.'

Alexander is also known by the name Abhiik Kumar.

D. The New South Wales Railway Workers Union is threatening to stop the train carrying the delegates to Bowral. This is to demonstrate the shocking conditions for many workers at 'a number of stations'. The idea is to stop the train at one of these 'shocking stations' and presumably shake these leaders to the core about the state of Australian railways.

E. Three blank invitation cards to attend the PM's CHOGRM banquet were found in a hotel room occupied by a person 'identified as Helen M Bell (née Gundry)'. Neither she nor her husband are known to ASIO.[8]

A bunch of foreign students, a militant trade union, a religious sect missing a leader, some pissed off rail workers and a woman who may or may not pilfer stationery. The immediate threats seem ridiculously benign, but Sheather decides to pursue them nonetheless. They are also the forerunners of a trove of less recent ASIO intelligence that will burst to the forefront of Sheather's investigation in the next 24 hours.

Tuesday 14 February 1978

Wednesday 15 February 1978

By the second day of the investigation, a pattern of events — a mixture of breaks, good policing, fatal mistakes, misinformation and disinformation — is established that will characterise and haunt the investigation for the next four months, until it becomes completely derailed on 15 June.

The problem with misinformation is that it's sometimes hard to distinguish from information. If you're in Sheather's task force you have to make a decision whether Mr Sutton, an explosives engineer employed in Adelaide, is correct in believing that 'from details he has heard in news broadcasts' the explosives used are the same as those stolen recently from his employer's warehouse in South Australia 1500 kilometres away and that this is a useful lead that should be pursued.¹ Similarly, is one to rely on the tip-off volunteered by Mr Robert Trotter (a draftsman and cab driver for Legion) who swears he saw Tim Anderson (PR spokesperson for the Ananda Marga and fellow cab driver) loitering in his cab outside the Hilton with a passenger yet with the lights turned off at 1 am on Sunday the 12th?²

While the latter seems like powerful circumstantial evidence, one needs to remember that at a press conference the day before, India's Prime Minister Desai had cheerfully aired his belief that he was the target of the bombing and that the Ananda Marga were to blame. At the same time, a lean, bespectacled and bearded 26-year-old Tim Anderson, in his role as spokesperson and secretary of that religious sect, has had his own well-attended and well-publicised press conference stating that Ananda Marga members were greatly shocked by the bombing and extended sympathy to the families of the dead men. Maybe Trotter has simply married this well-known identity to the man he thinks he saw in the cab. Is it evidence?

At the Ananda Marga press conference Anderson also informs journalists that the Margiis suspect they have been infiltrated by ASIO and Commonwealth Police agents (which is absolutely true in the case of ASIO) and that they welcome this. They have nothing to hide. To have Ananda Marga connected with the

Wednesday 15 February 1978

Hilton bombing is unthinkable. He adds that they are aware there are elements attempting to destroy Ananda Marga and that these elements were responsible for terrorism around the world. This refers to an alliance of the Russian KGB and the Indian Central Bureau of Investigation (CBI). He ends by saying, 'The fact that Australia, which is the little brother of the United States, in Russia's eyes, is hosting the conference, is all the more reason for an attempt to undermine the aim of the conference.'[3]

The disinformation is easier to identify but equally time-consuming to address. For the most part this takes the form of a swathe of bomb hoaxes that begin to be called in; there are three on 15 February and within six weeks Sheather's team will have logged over 500 of them. It also takes the form of a steady stream of mentally disturbed individuals who confess enthusiastically to being the bomber.

Accelerating the rising tide of intelligence, both good and bad, is the sudden announcement of a $100 000 reward to be given jointly by the state and federal governments for information leading to an arrest. This is simply an astonishing sum of money for Australians in 1978. To put it in context, it is exactly the same amount of reward money that would be offered today, almost four decades on, for Australia's most serious crimes. Not only is it a wad of money that promises to attract crazies, it is guaranteed to be ineffective in producing informants who may be implicated in the crime but wish to name associates in exchange for immunity, as Premier Wran has warned there would be no 'immunity for people responsible for the bomb blast. There will be no compromise for a terrorist. There will be no mercy for people who plant bombs.'[4]

One imagines Fraser and Wran felt they needed to make a gesture of this size commensurate with the catastrophic explosion — but it is simply a fatal mistake. It will turn Sheather's tide of intelligence into a tsunami.

Making the day worse are the initial reports from the ballistics team — the Scientific Branch — stating that while they do not believe the bomb was a land mine or plastic explosive, they do believe the explosion was of such force to have blown things such as a timer to pieces. The violence of the explosion makes it difficult to find many traces of the actual bomb. Their best guess is that it was 'plas-gel', a malleable form of gelignite or sticks of gelignite — the latter procurable at that point from almost any large hardware store — weighing around 4.5 kilograms.

Despite an exhaustive fingertip search of the barricaded site the night of the bombing by the Scientific team and a large number of police, the operation is 'hampered due to the presence of refuse' from within the garbage truck. The items of interest that are discovered 'that might assist in establishing the means of detonation' are sent for further examination to the

Wednesday 15 February 1978

school of metallurgy at the University of New South Wales and to a Mr West at the Analytical Laboratories. Among the items are: 'sections of white and yellow insulated wire', fragments of 'black plastic insulating tape', 'a small unidentifiable spring', parts of batteries, bits of an electric hobby motor, watch batteries, samples and swabs from the garbage truck, pieces of metal, a man's gold wristwatch and a single leather glove.[5]

And then comes the break: news arrives from Bangkok. Three members of the Ananda Marga have been arrested in the Thai capital in possession of 'enough high explosive to blow up a ten-storey building'.[6] Two of the three are Australian: Timothy Thomas Hilton Jones, 25, and Caroline Lee Spark, 24. Also arrested is US citizen Sarah Child, 29.[7] All three were about to leave Bangkok for Australia but had been unable to get on a flight.

As this news breaks, Sheather receives a barrage of reports about the Margiis. On 7 February in Manila, Americans Stephen Dyer and Victoria Shepherd (both members of Ananda Marga) were caught in the act of stabbing an Indian Embassy employee.[8] On 8 February in West Germany, two Ananda Marga members, Helmut Klein Schmidt and Erica Rupert, set themselves on fire and burn to death.[9] It seems they are protesting the arrest in London on 1 November the previous year of three Margiis — Anthony Niall Kidd, Brian Shaw and Susan Waring, all British — on bombing charges and for conspiracy to murder a member of the Indian High Commission.[10]

It is thought that this spate of violent acts in Manila, West Germany and Thailand in less than two weeks is linked to the fact that the imprisoned Ananda Marga leader Sarkar (Baba), a god to sect members, had his appeal denied in India on 2 February.[11]

Sheather must be staring at this information as one might stare at an unexpected visitor from a parallel dimension. Who are these people? What is going on? He must also be staring hard at those dates. Sarkar's appeal is denied in India on 2 February; on 7 February two Margiis are arrested for stabbing an Indian official in Manila; on 8 February two Margiis self-immolate in West Germany; on 15 February three Margiis are arrested in Thailand with high explosives. The bombing of the Hilton on 13 February sits neatly within these dates. The Indian PM was inside the hotel. Is there a link?

Coming across this material in the archive I actually feel a rush of adrenalin, as if I were one of Sheather's team making this discovery. If not exactly concrete evidence, it surely suggests a motive. It's provocative. Ten members of the Ananda Marga have been caught either planning or committing acts of extreme violence in four completely different countries — England, the Philippines, Thailand and West Germany. The latter three seem clearly motivated by the denial of Sarkar's appeal. Surely the Hilton must be part of a wave of Margii violence protesting against Sarkar's continued incarceration?

Needless to say, Norm will investigate this path — indeed, how can he avoid it? The Ananda Marga have thrust themselves forward as prime suspects. To be willing to touch a naked flame to your own petrol-soaked skin takes a certain kind of terrifying belief. What could explain it? To save a child? A lover? A country? To free your god? These acts are extreme. They cannot be ignored.

Norm will not, however, close off other inquiries nor completely discount the idea that the Hilton is simply a coincidence.

He contacts ASIO. Do they have someone working undercover within the organisation? Yes, they do. Had they received any information about these attacks in other countries? Anything about actions protesting the denial of Sarkar's appeal?

I imagine the ASIO officer takes a moment to consider how he will answer these queries. This is going to take some time. He needs to takes Norm back to when Ananda Marga first appeared in Australia. If the members of this religious sect are suspects, Norm needs to know more about them. And if he wants to know who within the sect could be responsible, if indeed they are, and how he might catch them, he's going to need the patience of Job.

Enter the
Ananda Marga

The Ananda Marga, comes onto the radar of Australian authorities in May 1976. A report entitled 'A Note on Anand Marg [sic]' is sent from the Indian Central Bureau of Investigation (CBI) to ASIO via Interpol.[1] The unnamed author is clearly hostile to the sect but nonetheless provides a detailed report of the religion's origins. Literally meaning 'Path of Bliss', Ananda Marga is founded in 1955 in Jamalpur in the state of Bihar by 31-year-old PR Sarkar, then a clerk at a local railway workshop. The sect is founded on a complex and detailed philosophy that eschews both communism and capitalism for a third path known as universalism. Like other Indian religious practices, its adherents practise yoga, meditation and vegetarianism and it has a hierarchised structure of followers with different cadres of disciples — in the Margiis case with the avadhuts and the acharyas at the top. Avadhut is a Sanskrit word for a mystic or saint, and acharya, also Sanskrit, means a teacher, a highly learned person or a leader of a sect. Both appellations and roles were common to a range of Indian religions.

The sect and Sarkar hold a great attraction for young Indians attending college and over the years the membership grows. Along with the Ananda Marga, Sarkar founds a philosophy called Prout (Progressive Utilisation Theory), 'a comprehensive socio-economic political philosophy [which] envisages a Proutist government that would take society towards "universalism"'.[2] Prout is also established as an organisation. Although the Ananda Marga and Prout share similar tenets, they can and do have separate memberships and indeed different aims.

To define them crudely, the former might be regarded as the practitioners of spiritual philosophy and the latter as those who undertake practical and proactive steps towards social reform.[3] Up until the mid to late 1960s the sect is mainly confined to India, but then starts to send out disciples to an increasing number of countries — the USA, Germany, the UK, Italy, Sweden, Thailand, the Philippines, New Zealand and Australia. These disciples are for the most part white, Western and well educated, having joined the Path of Bliss after visiting Sarkar in India. The disciples scatter to the four corners of the globe and establish yoga societies, schools, meditation centres and relief centres in disaster-hit areas. These sites in turn collect funds and followers. The religion grows.

In 1971 local police raid the Ananda Marga headquarters in Ranch, Bihar State, and Sarkar's residence. The Indian police allege that in the course of the searches they discover bombs, firearms and 'lethal weapons'.[4] During this investigation the police receive further information connecting Sarkar to a hitherto unsolved multiple murder in which six tortured and mutilated bodies were found tied to trees deep in a forest. The murder case is re-opened and on intelligence from ex-sect members, including Sarkar's ex-wife, Sarkar is arrested for the murders. The victims, all Ananda Marga disciples who had become disenchanted with the sect, were part of a killing spree allegedly carried out by Sarkar and his followers. Sarkar is put on trial, found guilty and jailed.

Thereafter, so goes the report, once all legal means to release Sarkar have failed, the fanatical members of the sect mount a violent campaign to secure their leader's freedom. Amongst other things they are accused of a successful 1975 grenade attack against a senior Indian government minister that killed him and two others, and a failed attempt on the life of the Chief Justice of India when sect members were caught throwing grenades into his car. Fortunately, the grenades did not explode.

The Indian authorities warn Interpol that 'until 1975, the criminal activities of the fanatical group of Anand Margiis [sic] have been confined to India'. However, they add — and now one can get a sense of how they really feel —:

> It would be strange if amongst these disciples, there are not some, who like the more fanatical type of Avadhuts in India, have not been so brainwashed and indoctrinated as to be willing to participate in any plans of violent activities which would be spectacular such as causing explosions, hostage taking, causing physical harm to Indian dignitaries residing in or visiting a foreign country or staging violent incidents in the country where these units are located to attract world attention and to pressurise the government of India to release their leader.[5]

They refer to an 'incident' in New Zealand involving six Margiis — two American nationals, two citizens of New Zealand (one of Indian origin), one Italian national and one Australian citizen, which 'should be an eye-opener'. The Margiis are reported to have stolen explosives, kidnapped a police officer and planned to blow up the Indian High Commission. The Americans are deported and the others imprisoned for between two and four years.

Our unnamed Indian source ends with this warning:

> It will be seen from the above that it is very necessary that the police services, specially of those countries where Anand Marga [sic] activities have been noticed in any form, should not be deceived by the outwardly innocuous façade of the local Anand Marg [sic] units being engaged in the propagation of yoga, or spiritualism or social service. They are capable of the most violent and outrageous crime on the command of their leader presently in jail. It is not necessary that they receive such a command personally from the leader. For them it is enough to be told by any one of the Avadhuts that PR Sarkar has desired it.[6]

Stirring stuff, and if the Margiis did plant the bomb at the Hilton two years later, wonderfully prophetic. But — and this is a big but — from the get-go Sarkar has proclaimed not only his innocence but that the Indian Government, under the leadership of Indira Gandhi, has been out to get him and his followers by any means possible. On 4 July 1975, her government declares a State of Emergency and bans the Ananda Marga from operating in India on the basis that their activities are prejudicial to the national interest. Sect members argue that Sarkar has been set up for the murders and all the attacks in India blamed on the Margiis have in fact been carried out by the Indian secret service.

It is here that things get even more complicated. One of the most confounding aspects of the sect in the mid to late 1970s is its members' extremely vocal and increasingly strident assertions that the acts of violence carried out in the name of the Margiis are in fact part of an elaborate conspiracy driven by the Indian CBI in cahoots with the KGB to discredit the religion on a global scale.

In the Ananda Marga's allegations this conspiracy takes the form of the Indian CBI, possibly with the KGB, impersonating a violent inner cell or sister group of Ananda Marga or Prout called UPRF (Universal Proutist Revolutionary Federation), who commit violence or threaten violence against Indian officials or institutions in Australia and around the world in the guise of a continuing campaign to have Sarkar released from jail. These acts and threats of violence are not supported by the Margiis or Proutists and are in fact orchestrated in such a way as to erode the credibility of the sect — who oppose violence — and thereby damage their legitimate and legal attempts to have Sarkar released.

In the opinion of the Indian CBI and the Indian Government, this scenario is a complete invention — a kind of double blind to terrorise the Indian

Government and simultaneously curry favour with adherents, particularly the growing counter-culture movement in the West. What better way to attract adherents than to present the sect as virtuous and persecuted?

So far, so good. The finger-pointing is nicely balanced. It's clear to Norm that ASIO and the Australian Government don't simply take the Indian Government's accusations at face value. Despite India's banning of the sect in 1975, the Ananda Marga in Australia, and indeed in most of the West, is recognised as a legitimate religion. In Australia, state and federal governments extend the sect financial assistance for their schools in New South Wales, Tasmania and Western Australia, and register their marriage celebrants. Who is to say what Indira Gandhi's government was really up to when it imposed a State of Emergency from 1975 to 1977? Perhaps they were attempting to discredit the sect. It's possible.

It's in 1977 that things get even more confounding. Early in the year Gandhi's government — which instigated the State of Emergency for two years, during which the Margiis and other groups were banned — is crushed by Desai's Janata Party in a victory of democracy over dictatorship.[7] On winning the election, Desai's government immediately lifts the ban on the sect and agrees to review Sarkar's conviction. Indeed so committed is this government to righting the wrongs of the previous government that they arrest Indira Gandhi herself and get rid of 75 per cent of the secret service personnel.[8]

However, while the position of Sarkar and the Ananda Marga is decidedly improving, they are dealt a severe setback in July 1977 when the attempt to have Sarkar's case re-opened unexpectedly fails.

At that moment the ground rules completely shift. Prior to the ban being lifted, almost all the protest activities associated with the sect in Australia and the West have taken the form of demonstrations, posters and graffiti. After the July 1977 ruling, things abruptly change. A wave of violence and threats of violence rains down on Indian officials across the world. Accompanying this is the same pattern of denial from Margii spokesmen.

One of the oddities about these acts of violence and the declarations of denial that flare suddenly in 1977 is that despite the radical change of government in India, the Ananda Marga continue to claim that they are being set up and maligned by the same enemy government agents. In short, that the instigators behind the violence remain the Indian CBI and the KGB.

An Australian campaign of terror

In Australia on 24 August 1977, a few weeks after Sarkar failed to have his case re-opened in India, Ananda Marga member Paul Alister, then going by the name O'Callaghan, walks into the Air India building on Elizabeth Street in the Sydney CBD, places a pig's head on the counter and begins throwing plastic bags filled with blood on the ceiling, walls and carpet (fine $600 or 120 days in prison) and on the trousers (fine $100 or 60 days in prison) of the unfortunate staff member at reception.[1] Alister is subsequently arrested. Two days later a bag containing another pig's head is found inside the Indian Consulate General's office on the tenth floor of Caltex House. The next day a plate-glass window at the front of the Sydney Air India office is smashed. On the same day an Air India employee is told that there is a bomb on Air India flight AI 1415 leaving Sydney.

A letter purporting to be from the Universal Proutist Revolutionary Federation (UPRF) claims responsibility for the Air India attacks. The letter is almost comically malevolent, made up of words cut out of newspapers. It states that if PR Sarkar is not released, 'such action and more will continue'.[2] This is the first time the UPRF claims responsibility for an act of violence in Australia. Special Branch is alerted.

Two days later, on 29 August, a fire breaks out at the chancery of the Indian High Commission in Canberra. Then on 6 September another letter arrives from UPRF claiming responsibility for the fire and stating their intention to escalate operations and 'to begin assassinations of Indian government representatives and lackeys unless Shrii PR Sarkar is immediately and unconditionally released'.[3] Unlike the first, this one (postmarked Canberra) arrives at the Ananda Marga headquarters in Sydney. Tim Anderson, the Margiis' spokesperson, sends the letter straight to the police 'dissociating [the sect from] the fire and [denying] knowledge of the fire'.[4]

Harder to deny is what happens at the Indian High Commission in Canberra the following week, when military attaché Colonel Iqbal Singh is stabbed and he and his wife are abducted from their home. (Singh and his wife escape.) Ananda Marga member John William Duff is charged by the police over the attack and the attempted abduction.[5] This incident spikes the attention of police and government alike. Attacks seem to be escalating exponentially.[6] Special Branch in every state begin to carefully collate reports. The federal government asks for a review and sets up a task force to investigate. ASIO starts sniffing around and begins to run agents (i.e. to recruit informants) within the Ananda Marga.[7]

Throughout September 1977 waves of letters from UPRF land at the homes and offices of Indian officials and at newspapers. Bricks go through windows. Indian officials are knifed by unidentified assailants. Threatening phone calls are made. The victims include Indian doctors, solicitors, nurses, consuls and their wives and children.[8] The message in the letters is consistent: 'Our programme is clear and simple — regular and systematic assassination of any worker in your high commissions, consulates, trade offices and Air India throughout the world until Shrii PR [Sarkar] is unconditionally released.'[9] The letters, which frequently turn up at home addresses, are particularly unpleasant — apart from the usual demand for the release of Sarkar, and $100 000 to be paid to the Ananda Marga, they also include, as Special Branch Detective Toms delicately puts it, threats of 'rape-death'.[10] One letter disgorges pornographic clippings and another includes, along with a death list of 30 Indian doctors, solicitors and businessmen, warnings that 'we will start with your kids — prustitute [sic] and kill' and signs off with 'Do not panic. Our attack will be anyday [sic] even after months when I diots ci re you [sic] will think everything has settled. We will get you — your embasy [sic] cools how long police stand by?'[11]

While reports start to trickle in about similar attacks and similar letters around the world, Special Branch focuses on what is occurring in Australia. This will prove to be highly problematic in the months to come.

By the end of September 1977 the Indian expat population in Australia is completely terrorised. Whether it's the Ananda Marga or, as the sect claims, the Indian secret service who is reigning down the terror, the results are the same. From Mr Chand, the 'excitable' house-boy at the Indian consul's house, to Mrs Gupte, the wife of the Indian Government tourist bureau attaché, to the 18-year-old brother of Miss Alag, a nurse, all are in a panic.[12] CHOGRM is less than five months away and action needs to be taken.

Under the command of Inspector Perrin, Special Branch become hyper-vigilant. Officers are sent out to watch Ananda Marga premises and to collect statements from Indian nationals who have been threatened or attacked. They carefully type up detailed reports. There are hundreds of pages from Special Branch relating to the threats against Indians and while there are many officers involved, the names of DC Helson, DC Henderson and DC Krawczyk are most prominent. They are the ones who interview most of the terrified Indian nationals, and they are the ones who haunt the exterior of the Ananda Marga headquarters, noting comings and goings. They trawl through the sect members' bank accounts and tenancy agreements.

From what I can ascertain, Special Branch is being quite thorough and fair-minded. They appear to be taking the sect's assertion that they are being framed seriously, and write copious notes on the elaborate forensic tests that the letters are subjected to in order to determine their point of origin. They also regard some of the claims by Indian nationals with scepticism. For example, after one reported attack in Canberra, Detective Toms writes that, 'owing to the apparent fear, and confused mental state, of the occupants there are some doubts that the actual reported incidents [a man throwing projectiles at the building] did actually occur'.[13]

It's hard to imagine who would be more likely to write these absurdly misspelled moustache-twirling provocations — an Indian CBI agent or a Western-born member of an Indian cult? Both would have been very well educated. Almost all Australian members of the Ananda Marga are drawn from universities, and CBI recruits are co-opted from the highest ranks of Indian society. There is something in the letters that smacks of undergraduate humour — a kind of parody of what one expects a revolutionary religious zealot to come up with. Trying to fathom the truth of the threats and denials becomes a mind-bending exercise. Does 'You are dead one by one your daughters will earn for us as above'[14] sound more like an Indian spy impersonating a Western member of an Indian sect or a Western member of an Indian sect impersonating an Indian spy impersonating a Western member of the sect? What is to be achieved by terrorising the expat Indian population?

There is little time to allow such thoughts to bloom. After the stabbing and attempted kidnapping of Colonel Singh, Prime Minister Fraser weighs into the debate. In his opinion, while ideally an attempt should be made to disperse the violent element of the Ananda Marga — if it exists — it is clear that such an element is 'difficult to pinpoint'.[15] That said, under the circumstances they simply have to take action 'on the assumption that there [is] a group' attempting 'to precipitate violence against Indian officials, as a means of pressure on the Indian Government to release the leader of Ananda Marga who has been imprisoned on murder charges'.[16]

Fraser calls a meeting of all Commonwealth and state police, including Special Branch, and intelligence (ASIO) officers, along with a visiting Indian expert, for 28 September 1977. For Fraser, the information collated at this meeting confirms 'the depth of the problem'. In response he asks that all agencies agree that 'the pursuit, collection and interchange of information on Ananda Marga be constant and intensive to permit adequate assessment of the threat' and that they set up a system of regular cooperation and coordination. Fraser indicates that he wants 'sound information' that would give the government a 'more precise picture of the workings' of the Ananda Marga in Australia. Both the federal and state governments provide support — both financial and in the form of licences — for a broad range of Ananda Marga activities including preschools, marriage celebrants and so on. Fraser wants to suspend any support until there is an urgent examination of the sect's activities.[17]

By early October the Indian High Commission and Consul General are in urgent talks with both state and federal ministers about the spate of attacks. Detective Constables Jan Krawczyk and CL Helson of Special Branch write up an exhaustive report of 43 separate incidents of actual or threatened violence upon Australia-based Indian nationals over a period of three weeks. But despite all the threats being made in the name of Ananda Marga, the detectives keep an open mind as to the identity of the perpetrators, stating, 'All possible inquiries are being made.'[18]

At the same time, ASIO's covert operatives begin to talk.

Abhiik Kumar

Norm Sheather, in the first heady days of the investigation, is still embedded in the recent past, stretching his mind around the perplexing events of 1977. Who was making all these threats and committing all these acts of violence against Indian nationals in Australia?

What did the Indian Government have to gain by pretending to be Margiis or Proutists and threatening their own citizens with 'rape-death'? To ensure Sarkar stayed in jail? To justify putting him there? To discredit a marginal cult?

The US Central Intelligence Agency (CIA) certainly has no qualms about including the Margiis on its greatest hits list that year. In a recently declassified document produced by the CIA's National Foreign Assessment Center entitled 'International Terrorism in 1977', the sect is contextualised alongside other groups such as the radical Popular Front for the Liberation of

Palestine, the Japanese Red Army and the remnants of the Baader-Meinhof gang. It's highly probable that ASIO would have been forwarded a copy of this document and that some mention of it would have been made in the briefing Sheather received after the Hilton bombing. Interestingly, while the CIA perceived an increasing trend 'towards cooperation' between international terrorist groups, citing the activities of Carlos the Jackal facilitating contacts between terrorist bands, they perceived no such behaviour in the Ananda Marga. It was an altogether different fish.

> Violence-prone members of the Ananda Marg [sic], an Indian religious sect, conducted attacks on Indian diplomats on several continents, including the United States. To date, the group has not used weapons other than knives, although several of its sympathizers in Asia have been detained on charges of illegal possession of explosives. The group has not attacked non-Indian citizens, but its international membership suggests connections with a farflung support apparatus, and its future actions could involve unintentional victimization of other nations. Its idiosyncratic, parochial motives, however, make it unlikely that the organization would be willing to cooperate with other terrorist groups.[1]

'Its idiosyncratic parochial motives' also make it a difficult organisation to fathom and to penetrate. ASIO's undercover agents begin to roam around the edges, attending meditation and yoga sessions. Their encounters with members are slightly unnerving — these aren't laid-back hippies preaching free love. Many who have committed to the sect have cut themselves off completely from their families and their former lives. There is an intellectual quality to their belief system, which is rigid, controlled and tightly disciplined. It is a strictly hierarchic sect, in which orders come from the top down. The top, of course, being Sarkar (Baba), imprisoned in India. And who does Sarkar speak to about things in Australia? To the spiritual leader of the Ananda Marga in Australasia: Abhiik Kumar.

This name is probably unfamiliar to anyone who followed the sagas of Margiis Alister, Anderson and Dunn. Indeed in all the books, articles, multiple films, both documentary and dramatised, about the ins and outs of the case, decrying injustice, demanding royal commissions, arguing conspiracy over all the years, there is barely any mention of him.

And yet there he is, centre stage, the focus of inquiries in late 1977. Well, when I say centre stage, he is admittedly hard to make out at first, concealed as he is behind scrim and smoke. Even for ardent Australian devotees of the sect in 1977 he is an elusive character, revered, if not often seen. There is first up the matter of his name. Or rather, his names. He is Acharya Abhiik Kumar to the faithful, but he travels during mid to late 1977 under the name Jason Holman Alexander. That's the name he adopted in March that year, changing it from Jon Hoffman by deed poll.[2]

Hoffman, born in the USA, comes to Australia to increase Ananda Marga membership in the early 1970s not long after Sarkar's original imprisonment. He has another occasional name of Mark Randall and he has other names he will adopt officially and otherwise in the future, such as AK Brahmacarii,[3] Stephen James Manly, David Hart and Michael Brandon. But right now, as ASIO and Special Branch start to pierce the gloaming, and as Norm starts to see, his names are Alexander and/or Kumar.

The first official report on him from ASIO lays out the known facts:

> Alexander lives in Newtown. He has had 24 overseas trips in the last 2 years, and he possibly went to the [Ananda Marga London?] conference in July 1977. Sources of his — and indeed the organisation's — finances are unknown. Alexander has the power to override decisions of the committee at any time on any matter. Ananda Marga membership in New South Wales is estimated at 200.[4]

It's not much to go on and the membership is reverential. When engaged in chitchat they all reiterate the public statements — Margiis deplore all violence and these actions in the name of UPRF are not condoned by them.

However, the attack on Colonel Singh and his wife in September draws not only Prime Minister Fraser's attention, it also draws out a former sect member who has information to impart. While his name is completely erased from the archive it is clear that he somehow contacted or was contacted by ASIO and arranged to speak to them on two separate occasions, 24 and 27 October 1977.

> Subject informs us that he had been involved with the Ananda Marga for the last three or so years and had come to the conclusion that it was a dangerous organisation. He said he now wished to impart certain information concerning Ananda Marga because he felt the competent authorities in this country ought to know about it. He then proceeded to narrate his experience with the Ananda Marga.[5]

It's quite a story, both detailed and charmingly domestic before it veers into the dark. It starts in 1974, shortly after his young son joins the Margiis' Sunrise School in North Sydney. One day at a school fete he and his wife meet Eric Fouter, a member of the sect who invites the couple to attend an Ananda Marga meeting. After this other members take a great deal of interest in them and they are invited to join the organisation. They agree to join because 'they felt it might help their son at school'.

Later that year he is approached by Abhiik Kumar, who asks if he would help run their 100-acre farm in Queensland. He agrees to do this on a short-term basis. By the end of the year he is asked to assist with a feasibility study relating to setting up health food shops across Australia. Again he agrees and does so for a while before giving up 'through utter frustration'. About the same time he is approached by 'Kapil' (probably Hanspeter Arn, a Swiss national) about some of the 'lads' in the organisation getting some training in self-defence on the farm in Queensland. This time the subject declines because 'a person known as Katutuvera', whom he describes 'as a psychopath', insists that the trainees should learn how to 'kill an opponent'. Despite his refusal to participate, he thinks that the training did eventually take place in June 1975.

Over the course of the two days, the subject's story grows in credibility. He relates detailed and hitherto unpublicised information about the New Zealand explosives theft and kidnapping in 1975, and about the inner workings of the sect. The sect's impenetrability owes much to the particularities of its recruitment processes. Only friends of current Margiis are asked to join, and then undergo a rigorous process of induction. This involves a month of rigid discipline, intensive fasting, instruction and cold showers at one of the sect's schools. After this recruits are required to sever all contact with their own family and surrender all their possessions. The latter then becomes the primary source of Ananda Marga's resources. Outstanding graduates are then selected for further 'severe' and rigorous training, which 'involves unquestioned obedience to the Ananda Marga leadership'.

While embarking on this path, and after almost 18 months of membership, the subject gradually begins to be groomed by Kumar himself and admitted into the inner workings of the group. In late 1975 he is summoned to meet Abhiik Kumar. The sect leader is impressed by the subject's staunch anti-communism, which reflects very much the position of Ananda Marga. He then asks him how far he would be prepared to go in the fight against communism and 'whether or not he would be prepared to kill in the process'. That would depend, he replies, on 'whether or not Australia was threatened or endangered by the communists'.

A few days later the subject is summoned once again to Kumar's office. Abhiik asks the subject whether he is willing to 'cooperate in organising a political group known as Prout'. This group, of which Kapil is a member, is to be separate from Ananda Marga and its task is to nominate candidates for election to parliament and to infiltrate organisations such as trade unions, Friends of the Earth and conservation groups. I'm too busy, says the subject. Kumar then wants to know what he feels about a pornographic film being screened at a Sydney theatre. He thinks such films should be banned. Ring them up, Kumar suggests, and threaten 'to have the theatre bombed unless the film is withdrawn'. The subject replies, 'I'm not sure I want to go that far.'

'You know that Baba was imprisoned in India because the bodies of defectors were found,' says Kumar, and then adds, 'It would be much easier to dispose of such bodies in Australia.'

The subject knows this is an explicit warning and he sets about gradually extricating himself from the sect, being careful not to antagonise them. Months pass until he ceases attending meetings altogether. It is then that Kapil reappears. He wants to know if the subject is still one of them. Of course he is, the subject replies. What does he know about explosives? Enough, he says, as he had had some training in chemistry. Then ensues a conversation about blowing up the Indian High Commission in order to bring about pressure to 'secure the release' of Baba. The subject, while expressing disapproval for the plot, also — probably wisely — treats the whole thing 'like a big joke', while he asserts that 'he did not believe in achieving ends by such violent means'. He also adds that 'he felt that the Ananda Marga members were not the sort of people who were capable of such an act'. Indeed he later tells the ASIO agents that 'he used to laugh about suppositions that the Ananda Marga could carry out bombings and was sure that it would have been a hopeless bungle had they tried'.

The violence in New Zealand in which five Margiis are caught changes his mind. He realises that the bulk of the membership has little idea about the inner workings of the elite. He believes that it can function in such a clandestine manner because it operates behind the respectable façade of a religious charity. Abhiik Kumar is the absolute leader in Australia and:

> ... a violent man by nature. KUMARA [sic] is the guiding genius ... He is an American who seems to have no difficulty when travelling to or from Australia or elsewhere ... [Kumara is] the 'king pin' of the Ananda Marga in Australia and a very clever person. He has a black beard and always wears an orange turban ...The hierarchy of the Ananda Marga exists in name only and is nothing but a front for the organisation which functions solely in accordance with the wishes and orders of KUMARA. However, there is a President of Ananda Marga for Australia and other nominal

members of the leadership, *but these are appointed and dismissed by Kumara at will.* The president is known as 'Govinda' [Timothy Anderson] and is resident in Sydney.

Subject [mentions] he has found KUMARA capable of incredible mind reading and possessed of a highly developed sense of intuition.

According to information obtained from Kumara himself ... Australia has been selected as a base from which Ananda Marga operations can be mounted ... because of its lenient travel control procedures and tolerance of so called charitable organisations.[6]

This tolerance is clearly running short by the end of 1977. As the task force collates its findings, it incorporates an increasing number of reports about the violence targeting Indian nationals coming in from other countries. In August a number of Indian officials are physically attacked in the UK. In October three Margiis are arrested for an attack on Indian nationals in London and attempting to blow up the embassy. The same month in New York there is an attempt to fire-bomb the Air India offices. November brings an explosion in the Indian Embassy in Katmandu and an explosive device thrown at the Indian ambassador's residence in Copenhagen. The New York City Police Department Intelligence Division sends further reports of an attempt to stab an Air India employee in Los Angeles, and the stabbing of an embassy official (Silla Koteswar, 25) in Washington DC. The NYC police report states:

> In each of the above incidents, letters have been sent to Indian officials by a group calling themselves the Universal Proutist Revolutionary Federation (UPRF). Each letter demands the immediate release of their leader, PR Sarkar, and threatens violence if this is not accomplished.
>
> Although the Ananda Marga Yoga Society vehemently denies any association with the UPRF, the Indian officials feel the UPRF is in fact the Anand Marg [sic], as both desire the release of PR Sarkar. More terrorist incidents by this group are expected, both here and abroad.[7]

While the attacks are familiar, it's the astonishing consistency of the denials that begins to sow doubts about the Ananda Marga. It's hard to imagine how a government agency, such as the Indian CBI or the KGB could be so effortlessly adept at coordinating these acts of violence across continents. It's also hard to figure out how it would work logistically. According to the Margiis, an Indian government agent (or KGB agent?) would be operational in (travel to?) a foreign country (the USA, the UK, Sweden, Norway, Australia, etc.)

and then stab, attack, fire-bomb an Indian national — then hurry home (go underground?) to (Russia? India?) at the same time writing up and carefully sending off a letter claiming the violence in the name of the Universal Proutist Revolutionary Federation — all to discredit the Ananda Marga. Whew! Remember this is the Indian Government undertaking an extraordinary clandestine global campaign of terror against its own citizens. It's a lot of time, money and effort, not to mention the potentially catastrophic diplomatic consequences if caught, to devote to ensuring an ex–civil servant heading a minor religious sect stays in jail. Hard to explain, too, are the incidents such as those in London or Australia where identified Margii members are actually caught in the act.

ASIO continues to collect information from former Margiis, who add to a picture of zealotry. One ex–sect member recounts that 'Abhiik told him in conversation that the end justifies the means. If aims cannot be achieved by peaceful means, then there was no alternative but to use violence. In short, Abhiik considered violence as a means to an end and this apparently alarmed [redacted] and hastened his exit.'[8]

The seriousness of the threat the Australian Government is feeling is summed up in the secret report compiled for federal Cabinet late in 1977, only a few months before CHOGRM. The report, declassified in 2009, is the findings of the task force, made up of representatives of the departments of Administrative Affairs, Prime Minister and Cabinet, Foreign Affairs, Education, Immigration and Ethnic Affairs and the Attorney-General, as well as ASIO and the Commonwealth Police — along with responses from state premiers. The report's main purpose is to 'seek Cabinet endorsement to certain measures to restrict and endeavour to halt the acts and threats of violence … against Indian nationals in Australia'.[9]

The members of the task force are clearly disturbed by what has occurred over the last five months. Adding to their concern is that:

> … it has recently been reliably reported from ASIO that Ananda Marga intends to hold a conference from 23rd to 29th January, 1978, at the Seventh Day Adventist Youth Camp at Crosslands [New South Wales] to which New Zealand and other overseas visitors are expected.[10]

The task force goes on to assert:

> … while ASIO and the Police are making every endeavour to ascertain details of the proposed conference, the interdepartmental task force has given urgent further consideration to action to restrict and endeavour to halt activities by Ananda Marga. This has been done in light of

the knowledge that the Indian Prime Minister is expected to visit Australia in February next, 1978.[11]

Their opinion is that 'Proutist organisations are integrated with Ananda Marga, both in relation to their common hierarchy and the advocacy of violent means as evinced by some of their publications'.[12] The suspicion is that those who are perpetuating the violence in the name of UPRF are in fact members of Prout operating as a splinter group within Ananda Marga. It is also possible that the bulk of the Ananda Marga membership is unaware of the existence of this splinter group.

What the task force proposes to do seems perplexing at first and rather underwhelming. In order to be 'consistent in achieving effective governmental action as action by the Immigration and Education authorities, there is a need to terminate formal governmental recognition of Ananda Marga as a recognised denomination for the purposes of the *Marriage Act*'.

The immediate effect of this will be the automatic deregistration of the four existing Margii marriage celebrants as 'ministers of religion'. It becomes clear that this a highly provocative act. Ananda Marga at that time is not registered as a charity and its only formal recognition as a religion is the licensing of its marriage celebrants. Of the four who are to be deregistered as ministers of religion, only one is named:

Brahmacarii Abhiik Kumara (Jason Alexander, formerly known as John Hoffman) a former US citizen, naturalised Australian in March 1977, an Ananda Marga leader (Spiritual Director for Australasia).[13]

The task force members acknowledge that they:

> ... have taken into account the possibility that this governmental action may provoke the Ananda Marga or elements within it to attempt to mount a legal challenge ... and possibly go so far as further acts of violence against Indian government representatives in Australia.[14]

They also recommend that a suspension of all new requests for government support or recognition of Ananda Marga be continued until 31 March 1978 and that 'in view of the current assessment of the nature of Ananda Marga and in view of the information that they are planning to hold a conference in Sydney from 23 to 29 January next, which will be shortly before a Commonwealth Heads of Government conference in Sydney, the Task Force was of the view' to continue the ban authorising or permitting 'entry to Australia of foreign members of Ananda Marga or foreign persons actively involved with it'.[15]

While these recommendations may seem draconian, there's a clear sense in the report that they are born out of frustration and a genuine fear of what some elements of this sect may be capable of. Despite vast increases in police protection for Indian officials in Australia, including the visiting Indian cricket team, the report admits that while this is 'an essential protective action by the government [that] needs to be continued', it 'does not in itself halt the continuing threat of the violent element within Ananda Marga to attack Indian establishments in Australia'.[16]

There is recognition, too, of the significant legal and human rights problems for the government should they decide to introduce legislation to ban the organisation outright, particularly when that organisation claims to be religious and carries out social welfare work. It is, however, something they are inclined to consider should the pattern of violence continue. In the meantime:

> ASIO and the police forces (Commonwealth,
> State and Territorial) are continuing, as vigorously
> as possible, their enquiries into Ananda Marga
> and, in particular, the violent element and
> the existence and nature of a possible Proutist
> organisation within Ananda Marga.[17]

Another recommendation is that officers from the Administrative Services Department and officers from the Department of Education have talks with the leaders of the Ananda Marga (they note that the public relations officer Tim Anderson has sought this) 'to discuss with them the problem of the consistent pattern of violence or threats of violence associated with members of the Ananda Marga and the apparent link between a possible UPRF and Ananda Marga'.[18]

They want to put to them:

(i) The fact that their members have been involved in a consistent world pattern of violence and threats of violence and inviting them to explain how their organisation proposes to control this and to halt further acts and threats of violence; and

(ii) In light of this fact, how would [they] sustain continuance of applications for education grants and concessions.[19]

It's a neat tactic — predicated on the idea that most of the Margii membership do not condone, and indeed are not aware of, the violent acts of the inner cell of Proutists, and they will have more clout in reining them in than outside forces — particularly if they are concerned that financial assistance, for example supporting the schools their kids go to, is taken away.

As Christmas of 1977 approaches, and with

CHOGRM seven weeks away, the summation of the task force is this:

> Either the talks will achieve the cooperation of the leaders to curtail the violence of their members or, if violence continues, the government will be in a position to act more strongly against the organisation.[20]

Of course this is all absolutely hush-hush, but the one decision that does become public knowledge is the banning of foreign members of the sect from entering Australia until after CHOGRM. The task force had been correct to consider the human rights implications of adopting a hard line with the Margiis. The reaction to this compromise decision, falling far short of banning the sect outright, is condemned in an editorial in the *Sydney Morning Herald*:

> It is hard to imagine a worse case of guilt by association. Where will it end? What other members of a religious sect, or a political party — or those who may be 'involved' with them, whatever that means — are going to fall foul of our immigration authorities? Are hundreds of transcendental meditators, avowedly non-violent, going to have their movements circumscribed just because a handful of meditators are alleged

to have resorted to violence? Indian diplomats and businesses in Australia deserve sympathy, of course, for the violence they have suffered; but Australia should be careful not to give the appearance of swatting a fly with a sledge hammer. It should also make absolutely certain that it is aiming at the right target.[21]

So, what Norm wants to know is what happened next. Were talks held? Was there more violence? The answer to both is no.

It all goes quiet

Weirdly, almost by magic, the moment the top secret task force report is being compiled in late November 1977, all the violence stops. Stops not just in Australia, but everywhere else in the world. Up to that point, since late July 1977, when Sarkar's first appeal was unsuccessful, to late November, there have been acts of violence or threats of violence either by Margiis or in their name in a dozen countries every two or three days — sometimes every day.

Then abruptly, between 28 November 1977[1] and 7 February 1978, when an even greater wave of violence is unleashed, there is no recorded act of violence or threat of violence towards an Indian national anywhere in the world. The only thing to change in this 10-week window is that Sarkar's second appeal is denied on 2 February 1978.

So what were the authorities doing during those

two months? Doing what spies and secret police do best: spying.

December 1977 and January 1978 see the two agencies charged with leading the surveillance on the sect — ASIO and New South Wales Special Branch — in covert operations heaven. There are wire-taps on Ananda Marga headquarters in every state. There are listening devices planted in their meeting places as well as in meditation and yoga centres. Cars are stationed outside gatherings, camps and training grounds and careful notes taken of each member's comings and goings. While there is information collected from Ananda Marga in Melbourne, Adelaide, Canberra and Perth, Sydney is the epicentre. ASIO regards it as 'the focal point of Ananda Marga activity in Australia and also the location of most Margiis suspected of being capable of being involved in politically motivated violence'.[2]

Norm Sheather and the Hilton task force pore over the surveillance material ASIO and Special Branch gathered in the months leading up to the bombing. It's hyper-detailed, consisting of members' names, bank accounts, property holdings, photographs and transcripts of wire-taps. There are elaborate lists of dates and times, of members' movements at a variety of Margii activities throughout January. All this material seems to indicate that something is going on. Just what that something may be is more difficult to ascertain.

While they are carefully monitoring the imminent camp to be held at the Seventh Day Adventists' Crosslands Youth and Convention Centre at Galston from 23 to 29 January, Special Branch gets a tip-off about another camp to be held earlier in January.

> Ananda Marga Inquiry — information received from reliable source concerning Paul Maurice O'Callaghan and an unknown female attending a VSS training camp at Anandapalli.

This camp, to be held on the sect's property in Queensland, is to run from 9 to 16 January. The report goes on to confidently assert that:

> … the initials VSS represent Volunteer Social Service, however information received from another reliable source on an earlier date (running sheets submitted) reveal that this is in fact a Para-Military Wing.[3]

While this seems deeply intriguing — and possibly unsubstantiated — nothing comes of the tip-off.

The material relating to the surveillance of the late January conference is much more thorough and far less speculative. It is also difficult to analyse. As Norm and the team wade through the reams of surveillance notes, it's hard to decipher whether the evidence indicates signs of a terrorist training camp or the dull machinations of a group of rigid if somewhat paranoid religious devotees. Among the many items is a meticulously typed series of rosters for the weekly kitchen duties (breakfast, lunch and dinner) for the duration of the camp.[4] Next is a 'Prout Publications Price List'. While this list includes potentially suspicious titles, such as '*Prout's Revolutionary Strategy* $1' and '*Universalism — A Revolutionary Force* 75c', they sit next to the benign '*The Way of Peace* $2'.[5]

Of more interest are the notes relating to the security procedures the Ananda Marga deploy during the Crosslands camp. Crosslands is the perfect site for the security conscious. It sits in a corner of the Berowra Valley at Galston, just north of Sydney. Two of its three sides are bordered by water. The third side — the hypotenuse — is covered in dense bush with one main entrance. There is a bush track that allows access to the bush chapel (Bottom Gate). It is also protected by God. Owned by the Seventh Day Adventists, it is exclusively offered for rent to groups who wish to use it as a spiritual retreat.

The first document, No. 9 in the dossier, is a list of those Ananda Marga members allocated to guard duty at the two gates to the camp. There is a guard for each of the gates, rotated each hour on a 24-hour cycle. For example:

A.M Bottom Gate
12-1 MARILEV
1-2 VIVEK
2-3 BHARAT
3-4 JAMAD
4-5 MOHAN

And so on.[6] Thus on any day, guard duty involves 24 different sect members. The accompanying document, 'a copy of a typed article issued by VSS Chief secretary, concerning POINTS FOR SENTRY', runs over three pages and lays out detailed instructions for ensuring the security of the camp.

> When a car comes, walk out 9 in[ches] in front
> of it and see who they are. If Margiis allow them
> to enter. If state police doing their regular run
> (looking for stolen cars), let them through but
> the sentry at the top notify the one at the bottom
> gate … if they are commonwealth police, <u>don't</u>
> let them in unless they have a warrant. If they
> are tourists etc, politely tell them it is a closed
> retreat and tell them to turn back. — If any
> police — state or Commonwealth — come with
> a warrant, ask to see it and don't let them enter
> until you have a) taken the names and addresses
> of the policemen and b) what the warrant is
> for. You then let them in and if you are at the

It all goes quiet

top gate, notify the bottom sentry … if you have been told that they have a warrant also get Narada or Dada … if the top sentry calls down to say that unwanted persons forced their way through and are on the way down then the bottom sentry must lock the gate and taking the key out, notify Narada or Dada … always speak politely to howeveer [sic] you come in contact with on sentry, but be strong and firm in your stand if demanding a warrant or not letting them through. Don't be bluffed! + Remember vigilance is the price of liberty, always remain alert and serious about your work, don't take it lightly and space out.[7]

Is this evidence that the Margiis have something to hide? Like a plot to blow up the Hilton as the Indian Prime Minister arrives on the eve of CHOGRM? Or does it mean absolutely nothing — just a bunch of young believers fed up with police harassment and asserting their civil rights?

What about document No. 17? 'A receipt from Wormald International Electronics, dated 11.1.78 payable to DAMBIEC, of 14 Binning Street Erskineville 2043, in the amount of $80.00 payable by cheque No. 13956'.[8] Parts for a timer for a bomb? Or a sophisticated baby monitor?

Like so many bits of the information they collect,

most of it is irritatingly ambiguous, like a Necker cube — one second a solid object, the next it flips and presents itself just as convincingly in reverse. Norm notes the names on the bottom of the dossier of documents collated over the duration of the Crosslands camp — Special Branch detectives Krawczyk and Henderson. He remembers their names from their work in tracking the wave of violence directed at Indian nationals for the task force. One can sense how deeply committed to the case they are, how vigilant, and how they must long for that hard clear unequivocal piece of evidence to provide a reason to storm the gates and catch the Margiis in the act. The incredulous denials from the Margii spokespersons around the globe must have them fed up to the back teeth. Norm has to remind himself that all this intense focus, all the resources expended over the last few months, predates the bombing at the Hilton. Yet as he looks through these pages of notes he finds nothing.

The problem with all this material acquired through technical coverage is that it lacks a 'human source', as ASIO puts it, to interpret it.[9]

ASIO starts to gather informants in late November, around the time the 1977 wave of violence is peaking. They are deliberately vague on the details they give to Norm and the Hilton task force. Yes, they have agents inside the Ananda Marga. No, the police can't know their names.

These agents are off limits to Norm. They have only been active for a few months and their coverage has been limited. None of them had any forewarning about the Hilton bombing. It's critical at this stage that they don't do anything to jeopardise their cover that might yield rich intelligence in the future.

The existence of these shadowy agents, sex unknown, some of whom, Norm realises, may already have been interviewed by his task force in the round-up of suspects after the bombing, must unnerve even the most unflappable of policemen. Even ASIO admits in its training manual that it 'faces obvious difficulties in using human sources to monitor violent organisations'. Obvious difficulties — such as where an undercover agent draws the line when acts of physical violence are being planned.

> On the one hand, an ASIO source operating within a violent organisation has to maintain cover, and this will involve at least some commitment by word or deed to the objectives of the target organisation. Also, there is the possibility that, if the agent refuses to become involved in planning or executing acts of violence, others will be approached, and ASIO will lose both vital intelligence and the opportunity to exert some influence over events. On the other hand ASIO must not allow its agents to become *agents provocateurs*.[10]

Of course it's only a difficult line if it is certain that the source is infiltrating a violent organisation, but the hard evidence for this is currently beyond ASIO's grasp. As yet these newly minted covert Margiis have only orbited on the margins of the sect. Those at the core of power — Kumar certainly, Kapil maybe, Anderson who knows? — have been members for years. Who exactly is a member of Ananda Marga or Prout or both is complicated. The religion is complicated and there is much to get one's head around.

The other problem, and this surely gives Norm disquiet, is that the day after the Hilton bombing Tim Anderson clearly and publicly states that the sect knows it has been infiltrated by ASIO agents. This hardly provides much confidence in the intelligence these ASIO operatives would be able to gather at this stage. The danger too is that often the information agents collect is hearsay, and police know how useless this is in attempting to obtain a conviction. This is where the volume of technical surveillance provided by Special Branch could prove invaluable should it uncover concrete evidence to be used by some future prosecutor.

In theory the human sources and technical sources should complement each other in any clandestine operation. So too should the work of the police and the secret service — the flow of information should be harmonious, organic and productive.

And so it seemed it was — right up until the moment the bomb ripped Alec Carter and William Favell apart on 13 February 1978.

As Norm is taken through the months of surveillance work, what is clear is that they all failed. Despite the task force, the top secret Cabinet reports, the covert agents, the extra protection, the vast security protocols surrounding the CHOGRM — the sheer manpower focused on preventing a terrorist act at the conference had been for nought.

Someone missed something. Someone put a bomb in the bin. While in the days directly after the bombing the shock keeps the blame-game to a minimum, the shame all the agencies feel must be palpable. Were they looking at the wrong targets? The wrong group? What do our friends Detectives Krawczyk, Helson and Henderson of New South Wales Special Branch feel that morning in the aftermath of the carnage, knowing that there was a warning call to their office minutes before the blast? True it came too late for anyone to have been saved, but the fact that the diligent Suzanne Jones put the caller through to Special Branch between 12.35 and 12.40 am and the phone rang and rang in that empty office must cut pretty close to the bone.

It's easy to make cartoon baddies or Inspector Plods of these men. But, like Norm, I have read their reports and seen the months and months they put in building an incredibly detailed portrait of the sect's operations in Australia. It's hard to view these Special Branch officers as anything but earnest, diligent and committed to the job. Possibly over-focused on detail, but the job of grasping the overview, the global perspective, is the role of those higher up the food chain — ASIO, the Department of Foreign Affairs, the Commonwealth Police. Does Special Branch blame them? Norm Sheather may or may not detect this whiff of bile early in his investigation, but it will seep out in days to come and like acid eat away at any semblance of agency cooperation, eventually destroying any chance to try the case. But this is still to come.

What Norm notes straightaway is what they all missed. Not so much the elephant in the room but the absence of it. Where in all this covert surveillance is Abhiik Kumar? Where is the man who is clearly regarded by all the agencies involved in the government task force in 1977 as the one, of all the sect members, to watch? Where is the man who made all those worrisome allusions to violence — the man of many names and many passports, the man who is the absolute spiritual leader of the Australasian Margiis, the one with the direct line to the imprisoned Sarkar, in whose cause all this violence is carried out?

It seems that for the last eight months or so no one is exactly sure, beyond 'travelling internationally'. He is not present in any of the Special Branch surveillance targeting Margii headquarters in Sydney, nor does he feature in any of the debriefings of ASIO's Margii operatives. Through December and January he is not in the country.

Then on Sunday 12 February he spectacularly reappears centre stage, in full kit with dark beard and turban. ASIO wire-taps a hissy fit he has with Tim Anderson, who tells him that the Ananda Marga protest against the Indian Prime Minister should take place at the Hilton Hotel's George Street entrance. Kumar shouts him down, he's joining the sect at the airport where they will present Desai with a petition advocating Sarkar's release. Tim ignores him and heads to the Hilton.[11] That day there are photographs of Kumar and fellow sect members taken by Special Branch which consist of a series of long-lensed snaps of Kumar, his tall willowy turban-topped frame bobbing above a group of Margiis milling at Kingsford Smith airport.[12]

While Kumar's reappearance is unexpected and flamboyant, it is also less than 12 hours before the bomb goes off. This would seem — if indeed the Ananda Marga is innocent of the crime — to be a spectacularly bad time to resume the reins of the sect. Of course if they (or Proutists) did plant the bomb, the timing is just about perfect. If you are orchestrating an international reign of terror against Indian nationals in order to free your god, it's not something that you're likely to miss.

And before that? Where was Kumar exactly? It astonishes Norm that no one has been tracking his movements. It is something he addresses immediately.

He tempers this with the knowledge that despite all the forensic surveillance of this sect over months and months, there is not a sliver of evidence to tie the Margiis to the bombing. Except for the possible sighting by a fellow taxi driver of Anderson parked in his taxi near the Hilton the Saturday night before the bomb went off.[13] He remains convinced that he needs to keep the minds of his task force investigators open to other possibilities until something sways him one way or the other.

This is not a pathway that will be adopted by those most professionally battered by the blast. Within days Special Branch officers will embark on a dizzyingly maverick and misguided quest. It will be the undoing of Sheather, his team, and the case.

It all goes quiet

'The blast that shook Australia'

On the third day of the Hilton task force's existence, Norm must feel close to success, or at the very least confident in his captaincy and the direction he has set with his crew. However, at sea nothing is certain.

In the case of the Hilton bombing, Norm Sheather's sea is the unruly and emotional reactions that the blast has set off in the pentagram of institutions and organisations that surround the investigation. These five are the government, the press, ASIO, Special Branch, and the Hilton task force itself with its 58 detectives. A fatal bombing at an international political gathering has set forces in motion that, in turn, set off others; all manner of old wounds and agendas flare up. People can respond very badly or foolishly when they are terrorised.

For a moment let's leave Norm Sheather and the Hilton detectives hunting down the movements of Abhiik Kumar over the last eight or so months, interrogating suspects and waiting for Interpol requests for terrorists' MOs to come in. Let's see what's going on in the public arena. Let's test the public mood.

To be frank, three days post-bombing the mood is far from good. For the first 36 hours the Australian people reel in shock. The *Sydney Morning Herald*'s editorial sums up the public horror:

> Australia is not entirely a stranger to isolated acts of terrorism but there was an ugly new dimension to the Sydney bomb outrage. This kind of reckless political violence, careless of what innocent victims suffer, is a pattern familiar to many countries but from which Australia had hitherto been almost free.[1]

Throughout the country the bombing is regarded as a game changer — a moment the nation is thrust violently into the global arena of terrorism. Within days the government is copping criticism for its failure to protect its citizens. First, of course, there is a chorus of attacks about the inadequacy of the security for CHOGRM and the hotel. Then, attacked with equal vehemence, is Fraser's decision to call in the Army to provide security for the international guests in the following days. Everything the federal and state governments do in the days following the blast is regarded as misguided, kneejerk or corrupt by someone in the media. The conservative elements in the Australian press accuse the South Australian and New South Wales premiers of undermining the power of Special Branch in South Australia and ASIO in New South Wales because they have been investigating allegations that both agencies were keeping 'dirt files' on private individuals.[2] When New South Wales Premier Neville Wran drops the inquiry into ASIO in the immediate wake of the bombing, the more liberal elements of the press are critical. This inquiry, about events in the early 1970s concerning ASIO and a Liberal party politician, Peter Coleman, has nothing to do with New South Wales Special Branch and is not an attempt to shut ASIO down. Nevertheless, from this point onward arguments will be made that dropping the inquiry is proof that ASIO and New South Wales Special Branch planted the bombs themselves.[3]

There are a few things to remember about the late 1970s in Australia. The first is that people on the left hated Prime Minister Malcolm Fraser with a passion that I doubt has been matched before or since. I mean hated him like spurned lovers, or like betrayed and vengeful Shakespearean characters. Think Medea. Think Macbeth. Big hate. Fraser was regarded as the illegitimate ruler who had snatched power from the forward-thinking Labor leader Gough Whitlam in 1975 in the most unsportsmanlike, underhanded and dastardly manner. The Dismissal sat fresh, raw and oozing in the minds of the left. My mother was one of the true believers who was so enraged that night of 11 November 1975 that she left my elder brother and me without a babysitter so she could attend a hastily organised protest at the Royal Motor Yacht Club in Newport where Fraser's equally loathed henchman, Governor-General John Kerr, was heading for dinner.

Even a little over two years later, in February 1978, these true believers were having no difficulty maintaining their rage.

The other thing to remember is that papers such as *Nation Review* and the *National Times* were made up of bright, intelligent new voices. They weren't just a bunch of scruffy ratbags — they were well-educated, thoughtful and credible. Emerging in the early 1970s these journalists instigated dozens of explosive investigations revealing corruption in big business, among politicians and within the police. The 'first comprehensive account of the Hilton Hotel bombing' in the now legendary *National Times* was written by Paul Kelly, David Leitch, Anne Summers, Andrew Clark, David Hickie and Evan Whitton.[4] The special report titled 'The Blast that Shook Australia' is convincing and disturbing:

> A threat psychology, provoked by a tragic bomb attack still totally unexplained, is abroad again in Australia. For the first time in our peacetime history military forces were deployed last week to support the civil authorities. This was the real precedent and lasting legacy of Malcolm Fraser's initiative in calling together Commonwealth region leaders (CHOGRM) at Sydney's Hilton Hotel and at Bowral.[5]

For this new breed of journalist it is not the loss of innocence that is of concern but '[t]he psychological effect of the bombing' on the government and the population; the response to the crisis 'has transformed the meaning of security protection for VIPs in Australia'.

For the journalists this has generated two troublesome tendencies since the Monday blast:

1. The way the bomb blast transformed the political climate in favour of strong security measures advocated by the Prime Minister and against the softer 'civil liberties' line espoused by Labor premiers Wran and Dunstan; and
2. How swiftly the legal and constitutional processes were effected to make the entire military apparatus available to the government to quell domestic disturbance.

The report is full of detail and analysis that on a minute level seems very well considered, but on another level, through a headline like 'Bombing a Boost for ASIO',[6] it helps create the crucible that will forge the conspiracy that the secret and not-so-secret services — ASIO, Special Branch, the military and potentially Fraser himself — colluded and planted the bomb so they could maintain and extend their power.

The other aspect of this report is that the authorities are characterised as buffoons, which undermines the idea that 'they' hatched a sleek, sophisticated and malevolent plan to place the bomb themselves. The authors assert there was:

> This uncertainty, arising from the total lack of clues to who placed the Hilton bomb, combined with official confusion and military inexperience, gave the week-long security measures a continuing note of farce. Just as it was possible for unauthorised visitors to walk into the Hilton's security areas, so it would have been equally possible for a determined assassin to do his job at Bowral despite the army.[7]

Not that the mainstream press is much kinder to Fraser — they also see the Army call-out as absurd and misjudged: 'In the over-reactions at Bowral we looked faintly ridiculous — babes in the woods.'[8] Overlaying this disapproval are the unambiguous images of three little girls — Christine and Susan Carter, aged seven and nine, and Cassandra Favell, seven[9] — at their respective fathers' funerals on 17 February, and the stark headlines, five days later, reporting that young Constable Paul Burmistriw had died from the injuries he received in the blast.

In a state of shock and collective pain in the days after the bombing, the public demands swift action, which is counter to the slow gathering of evidence by investigating police. The frustration is palpable in the papers, which complain loudly and regularly with headlines such as '"Ring us" plea to bomb warning man'[10] and 'Police frustrated in bomb investigations'[11] and accompanying articles that depict the Hilton task force as being at the mercy of the public, who either fail to give them leads or waste valuable police time by making bomb hoax calls.

Fraser does what anyone else in his position would do when harassed from all quarters — he decides to hold an inquiry. The inquiry, announced 12 days after the bombing, is to be expensive and extensive and helmed by the best expert one can get. In the time-honoured Aussie tradition of getting someone from overseas — preferably white and male and from the UK — to come over and sort us out, Fraser appoints Sir Robert Marks, former head of Scotland Yard, to come and take names and find someone to blame.[12] At the very least, it takes the heat off the government.

Thursday 16 February 1978

Meanwhile, Norm and the Hilton task force, buffeted by the sea of government, public and media reactions, also respond to different internal tides and unexpected waves. Three days in and Norm is taking the long view. Different lines of investigation begin to solidify into three broad areas. First, those detectives pursuing rigorously what can best be called the usual suspects. Second, those detectives responding to evidence gathered from the blast, including the evidence contained in hundreds of witness statements and information from the public, and third, the detectives getting to the bottom of the cluster of international violent acts surrounding the Hilton bombing allegedly carried out by the Ananda Marga.

While Norm is briefed on the course of all three, it is the latter that he steers most directly.

For those who have long believed that the Ananda Marga were singularly targeted, hounded, persecuted and stitched up, it may be surprising how thoroughly the police pursued other lines of inquiry. While there is a potent and compelling sense in the media that the Hilton bombing is a defining historical moment in which Australia is thrust into the horrors of international terrorism, it is also true that there was a fairly long-ish and diverse list of individuals and groups who could have been responsible. A wonderfully subtitled article 'Cowardly killer that knows no innocents: Australia in Bomb Club', published the weekend after the bombing, states brightly, 'Security police say there are several hundred people in Sydney alone who could have conceivably been involved in bombing incidents.'[1] This includes 'Certain members of our fledgling and crackpot National Socialist (Nazi) movements' or 'the anarchro-syndacalists [sic] and others on the far Left'. There were also the Yugoslav and Croat communities in Australia who 'brought their native animosities here' and have been attempting to blow each other up for years. A number of these community members were interrogated and checked for alibis. Slavko Fuskic is investigated because of his vocal attacks on Fraser and the Liberal government, and because he is an electrical fitter by trade.[2]

Another course of inquiry followed with vigour is a theory that the Malaysian Liberation Front operating in Australia was targeting Singapore's prime minister at CHOGRM. In response to an inquiry about a Singaporean student who arrived in Australia on 30 January 1978, the Singaporean intelligence service sent back an urgent telex warning that Ng Hiok Ngee was a member of a Marxist group plotting with Euro-communists to exert pressure on the Singaporean government 'to release hardcore communist detainees to rebuild the Communist United Front in Singapore'.[3] He is also accused of sending money to the Malayan National Liberation Army (MNLA) 'who are Communist Terrorists operating in the Malaysian jungle, engaged in insurgency to overthrow the elected governments of Malaysia and Singapore'. The tone of the telex from Singapore strongly suggests that Ngee is good for the Hilton bombing and should be locked up, although the most he is accused of is being a member of an illegal political party. Two days later he is hauled in and interrogated by the task force. His defence, that he is in Australia purely to visit his sister, is backed up by strong corroboration from the sister and her husband.[4]

Lebanese-born Baha Bayeh presents as a strong suspect in so far as he has convictions for assault and related offences and, exactly one year and one month before the Hilton bombing, 'was arrested at Waverley on the 13.1.77 by Detective Sergeant Hetherington for the offence of maliciously plac[ing a] bombing device to destroy a building'.[5] After investigation, he too is eliminated from the list.

What the Hilton task force is looking for is those who would have the most to gain from an act of terrorism. As Mr William Clifford of the Australian Institute of Criminology points out, 'The sad thing about terrorism is that it works ... Bombings are usually not at all personal. They are used to attract attention to particular causes or to destabilise the political climate.'[6] The *Herald*, quoting Clifford, expands on this, arguing that the 'callousness of bomb attacks by movements which seek mass support is difficult to explain, except on the theory that governments are finally blamed for the failure to create safe, stable societies'.

Clifford's take on where the blame lies differs from every other publicly reported opinion:

> This week ... there was room for improvement in the national coordination between Australia's police and security forces ... But the real need, the Criminology Institute Director believes, is not for more police and more Special Branch surveillance — a topic quickly taken up by conservatives in the wake of the bomb attack. 'What is really needed in Australia,' Mr Clifford is reported as saying, 'is greater cooperation between

the public and the police. People should be much more security-conscious and aware of the dangers in their cities ... Disregarding the police performance, a number of aspects of the Hilton bombing indicated that people generally were just not alert to the risk.'

If Clifford is correct, the 'people' are certainly attempting to make up for their failings in the days following the bombing. The task force is besieged by information from the public and it is the responsibility of a section of detectives to pursue this information, whatever it may be. In the files is a long and detailed statement about a man behaving suspiciously around the Atomic Energy Commission,[7] another relates the sighting of an old noisy car crossing the Harbour Bridge with three male occupants and Western Australian licence plates.[8] It's all too easy in hindsight to regard these as petty and inconsequential, but big crimes are often solved with exactly these kinds of random sources of information. The Yorkshire Ripper was caught through a vehicle registration check. The Hilton task force has to receive information with open arms. They set up a desk inside the Hilton lobby manned by Special Branch officers for the sole purpose of providing an easy portal for the public to pour forth their tips, sightings and theories.

So when Richard Seary walks through the smashed exterior of the Hilton Hotel on the afternoon

Thursday 16 February 1978

of Thursday 16 February and comes up to the desk with a story to tell, Special Branch Detective Sergeant Ireland listens and transcribes it.

Did the Hare Krishnas do it?

What Seary discloses to Detective Sergeant Ireland has enough merit to start moving him up the chain of command. He is asked to repeat his allegations on 22 February 1978 — this time to two other Special Branch officers, Detective Senior Constables Inkster and Hardy.

Richard Seary will become one of the most notorious witnesses in Australian criminal history thanks to his involvement in various court cases and inquiries surrounding the Hilton bombing, including the official inquest in 1982. Because of this, it is fascinating to observe his entrance onto the stage; to see not how he was viewed in retrospect, once the spotlight glared down on him, but how he sat among all the other hubbub going on at the time.

In the future much will be made of the fact that immediately before he fronts the police desk three days after the blast, Seary had been to see the first *Star Wars* at the Hoyts cinema complex further down George Street. The implication being, I suppose, that he was all hopped up on Goodies and Baddies and living in a complete fantasy world. In reality there can't have been that many people in Sydney who hadn't seen *Star Wars* at this point.

More pertinent is the potential connection between the timing of his statement to the police and the announcement of the astronomical reward that same morning. I would imagine that anyone who believed they had even a snippet of information about the Hilton bombing would have been lured out when this bait was dangled.

Yet another accusation to be made against Seary is that the allegations he makes to the police that day are full of bizarre and colourful oddities. However, reading over it now, Seary's statement comes across as rather boring and long-winded, as if from an over-earnest but upstanding member of the public.

He introduces himself thus: 'I am a drug counsellor at the Wayside Chapel at Kings Cross and I have been engaged in this work for the past 14 months.'[1] He goes on to relate a visit he made to a Hare Krishna gathering at Belmore Park in Sydney on 3 February 1978. The Hare Krishnas are a religious sect popular among Westerners, founded in 1966 by an Indian swami based in New York City. Seary told the police he had been invited to the gathering of four or five thousand people because he was a former member of the sect, and he was interested in what was going on. There he sees an old friend called David. They chat and then David leaves. After this, a stranger, a Krishna called Bala Deva, approaches him. Deva knows Seary's former sect name, 'Pandu', and strikes up a conversation. He knows that Seary had been an opal miner at Lightning Ridge and wants to know all the ins and outs of what kinds of explosives he used, how you obtained them, and whether they were safe to handle. Seary reports all this with the monotony of a head prefect dobbing on a wayward student.

> He said, 'You're mining, aren't you.' I said, 'Not any more. I haven't mined for about a year.' He said, 'What sort of mining?' I said, 'Opal mining.' He said, 'Do you use explosives?' I said, 'Yes.' He said, 'What sort?' I said, 'Nitropril or gelignite.' He said, 'What's nitropril?' I said, 'It's a nitre [sic] glycerine solution suspended in a neutral base which gives it the appearance of small gray pebbles.' He said, 'How does it work?'[2]

And so on and so on. The Krishna Deva does not say he is intending to buy or use explosives of any kind.

Did the Hare Krishnas do it?

He does not say he is intending to blow anything up — let alone CHOGRM or the Hilton. This is the worst that Seary says of Deva: 'I would recognise him again if I saw him. I would say that this person I was talking to was very interested in explosives and mining but he obviously didn't know anything about it.'

What piques the interest of the Special Branch officers is how Seary contextualises this conversation with Deva. He tells the police that when he had been a member of the Hare Krishnas he had 'heard talk of a radical member of the sect' advocating a plot to bomb the Homebush Bay meatworks. There was mention of a similar plan in New Zealand in which two members had died while building a bomb to be planted in a meat-packing factory. He says that he had eventually left the sect in Brisbane after becoming disenchanted with the leadership. This leadership tended towards violence, directed at the more peaceful members, particularly on the part of some of the 'more radical' members, mainly the Americans, many of whom were Vietnam veterans …

Seary rounds all this off by stating that he believes that some members of the Hare Krishnas were capable of the Hilton bombing. He offers to provide information to Special Branch if they want some insights into the organisation. Furthermore, he claims that some senior members of the sect who had been at Belmore Park had come from overseas and were in Sydney several days before the Hilton bombing and left two or three days after it ... The only possible motive he can provide for Hare Krishna involvement in the bombing is that it would have been directed against the Prime Minister of Singapore, 'as a number of sect members had been imprisoned in that country'.[3]

As vague, if overly detailed, as Seary's statement is in its allegations, it does have enough references to explosives and suggestions that this Deva could be a potential member of the new 'Bomb Club' to warrant attention.

Seary's assertions are typed up in the running sheets. Next they are considered by long-suffering Hilton task force member Detective Sergeant Bruce Jackson, whose job it is to sift through the mountain of information received and identify 'which matters ... called for further investigation'. Such information could include rants from a certain Mrs A, who thinks her 'Euro-Indian neighbours' whom 'I do not know [and] do not wish to'[4] are putting 'shocking' literature in her letterbox, to the delusional confessions of the mentally ill. Jackson selects Seary's statement for review and it is sent to Norm Sheather for consideration.

As will be said in one of the many official inquiries years later, 'It is evident that the members of the Hilton bomb squad were unimpressed with the information.'[5] Norm's immediate reaction is to dismiss the tale outright. There has never been a whiff of violence, alleged or otherwise, associated with the Hare Krishnas in Australia, which for Sheather makes them unlikely suspects.

As an exhaustive inquiry seven years later put it:

> Detective Inspector Sheather was satisfied that the description given by Seary of Bala Deva as a man '25 to 26 years old, 170 centimetres tall, slim to medium build, large nose, pimply face, looks slightly Jewish, mousy brown hair which possibly was a wig' was too uncertain, and that there was no suggestion in the police files, or within police experience, of any involvement of the Hare Krishna in terrorist activity. As a consequence the allegations were not pursued.[6]

And that is that. I imagine Norm simply put Richard Seary from his mind and did not expect he would ever encounter him again. If someone had told Norm that in less than four weeks this man would actually be working for the police force on the Hilton bombing investigation without his knowledge or approval, he may have simply retired early or demanded a transfer — anything to avoid the horrors he will be plunged into once he and his task force go over the falls with Seary.

But right now, the investigation is still fresh and Norm is otherwise absorbed. He is drawn away from the chaotic rapids of the intelligence coming in from crazies and eager beavers and moves towards the steady, heady stream of compelling intelligence pulling him back towards certain members of the Ananda Marga.

Did the Hare Krishnas do it?

The Bangkok Three

I imagine that there will be a certain point in the future when the past can no longer be researched physically. That time when things are simply collated in digital formats and live in the ether like fairies. When everything is stored somewhere, undeciphered and unedited, in vast underground storehouses in Utah or the like. There won't be things that sit in boxes for years unattended and unloved waiting to be discovered. Historians or researchers of the future perhaps won't be able to feel the rush of undoing the linen ties that enclose a stack of primary sources that suddenly spring open yielding pages that you can leaf through with your lint-free gloves. Part of the whole experience is the time it takes to discriminate and decide which page is significant, which you will take notes on, which will be set aside.

It's much the same way Norm has to function

each time the indefatigable detectives on his task force present the daily intelligence on the Hilton bombing to their boss. He is understandably alert to any mention of the Ananda Marga, given what he has learnt about their alleged violence in 1977 and given the coalescence of violent acts internationally surrounding the 13 February bombing in Sydney. So when a neat hand-written letter from a Ms or Mr AB pointing to a member of the sect as being good for the bombing is sent up the line to Norm, he does not downplay it as he did the Hare Krishna scenario sketched out by Richard Seary.

The letter is written entirely in capital letters.[1]

DEAR SIR,

AS YOU WILL APPRECIATE I HAVE NO WISH TO BECOME INVOLVED BUT FIGURE YOU OUGHT TO KNOW

THE PERSON YOU ARE LOOKING FOR WHO MADE THE BOMB AND KNOWS WHY IT WAS PLANTED AT THE HILTON HOTEL IN SYDNEY IS A GUY ANSWERING THE NAME JACK–MELEE–BEERE. I DO NOT KNOW IF HE TOOK IT DOWN TO SYDNEY. HE IS A SILENT MEMBER OF THE ANANDA MARGA SECT AND HAS A

NUMBER OF MISSIONS TO ACCOMPLISH BEFORE RETURNING.

The helpful AB states that 'I HAVE SEEN HIM MAKING EXPERIMENTAL BOMBS FOR PARTICULAR MISSIONS', that 'JACK IS AN ELECTRICIAN BY TRADE' and that if they need more information about plans for further attacks 'MAYBE HIS WIFE CAN HELP AS I KNOW SHE LIVES IN FEAR'.

AB signs off with:

> I WISH YOU LUCK IN STAMPING OUT THE PROPOSED ATTACKS, DEPORT HIM, FOR THEY WILL SEND SOMEONE ELSE AND WE WILL HAVE MORE INFORMATION AS WE ARE NOW CLOSER TO THE TOP.
> PERSONAL COLUMN FOR FURTHER INFORMATION IF YOU REQUIRE IT AND WE WILL REPLY. GOOD LUCK.

I really feel for policemen involved in major criminal investigations when I read things like this. Why the cloak and dagger? If you know something, why not just front up with the evidence? Make a statement? Be prepared to stand up in court? Their hearts must sink. Is it credible? What text should they place in the personal columns? 'Seeking AB who blew my mind on 16 Feb. I'd love to find out more about you and your interesting friends. Can we meet? CIBXXX ...'

Still, coy as this letter is, it is a tip-off that cannot be ignored given the unnerving alarm bells it sounds. No other tip-off, anonymous or otherwise, has made reference to potential future attacks. Sheather assigns detectives to investigate.[2]

At the same time he steps up the focus on the alleged violent acts by the Ananda Marga reported in Manila, West Germany and Bangkok immediately before and after the Sydney bombing. The two US-born Margiis arrested in the Manila knife attack on 7 February, and the three Margiis arrested in Thailand on 15 February (two Australians, and one American), are loudly proclaiming that they have been framed by the police forces in those countries.[3]

Not claiming foul play are Lakesh and Didi Uma, aka Helmut Klein Schmidt and Erica Rupert, who on 8 February, six days after Sarkar's appeal is denied, 'sacrificed themselves by fire in protest against continued incarceration of Baba, world hunger and as a reprisal for the arrest of sect members in London'.[4] These London sect members — Anthony Niall Kidd, Susan Waring and Brian Shaw, caught and arrested on 1 November at the tail end of the 1977 wave of violence against Indian nationals — are about to stand trial in the UK.

Sheather's list of confirmed members of the Ananda Marga caught red-handed in acts of extreme violence (which includes the Australian Margii John William Duff, accused of attempted abduction and stabbing the military attaché at the Indian High Commission in Canberra) is growing and he and the team turn their gaze outside Australia to see if they can begin to connect these scattered sect members. There are broad similarities between them. They are all Western. They are all under 32 years of age. Each separate group always has a mix of genders. Never just all women or all men. Why? Does it make them less noticeable? Just hippie couples, hippie friends wandering around. Perhaps that makes it hard to assume that such a group is about to stab someone, blow something up or indeed set themselves on fire. If the Ananda Marga is responsible for the Hilton, was a similar modus operandi used? Are they looking for male and female suspects?

Driving Norm forward is the vital evidence that has just arrived at headquarters: a copy of Abhiik Kumar's passport. It's like someone had just hauled the Rosetta stone up the stairs and left it in the middle of the floor — 'There you go lads, mystery solved.' While whoever filed the copy in the Hilton archive took pains to black out the origins of this wondrous document, it's pretty obviously from one of the ASIO agents embedded in the sect. It's a pretty nifty piece of spy work too — it can't be that easy to filch a sect leader's passport, take photographs of its many pages, then smuggle it out of sect headquarters and get it to your contact so they can send it to the Hilton task force. All I know for certain from the running sheets is that this operation took place between 8 pm on Thursday 16 February, three days after the bombing, and 8.30 the next morning.[5]

It must have been pretty scary. Imagine you're an ASIO operative embedded in a sect trying to worm your way up to the leader. Now you have to get hold of his passport without being seen, bearing in mind that the Margii headquarters in Newtown where both leader and said passport reside is a densely populated communal living space seething with paranoia. Remember Tim Anderson claimed in the Margii press conference the day after the blast that they believed the sect had already been infiltrated by ASIO. Adding to the tense atmosphere is the fact that the Newtown residence had been searched by Breaking Squad police on the night of 14 February. The Margiis must have been as twitchy as cats on a windy day.

I suppose the above could be fanciful speculation on my part and the passport could have simply been copied by a diligent Customs officer the day Kumar arrived back in Sydney just prior to the bombing, and then passed on to the Hilton task force. It's the assertion by the redacted author in the running sheets that it was obtained via an operation that occurred over the course of a Thursday night that makes me think it was obtained through covert means.

Whatever its origins, there it is on the morning of 17 February — 13 photocopied pages of the passport of the spiritual leader of the Ananda Marga in Australasia. Well, in actual fact, 13 photocopied pages of one of Kumar's many passports. He had one for each of his many names. This one is for Jason Holman Alexander, not Jon Hoffman or Michael Brandon or any of the others he is known to use.

Norm gets to see him close up for the first time, staring out of that square photograph. Thick black-framed glasses, bushy Ned Kelly beard, '1.80 m in height, brown eyes, brown hair. Born in Hartford on 21.11.49'. This makes him 28 years old.

The pages of this passport provide Norm Sheather with a fascinating if partial insight to where Kumar has actually been in the last eight months. While the notes accompanying the copied passport make it clear that certain of the entries cannot be deciphered owing to illegibility — for example, 'Page 7 bears five stamps of which only one is readable as follows: PERMITTED TO LAND SANTACRUZ AIRPORT BOMBAY DATE 22.9.77' — what it does reveal is illuminating. Where has Kumar been over the last eight months? Well, where hasn't he been.

Between the first legible entry of 8 June 1977 when he enters the USA, and the last on 8 February

1978 when he arrives in Kuala Lumpur, a period of exactly eight months, the team can identify stamps that have Abhiik Kumar entering or exiting 25 international airports or ports that include London, Sweden, Nepal, Bangkok, Hong Kong, Bombay, the USA and Felixstowe Port. This has to be put in context with the stamps that are illegible — which add up to a total of 18 unreadable entries that potentially almost double his activities. This would have him entering or exiting an international port on average every six days. This of course is only what *this* passport shows. It is more than possible that Kumar is using other passports under his other names.

This is something that the Margiis have always been upfront about. They often asserted that they changed their names and passports with such frequency in order to avoid harassment from various authorities. Given that Kumar aka Jason Holman Alexander changed his name from Jon Hoffman in 1977 but is also known at this point to use the names Mark Randall and Stephen James Manly, and is using a passport in the name of Michael Brandon by early 1978, he could well have used these passports in parallel with the one in the name of Alexander. Further evidence that it is possible he was travelling under a different name/s and passport/s is the large gaps in time and sudden leaps from continent to continent. There are no legible stamps at all for August 1977. He either stays in London for almost 11 weeks between his arrival on 8 July and his arrival in Bombay on 22 September — which seems a long time for our itchy-footed sect leader — or there are travels that can't be deciphered. Similarly, Kumar leaves Nepal on 24 September for destination unknown. There are then no legible stamps until he suddenly arrives in Sweden two and a half weeks later on 11 October.

So what? So the man is busy, he likes to travel — what does it prove? What can Norm actually tie to those readable dates and places? Quite a few things, actually. Kumar is in London at the time Margiis Kidd, Waring and Shaw are arrested for the attempted murder of the Indian ambassador. He is in India a few weeks before Sarkar's appeal is denied. He is in Bangkok eight days before Margiis Spark, Jones and Child are arrested in possession of explosives. He is back in Sydney the day before the Hilton.

While you can't prove anything exactly, what you can do is start to paint a picture in broad strokes. You can say, for example, that during those eight months Kumar was hopping around the globe, there is a record of him travelling to nearly every single country — the exceptions being Afghanistan and Canada — where there was a threat, an attack or a Margii arrest for violence against an Indian national. Bad timing? A coincidence?

Norm begins to drill down and sends two Special

Branch detectives assigned to the task force, Helson and Watson, to have a conference with the Indian vice-consul, Mr Alagh, at midday on 17 February. He asks Mr Alagh to forward a confidential message to India requesting information on Indian terrorists, the Ananda Marga, and the type of explosive devices used by same. The message reads as follows:

> Type of devices used by terrorists particularly the Indian sector of the Ananda Marga. It is requested that the reply include type, brand, colour etc, of wiring, explosive, timing device, battery, how detonated, and plan or photograph and modus operandi of terrorists and the usual way that they obtain explosives or any other information which may assist Sydney Police in their inquiries.[6]

Next, Norm turns his attention to the three Ananda Marga members arrested in Bangkok. While initially the proximity between the Bangkok arrest of Australians Spark and Jones, along with the American Sarah Child, and the Hilton bombing seems meaningful, it is swiftly established that neither Jones nor Spark has been in Australia for almost four years. It is true they all had tickets to Australia in their possession, however they were unable to get on a flight.[7] While Jones and Spark have been away for years, travelling in parts unknown, Norm is able to at least glean some information about who these young people are from their families in Australia.

What Norm and the team also learn is that the Thai police have credible information placing Abhiik Kumar with Spark, Child and Jones in Bangkok five days before their arrests. The Thais further suggest that Kumar is involved in the purchase of the explosives the trio are caught with.[8]

It is the parents of Timothy Jones who provide a potent if heartbreaking etch-a-sketch of the closed-off universe these young men and women inhabit. The report of the interview with Timothy's parents, conducted the day after their son, Spark and Child are arrested in Bangkok, is incredibly poignant.[9] Timothy's father is 'a chartered accountant [who with his wife] resides in an upper class area of Kew'. The telex sent to Norm begins, somewhat surprisingly:

> Parents freely admitted that their son was a member of Ananda Marga sect and had been so for a period of approximately five years, having to their belief now reached the level of Acharya. They then stated that they themselves take an active part in Ananda Marga (practising meditation and maintaining contact with David Mathew Meighan and Tim Anderson and attending other social functions i.e. christenings etc.) and receive Ananda Marga publications.

> On the question of their son upon arrest requesting that the appropriate authorities be contacted, parents stated this would be without doubt the Ananda Marga in Australia.

This portrait of intergenerational membership of Ananda Marga that seems to suggest an integrated and happy environment swiftly darkens when it is revealed that while the parents consider 'the Ananda Marga sect as a religious and peaceful organisation', they are very worried about their son's predicament in Bangkok and that the Australian Government may not be providing him with legal representation. If this is the case they state they are prepared to 'A. Lend money to Ananda Marga sect to cover legal costs and B. To pay expenses to provide legal representations from Australia.'

It turns out that Mr and Mrs Jones are willing (understandably) to do anything for their only son, from whom they are almost completely estranged: 'Jones' parents further stated they had not seen their son since 1974 … [and added] in the early stages of their son's involvement [with the sect] they experienced difficulty in maintaining contact with him'. It is only through a series of individuals connected to the sect, no doubt aided by their own active involvement, that they have managed to get information from him from time to time through an intermediary.[10]

I think of Mrs Jones attempting to meditate away

the strain of knowing her 25-year-old son is banged up on terrorism charges in a Bangkok cell. A son she raised and sent to Trinity Grammar — a boy whom she has not seen for five years and who refuses to visit or speak directly to his family. I think of how she and her husband must have had to ingratiate their way into the sect because it was the only way to gather crumbs of information about what Timothy was doing and whether he was safe ... One can say this, that even if the Margiis are innocent of all the crimes they have been accused of, they are clearly capable of inflicting an exquisite kind of pain on those who least deserve it.

Norm gets a photo of Timothy Thomas Hilton Jones. He looks like Jesus in a 1950s movie epic. Shoulder-length light brown hair, beard, big soulful eyes, clothed in some kind of robe-like apparel. He looks sweet. He, along with Child and Spark, is being detained in Bangkok for possessing 1300 grams of C4 explosives, detonators and a timing device. They are arrested based on information supplied by an undercover police officer who, according to a report sent from Thailand, 'stated he'd been told they [Jones, Child and Spark] planned to detonate an embassy in Bangkok'. The exact embassy was not identified but the trio had maps with the chanceries of the USA and Australia circled.[11]

The actions of the Bangkok Three are so close in time to the Hilton blast one can understand the task force's determination to seek connections between these Margiis and the Australian arm of the sect. Even the vocal claims made by Jones, Child and Spark that they have been framed by the Thai police mirror the frequent claims made by Margii spokespeople throughout 1977 that the sect was being set up.

Timothy Jones tells the Australian media that the explosive material had been planted on them to discredit the sect: 'Just outside the hotel the man approached us and said something in Thai ... I did not understand him. A moment later, police pounced on us and seized the over-sized shoulder bags we were carrying. Then they took us to our room at the hotel ... The police pulled stuff from our bags, and from drawers in the room. We had never seen it before. It was a plant, obviously.'[12]

In Manila, Shepherd and Dyer make almost identical claims of a frame-up, as do two of the three charged in London.

To Norm these implacable young people have an unnerving steeliness and a frictionless surface that appears impenetrable. Despite the crimes they are accused of, they seem unfazed. They argue in unison, regardless of the vast distances between them, that their respective arrests are simply evidence of the conspiracy against their leader and their religion. A conspiracy that has implicated the Margiis in violence since mid-1977 and has been masterminded by the Indian CBI, the KGB, ASIO, the CIA, and the police forces of England, Thailand and the Philippines. Despite the difficulty of imagining how such a group would work in unison, they do not falter. They stand as one.

It's a bit like the way cops stick together in the 'blue wall of silence' when criticised by outsiders. Does Norm get a whiff of this? Does he sense any similarities between the fierce loyalties of the Margiis and those within his own brotherhood? Maybe, maybe not. What is clear is that he's looking not just for connections between the Margiis named in the recent clusters of violence, but also for a way in. A chink, a foothold — something to connect them to Australia.

From Scotland Yard to Newtown

One of the task force detectives has alerted Norm to an article published in an Indian newspaper that states that Anthony Niall Kidd, one of the London Margiis responsible for stabbing the Indian High Commission official Mr Ahluwalia on 31 October 1977 and standing trial for bombing charges, had not only confessed to the crime but had also named Ananda Marga associates, thought to be American, Filipino and Australian and 'related his complete knowledge of the Ananda Marga sect'.[1] Norm immediately sends a telex to Scotland Yard outlining the details of the Hilton bombing and asking for everything they have from Kidd including 'details of the movements, including countries visited, by Kidd and his associates since June 1977. Also whether or not Kidd or his associates have visited Australia, and if so, the particulars of same.' He ends his telex with a final request:

> Information has been received by our office of the following persons having visited your country since June of last year and there is a possibility of an association with Kidd and his associates.
>
> 1. Jason Holman Alexander, previously known as Jon Hoffman, born 21.11.49, who had changed his name and became an Australian citizen on the 30th March 1977. Passport number Z2669601.
> 2. Timothy Edward Anderson, born 30.4.53, an Australian citizen.
> 3. Gary James Coyle, born 16.9.52, an Australian Citizen.
>
> All known leaders for Australasia sect of Ananda Marga. Please ascertain the movements of these three persons in your country since June 1977, and any background information you may have on them: TELEX SCOTLAND YARD UK. Signed N. Sheather. Inspector Third Class.[2]

As well as stepping up the focus on the international machinations of the sect, Norm ensures that the team keeps its eye on the domestic surveillance of the Ananda

Marga members. A list of 75 male members is sent to the Navy's military intelligence to discover whether any of them have received training in explosives.[3]

Norm also has the team pore over all the correspondence received from the Universal Proutist Revolutionary Federation (UPRF, in whose name the violence against Indian nationals is claimed) in Australia in 1977, hunting for a possible lead. Reading this material in the aftermath of the Hilton bombing it's hard not to be swayed by the astonishingly accurate warnings they contain. This letter sent on 27 September 1977 addressed to Prime Minister Morarji Desai is tantalising:

> The Universal Proutist Revolutionary Federation notes your callous refusal to release Shrii PR Sarkar, and points out that your resistance is, as warned, a death sentence to your overseas officials and lackeys …
>
> Let any government of the world spend three <u>hundred</u> million dollars on security, it will make no difference to us because we are ready to give our lives to this cause …
>
> Don't make the mistake of thinking security will protect your lackeys one iota — they are extremely vulnerable.
>
> There will be no more warnings, and kidnapping will not be attempted this time …

> As we are absolutely resolved and completely determined, the decision is only in your hands as to how much bloodshed there must be ... two deaths or two hundred ... the decision is yours and the blood is on your hands, Mr Desai. UPRF AUSTRALIA.

As suggestive as this letter and others are — think of the money spent on CHOGRM, the acts of self-immolation, the cessation of attacks between November 1977 and February 1978, the reference to Duff's attempted kidnapping of Colonel Singh and his wife and the apparent forewarning of the second wave of international attacks in February — they also mock and confuse. Copies of the letter above are sent to Air India in Sydney, Perth and Melbourne, and to the Indian High Commission and to the *Canberra Times*. Besides being able to ascertain they were sent at 11.30 am or 1.30 pm from Melbourne, it is impossible to trace the sender. Each time these letters arrive it must be remembered that the Ananda Marga in Australia denied their involvement and condemned their contents. Some letters, as mentioned earlier, were forwarded to the police by the Ananda Marga itself. In polite accompanying notes, often from Tim Anderson, it would be explained that the letter had arrived at their headquarters and they were alerting the authorities — reiterating that they did not support violence and had no knowledge of this UPRF group.

The task force assigns a full-time Observation Squad to keep watch outside the Ananda Marga headquarters in Newtown — still a cheap and semi-seedy inner-city suburb about four kilometres from the Hilton Hotel — throughout the end of February and early March. Members are watched coming and going as they undertake doorknock appeals for disaster relief throughout Sydney. There are numerous documents noting movements of members as well as attempts to interview associates of members.

In the reams of surveillance notes, some familiar names appear — those of Special Branch officers Watson, Helson, Henderson and Detective Constable Krawczyk. All of these police officers had been watching the Australian members of the sect long before the Hilton bombing. All were part of the stepped-up security measures enacted in anticipation of CHOGRM. These officers perhaps more than any others want to make an arrest — and perhaps hope to find evidence connecting Australian members of the sect to the bombing. Are they maddened by the lure of the circumstantial evidence? Are they ashamed of their failure? Norm Sheather is a fresh set of eyes; he started the day after the bombing and is untainted by anything that went before. These officers are burdened by having been charged to prevent the very thing that happened; rightly or wrongly, the effects of this burden will compel them towards a decision that will have catastrophic consequences for the case.

But this is all to come. By the end of February things start to open up to Norm, and what starts to flow in becomes a strong river of material pointing in the direction of the Margiis.

February to March 1978

To Norm's credit, despite the emergence of a strong suspect organisation, he continues not to place all his investigative eggs in the Ananda Marga basket. He keeps a robust number of officers exploring other leads. From late February to early March the Hilton task force investigates and discards dozens of names from the list of possible suspects.

For example, it is found to be unlikely that the bombing was undertaken by a militant Fijian trade unionist.[1] Likewise, while the three Singaporean students under suspicion (other than the student Ngee questioned and cleared immediately after the bombing) are found to be 'anti-Malaysia/Singapore government in outlook', it is acknowledged that 'this does not necessarily mean that any of these persons have been involved in any terrorist type of activity, or are in fact connected with any overseas group'.² A perky telex arrives from the Tongans in response to Norm Sheather's international call-out on 14 February requesting information about known terrorists who may fit the modus operandi involved in the Hilton bombing:

> REPLY FROM TONGA STATES NO TONGANS OVERSEAS WITH ANY DECLARED ANIMOSITY TO KING OR ROYAL FAMILY STOP NO TONGAN POLITICAL MOTIVE SUSPECTED END STOP.³

One of the suspect Croatians is found to have a solid alibi (he was in bed in Melbourne) and crossed off.⁴ There is one mentally ill gentleman who confesses to being the bomber⁵ and then another who sends a letter to Prime Minister Fraser, the Commissioner of the Commonwealth Police and the Attorney-General of Queensland:

> Statutory Declaration
>
> Subject
>
> Planting of militant Racist, Political and Industrial Terrorists as 'so called' union officials.

Planting of timebomb in garbage tin at Hilton Hotel Sydney, mailing of planted Explosives in parcels and envelopes in Australian mail and Planting of Militant Racist, Political and Industrial terrorists as so called combined mining and miners Federation Union officials by Utah Development Company's Gestapo Officials 'so called' Industrial advisors ... it is a premeditated crime against innocent people, against Australia as Nation.

And so it continues. Despite the florid accusations, Mr VS is nonetheless added to the list of people to be interviewed by the task force who, unsurprisingly, find 'that it is obvious that S ... is mentally deficient' and then he too gets crossed off.[6]

Along with the crazies there are also the home-grown xenophobes to contend with. As mentioned, Mrs A sends a long paranoid diatribe about a number of Indians in her street who she says are responsible for the terrorist act as evidenced by a leaflet she found in her letterbox.[7] A journalist from *The Age* newspaper calls from Port Moresby and relates an intensely complicated tale about a German prisoner who suicided in a PNG jail, the prisoner's wife and his criminal associate. The dead prisoner is alleged to have been a former member of the Baader-Meinhof gang and rumours spread in Port Moresby that he was the one responsible for the bombing.[8] A chap living in Indonesia shoots off a letter to the Australian Embassy in Jakarta, 'to inform you about the gang of terrorists which is responsible for bomb explosions at the Hilton Hotel'. This eclectic gang is made up of a Polynesian communist, a Japanese–Australian citizen who is a shipping expert, and a Malaysian journalist. The informant signs off cheerily, 'Hoping the Commonwealth conference will bring stability in South-East Asia and blessed by God.'[9] All these claims are looked into and dismissed.

The police are also methodically working to locate all the various protesters who were outside the Hilton on the day prior to the bombing. On 24 February one of the banner-wielding protesters is hauled in. He's cautioned and questioned. He is eagerly helpful, insisting that Detective Senior Constable Harvey, who is typing up his statement, add emphasis to his statement for effect: 'I was carrying a sign called "politicians are the pus" (please underline that — done) "of a suppurating society".' He goes on to add dramatically that he shoved his 'large and heavy' sign into the bin around 2.30 pm. 'It went in fairly easily with two heavy thrusts, right to the bottom. I am giving you this information because the Police want to know if there was a possibility of the bomb being there before.'[10]

The owner of the suspicious 1964 Mr Whippy ice-cream van sighted the night of the bombing is eventually tracked down. After weeks of media reporting, a teenage boy from Ashfield Boys High School sheepishly approaches the police and reveals the van is the property of his father, Angelo Parente, who speaks very little English. The van had broken down near the bomb site.[11]

In early March there is a flurry of excitement when the Hilton task force reveals a new lead. Because of the strength of the lead, and possibly the fact that all the recent international acts of violence have involved female suspects, the police decide to immediately alert the media and the public: 'Police investigating the Hilton bombing believe that a young woman seen carrying a small cardboard box near the hotel could help with their investigations.' The team go so far as to set up a full re-enactment outside the hotel 'of the dumping of the box into a kerbside garbage bin'. It's a good theory — this woman was seen by a dozen witnesses between 1.30 pm and 2.30 pm carrying a box. Norm is already thinking his bomber could be female. The 'suppurating pus' sign wielder is brought back in and he now swears that when he was doing his heavy thrusting with the sign that he 'struck a brown cardboard box at the bottom'.[12]

Despite the vagaries of the woman's description in the papers, she is identified straightaway. It turns out that she is 22-year-old 'Penny', a New Zealand resident who had flown to Sydney with the explicit intention of protesting at CHOGRM. She is described in the papers as 'a New Zealand woman known to be violently opposed to the abortion policies of the New Zealand government ... they believe [her presence in Sydney] could be linked with a pro-abortion demonstration against Mr Muldoon outside the Hilton Hotel on the Sunday before the bombing'. Some nark of a bloke she met the night she arrived rushes to the police to report that 'the woman was very hostile toward Mr Muldoon [whose] ... attitude towards abortion had caused misery to many women'.[13]

It's all over the next day when Penny, who is clearly not a shy girl, fronts up at the Wellington police station in New Zealand and demands to see the police. Within hours she is cleared of any involvement in the Hilton Hotel bombing.[14]

There's even a psychic who throws in his ten cents, holding a press conference at the airport. Mr Amery:

> ... claimed that he was a professional Mystic with certain psychic powers. He claimed that on Sunday 12.2.78 he and his wife had a premonition that Prime Minister MULDOON would be in danger at the Hilton Hotel. AMERY claims that both he and his wife were both in Queensland on 12.2.78 and that he actually telephoned the Hilton to warn Mr Muldoon, but nobody would put him through ... Amery stated

that he had no information about the bombing which could assist police, and that in fact his premonition was not that a bomb was at the Hilton, but the [sic] Prime Minister Muldoon was in some form of danger.

Perhaps what Mr Amery had detected was Penny's intense loathing for Piggy Muldoon and his anti-abortion stance. Or more likely, as the police and 'the members of the press who attended the interview' decide, 'AMERY was a bit of a nut case'.[15]

As all this trawling for, and clearing of, suspects grinds on, consuming wads of the task force's time, a thing of wonder is happening behind the scenes. Responses to the original telex that Sheather sent out to the police of the world asking for information on groups capable of similar acts of violence begin to roll in. One of the first comes from the French police, who send a sort of Baader-Meinhof showbag to Sheather consisting of wanted posters, a list of 90 known members and a booklet relating the history and crimes of the group in Europe.[16]

With this one exception, all the other responses from the international police departments are extraordinary in their consistency and indeed their breadth and detail. Keep in mind the original telex Norm sent seeking information did not speculate or offer possible theories or suspects. It simply asked: What do you know? Is there something this bombing at the Hilton reminds you of?

Over the next fortnight Norm Sheather's task force is sent telexes from police in the following countries: the UK, Afghanistan, India, Sweden, Thailand, Denmark, the USA, Norway, Germany and Canada. Each and every one of them independently identifies members of the Ananda Marga being caught or being suspects in a series of violent attacks or threats directed towards Indian nationals in their respective countries. Each also indicates that the bombing outside the Hilton bears certain similarities to the sect's violent operations in their own dominions.

The Metropolitan Police (the Met) in London send information regarding the attempted embassy bombing and attempted murder of the Indian ambassador in late 1977 by Margii members Kidd, Waring and Shaw. Norm and the task force already know about this case, but the Met expands on what they have, forwarding the fingerprints of the three, and adding more names to the list of suspects. There is the US-born Catalina Rivera Cabanatan, who is alleged to have been involved in the UK attack. The English police state that Cabanatan is a known associate of US-born Margii Stephen Holman, who Anthony Niall Kidd has fingered as the mastermind behind the London plot. Both Holman (the middle name of Abhiik Kumar's alias Jason Holman Alexander) and Cabanatan are known to have ties to US Margii Sarah Child, who was arrested in Thailand with the Australians Spark and Jones on 15 February. The British forward the passport applications of both, presumably obtained from the US authorities. Even in these plain orderly forms there is a sense of the nature of these young fundamentalists, as there was in the case of Australian Timothy Jones, who now sits in a Bangkok jail. I can tell you that both Stephen Holman and Catalina Cabanatan have beautiful cursive handwriting, that neither had been in their home country for years, and both had parents who were doctors — in Stephen's case it is Burton, his father, and in Catalina's, her mother Aurora.[17]

The information from the Afghanistan police relates to a threatening letter sent to the Indian ambassador in Kabul. This letter, postmarked Kabul, is actually sent as part of the first wave of threats and violence against Indian nationals in late 1977, but is only forwarded to the Australian police as part of this post–Hilton bombing request. The letter itself is reminiscent of the threatening letters written in the name of UPRF, except this one is exquisitely presented — it's a piece of calligraphy and laid out like a poem. The letter intones:

> You and three members
> of your embassy
> are marked for assassination

February to March 1978

one suicide squad is now leaving Nepal and will be there when you receive this Remember Canberra! We will not stop until Anandamurti is released by your government.[18]

It must boggle the minds of Norm Sheather and his colleagues that someone in Kabul would make reference to an attempted kidnapping in Canberra by Australian Margii John Duff. It really is as if Australia is the centre of this international terrorist storm.

As if to reinforce this, telexes and telegrams arrive within days of each other from the police in Stockholm, Denmark and Los Angeles, all providing considerable detail about attacks on Indian nationals, Air India offices or Indian embassies that were carried out in their cities (and others) late the previous year. What is new to the Hilton task force is the level of detail these various police organisations provide about the crimes being perpetrated. What's clear, too, is the frustration these police forces are feeling. They have strong suspicions that the Ananda Marga members in their countries are responsible: 'Evidence connecting the Ananda Marga with the incident was found ... A member ... Swami Dhritbodhananda was observed in the vicinity the night before the incident.'[19]

However, they often lack concrete evidence and the sect representatives in each country vehemently deny any involvement in acts of violence.

All of these international authorities, like their Australian counterparts, have been bombarded with letters from the UPRF claiming or threatening acts of violence. The letters are accompanied by public denials from the Swedish, Danish and American sect members, asserting that they didn't do whatever the letters threaten and that they have no connection to UPRF.

The other new intelligence that the Hilton task force receives provides a sense of the violent physical attacks that do occur.

> On 11.11.77 at 11.40 hrs a female oriental or Filipino, blk hair, brn eyes. 5' 2", 100 lbs., 22/25, entered the Los Angeles Air India Office and requested information on a trip to India. When employee Sudesh Mallick turned his back the female lunged at him with a military type knife with a 4-inch blade. The suspect dropped the knife and fled the building on foot.[20]

The LA police go on to report that similar attacks have occurred in New York City (20/10/77) and Washington DC (28/11/77). They also reiterate what the task force already knows: that one of their citizens has been arrested with two Australians in Thailand 'in possession of 1300 grams of C4 explosives, detonators and timing devices. Also in their possession was a Bangkok map with the United States and Australian chancelleries circled'.[21] The feeling emerging from all this information sharing is 'we're part of this too, the Margiis are good for these crimes'.

Particularly convinced are the police from Interpol in the Philippines, who have the two Margiis in custody over the stabbing in Manila on 7 February 1978. In their reply to Norm they write:

> We confirm attack of Jyoti Sarup Vaid, 45 years old Indian working with the Indian embassy in Manila as personnel secretary charge d'affairs at about 7.30 am ... he was stabbed on the back and chest by two American tourists. One male, identified as Steven Michael Dwyer [Stephen Dyer], 28 years old, single, a teacher, and the other a female identified as Victoria Sheppard [Shepherd], 31 years old, single, also a teacher: while they refused to confess, they were nonetheless charged for frustrated murder on the basis of positive identification made by the victim and witness. Assailants are said to be members of the Ananda Marga, an organisation allegedly engaged in assassination of respectable Indians abroad.[22]

They too are eager to help and send Norm's team fingerprints, photographs and police reports relating to the attack.

The tone that emerges from this cluster of responses is real concern about what could happen next. The whole thing has police around the world on edge. The Swedes have a Margii conference in Stockholm later that year and they are clearly nervous.

What must really get Norm's blood up, however, is some extraordinary intelligence he receives on 9 March 1978, which lassoes these far-flung events and people and pulls them inextricably together. The information is received from 'a reliable and confidential source relative to the inquiry concerning the Ananda Marga sect'. It's probable (but difficult to tell from the police running sheets) that the information comes through Interpol, possibly via ASIO, is passed on to Special Branch and thence to the Hilton task force.

The intelligence places key Ananda Marga members associated with these hitherto discrete violent acts in Bangkok, Manila and (potentially) Australia all together in India with the imprisoned Sarkar immediately prior to the denial of his appeal and the start of the second wave of violence.

It states:

This information indicates that between the 7th and 10th January, 1978 several leading Ananda

> Marga members passed through Bangkok en route to Kathmandu. Included amongst these were Timothy Hilton Jones (stationed in South Korea) [arrested in Thailand 15 February] Victoria Mary Sheppard [Shepherd] (probably stationed in the Philippines) [arrested in Manila 7 February] and Jason Holman Alexander (the spiritual director of Ananda Marga in Australia) [aka Abhiik Kumar].[23]

Just to be absolutely clear, Kumar spent January travelling with Shepherd and Jones, both of whom are now in jail — one for an act of violence in Manila, one for possessing explosives in Thailand — immediately after the trio met with Sarkar in India.

> Between 30th January and 7th February 1978 Jones, Sheppard [Shepherd], Alexander and two senior Ananda Marga Members from the United States Caroline Lee Spark and Sarah Childs [sic; also arrested in Thailand on 15 February] returned to Bangkok from Katmandu.[24]

To be even clearer, the Thai police have intelligence that places Kumar alongside Jones, Child and Spark in the purchase of the C4 explosives in the days prior to their arrest.

During the period 10th to 30th January, 1978 Spark, Alexander [Kumar] and Jones all had interviews with the Ananda Marga leader PR Sarkar, who is in gaol in Patna India and that at least Alexander and Jones spent some time together. It is therefore possible that a meeting or briefing of senior Ananda Marga leaders was held in India some time between 10th and 30th January, 1978.

On the 2nd February, 1978, an appeal by Sarkar was rejected, and it is thought that a series of violent or potentially violent incidents by Ananda Marga members throughout the world may begin.[25, 26]

The report then goes on to list the two self-immolations, the stabbing, the possession of explosives and the arrests. The analysis confidently asserts that the 'events in February 1978 are reminiscent of those which occurred between August and November 1977, following the rejection of an appeal for Sarkar's release in late July that year'.[27]

It is apparent that the unnamed informant thinks the connection between the violence in 1977, after Sarkar's first appeal is denied, and what is occurring now is obvious. In his or her view, the first wave was 'probably perpetrated by a group of senior Ananda Marga leaders who were attempting to force the Indian

Government to release their leader'. It thus follows that the 'events involving senior Ananda Marga members, coupled with the failure of Sarkar's [2 February appeal] indicates that a second series of violent attacks may have commenced'.[28]

The circumstantial evidence does indeed appear to be compelling and it's hard not to be overpowered by the desire to think, well, Abhiik Kumar (Alexander) was with all these Margiis who met with Sarkar in Patna jail, and Sarkar must have given the delegated sect leaders instructions on what to do if his second appeal failed. They wait in India until 2 February when the Indian Government denies the appeal. Next the Ananda Marga elite fly off to various destinations primed to bomb, stab or issue orders to other members to self-immolate. Many of them are apparently caught red-handed. How can all this be a coincidence? What were Kumar's instructions when he returned home the day before the Hilton bombing? A peaceful protest? Plant a bomb in a bin?

Problem is, compelling circumstantial scenarios are not a form of evidence that stands up in court. Until someone decides to confess or dob their spiritual comrades in, this intelligence is no better than gossip. It is equally possible that it is just scurrilous slander engendered by those forces (KGB, ASIO, CBI, CIA, Scotland Yard, etc.) intent on discrediting the sect. Even Sarkar weighs in from his jail cell, condemning these attacks and declaring that, in a fabulously convoluted argument, if these acts of violence do result in the Indian Government releasing him, he will not leave his cell in protest.

The only way to operate in this environment of strongly suggestive circumstantial evidence and total denial from the suspects is to be patient — to wait them out and wear them down. The big problem is time. If this is a second wave of violence and if the pattern of the year before is anything to go by, then things have barely begun. The police from countries in Europe, Asia and North America sense this. The missives that shudder out of the telex machine from them are redolent with anxiety and fear.

Adding to this rising level of concern is an urgent telex that arrives from Thailand:

> ... information was received from Airline security on 18th March 1978, that suspected terrorist members of Ananda Marga plan to sabotage the Indian and Republic of Korea Embassy in Bangkok in order to force Indian government to release the Chief of Ananda Marga detained in India. It is believed that members of Ananda Marga will sabotage Thai government premises or hijack Thai aircraft to force Thai government to release Bangkok detained terrorist group. The information is believed to be very reliable.[29]

The police in Australia immediately send patrols to airports to monitor Thai airlines and inform Qantas security.

Then it gets worse.

Another bomb

On Thursday 23 March, just five and a half weeks after the Hilton fatalities, there are separate phone calls made first to North Sydney police station and then to the Criminal Investigation Branch (CIB) headquarters. The anonymous caller says there is another bomb primed to go off at 7.40 pm.[1] It has been placed at the Indian High Commissioner's residence in Canberra.

There is a frantic search of the premises and nothing is found. However, unlike the hundreds of bomb threats received over the previous five and a half weeks, this one doesn't disappoint. On Saturday morning, 25 March, about 30 hours after the anonymous call, one of the policemen stationed at the High Commission (police protection has been provided for all senior Indian officials in the lead-up to and aftermath of CHOGRM) spies a length of wire and what looks like a detonator at the base of a tree in the garden. The

Canberra-based Commonwealth Police surge into the envoy's home and evacuate the High Commissioner, Mr Jagdish Ajmani, and his family and the staff from the residence. They then fan out and begin to search the grounds. After searching for about half an hour they discover a canvas haversack under a hedge.

The experts step in and extract it with a long hook then winch it up a line. Inside is a cut down carton 'previously used to contain 24 tins spaghetti from San Remo Macaroni Co.'.[2] The humble box holds a variety of batteries wired in series. The 'terminals of the 703 batteries were taped together and wired to the 2372 battery'.[3] Fifteen feet (4.5 metres) from the haversack, five sticks of gelignite are found, also taped together. All these are located a few metres from a cottage at the bottom of the garden. Inside the cottage are the housekeeper, his wife and their baby. After searching further the police realise that the High Commission backs onto a busy public park where Canberrans from the suburb of Red Hill like to walk their dogs. Anyone passing could have simply tossed the bomb over the back wall. The only good news is that while the alarm was wound up, the clock was not.[4]

The newspapers, no doubt longing for some update on the case, immediately tie the find to the Hilton: '… it is believed that the bomb could be similar to the one which exploded outside Sydney's Hilton Hotel last month, killing three people'.[5] They also make vague allusions to the Ananda Marga being long suspected of targeting and threatening Indian nationals. The paper quotes the High Commissioner, Mr Ajmani, as having 'no doubt who was responsible for the bomb. He said that the incident was typical of the terror some people were trying to use to force the Indian Government to release a certain person'.[6] The Australian Margiis go on the offensive and issue a statement strongly denying 'responsibility for, or any association with the planting of the bomb'. They go on to argue 'that it seemed significant that the bomb had been discovered about a week before the sect's leader was due before an Indian appeals court, seeking to reverse criminal convictions for which he was imprisoned more than six years ago'.[7]

The following day Mr Ajmani gives up on the niceties and directly accuses the Ananda Marga of planting the bomb at his house and at the Hilton.[8]

Behind the scenes the forensic analysis of the bomb itself is equally contradictory. The police have either diverted yet another tragedy or the device was never intended to explode. The Army ballistics unit, the Commonwealth Police and members of the task force carefully break down the bomb into its bibs and bobs. The clock, the gelignite, the detonators, the tape, the wires, the haversack, even the cardboard spaghetti box of 'normal brown corrugated type'[9] are described in comprehensive detail. All the components are easily accessible (Coles and Kmart stock most of the bits required) with the exception of some batteries of:

> ... unusual shape and size. One of the detonators is very badly corroded and appears to have been inserted into one of the sticks of gelignite for some time. The other detonator appears new. None of the components bear the marks of fingerprints.

What is clear is that whoever made it knew what they were doing.

> The device had been constructed in such a manner that it would have detonated had the circuit been completed, i.e. the hammer coming into contact with the bell dome. However due to some malfunction either when the bag was thrown into the grounds of the residence or the alarm lever having been left in the 'OFF' position, it failed to detonate.[10]

As the task force frantically examine this new bomb, looking for similarities between it and the detritus from the Hilton blast, they are acutely aware of how swiftly the level of threats is rising. Compared to the first wave of violence in 1977, this second wave is scrappier, nastier and more ambitious. These acts seem much more likely to result in civilian deaths and casualties. The threats are also coming in faster and faster. The team gets one lead a day after the Canberra bomb discovery. A young couple is reported being seen in the park behind the High Commission about half an hour before the bomb was found. The woman, described as slight, with shoulder-length brown hair, is said to have been carrying an army-style shoulder satchel similar to the one discovered in the grounds. Beyond that the descriptions are so general they could be anyone.[11]

If I were Norm I'd be conscious of how stretched things are getting. In attempting to solve a single violent crime — the Hilton bombing — he and his team are becoming embroiled in dozens of others. While he can collate the targets by nationality (Indian) and agencies (government), besides those they seem to be capable of occurring literally anywhere. There are thousands of Indian nationals holding government positions in foreign countries and thousands of members of the Ananda Marga around the world — you can hardly follow them all. Even if suspicions seem to point to Abhiik Kumar being associated with the members of the sect arrested overseas, there is nothing to say he is carrying out similar attacks in Australia. Even if he is, he could simply issue orders to others — and if so, who are they?

If things weren't complex enough, two very strange things happen. Completely out of the blue, *The*

Australian newspaper publishes an article declaring that it is possible that Mr Ajmani (or someone in his employ) planted the bomb with the express purpose of discrediting the Ananda Marga and disrupting Sarkar's final appeal process.[12] Although the Hilton task force has absolutely no evidence for this, the article claims a 'police source' stated that the Canberra-based Commonwealth Police (as distinct from the Sydney-based Hilton task force) and intelligence agents 'first agreed' it was definitely the work of the Ananda Marga. Now, however:

> ... after exhaustive investigations and interviews ... [they] believe the Ananda Marga was not responsible for that incident. Police sources stress that the sect's reputation for violence is well founded but on this occasion there is no evidence to implicate it ... Commonwealth authorities now believe it may have been the work of an Indian diplomat or intelligence agent working without the knowledge of the high commissioner.[13]

While it is hard to pinpoint what exactly motivated a police source to make a statement of this nature, it is most probably connected to the fact that three days after the bomb was found in Canberra, an employee of the Indian High Commission, Suresh Kumar, was found hanged.[14]

What does that mean? Was this chap guilty? Was he a secret agent for the Indian CBI? An Ananda Marga sympathiser? Or just a deeply unhappy man? Why would police, who have been so tight-lipped about their investigations up to this point, make such an assertion? Did Norm Sheather sanction it or did the Commonwealth Police (COMPOL) and ASIO just provide information to the press without consultation? Is this what they really think? Or is it disinformation intended to throw the Ananda Marga off the track? Is the federal government so fearful that they are seeking to defuse the situation by adopting a method of plausible deniability themselves?

I can tell you one thing: the same way a canary must have a first woozy sway before toppling to earth and causing miners to gasp and flee, this event is a precursor to the imminent and catastrophic implosion of relations between ASIO, the Hilton task force and the New South Wales Special Branch, previously united in their pursuit of the Hilton bombers. It's almost as if the Canberra bomb did explode, sending fragments of shrapnel into the investigation, which until now appeared to be going very well.

Keep in mind it's a little over two weeks since Norm got that beautiful intelligence tying those jet-setting senior Ananda Marga figures together and tracking them to India, then Bangkok, Manila and Australia. He must be feeling pretty good about how things are going. That it is possible that all the violence emanates from a tiny splinter cell within the larger organisation made up of elite long-termers way up the totem pole. Those with a direct line to Baba; those who go regularly to India, visiting him in jail, sitting at his feet in adoration and receiving his counsel. This is exactly what the original task force analysis stated in November 1977, and this is what recent intelligence fleshes out. But making this concrete is not easy. You certainly can't panic or do something reactive.

If a minority elite of the Margiis are playing a mind-bendingly sophisticated game, portraying the sect as oppressed, bullied and conspired against (and attracting huge numbers of new members in the process) while they are actually conducting a highly organised reign of terror in the name of the Universal Proutist Revolutionary Federation, it's going to be almost impossible to compel these individuals to confess.

Sheather has tried. In the days following the arrest of the Bangkok Three, he sends two task force members to Thailand to interview the suspects about their connections to the Australian Margiis and the Hilton. The task force offers them immunity, a free ride home and, who knows, perhaps some of that gigantic reward. Of course none of these inducements are going to fly — they are hardly going to appeal to earnest, highly disciplined young people willing to give up meat, money, careers, their entire families and, in some cases, their lives. By this stage five members have set themselves on fire in devotion to their cause.

Perhaps the wisest thing to do would be to wait them out — keep the gaze on the horizon. With all this information pouring in from international police, all these similar cases, something's got to give. Norm knows that ASIO has penetrated the sect — perhaps eventually these agents will crack the big time. What's needed is a cool head and a calm mind.

But fear and intense frustration are no allies of patience, and something fractures under the stress. That something is Special Branch.

Another bomb

Shadowlands

For reasons that can only truly be known by the detectives within this now-maligned group of police, whose actions now seem not only inexplicable but kind of insane, on 28 March 1978, six weeks after the Hilton bombing, Special Branch decide, without informing Norm Sheather or ASIO, to recruit and run their own secret agent inside the Margiis. An agent who will penetrate the sect and report exclusively to them. The person they select for the job is Richard Seary.[1]

It seems so completely mad, doesn't it? Why on earth would they recruit a man whose only contact with the Hilton team was to have wandered in off the street a few days after the bombing to point the finger at the Hare Krishnas? A claim that Sheather is completely unimpressed by. Why do detectives Krawczyk and Helson in particular, and to a lesser degree Watson,[2] think that recruiting this slightly odd young man is a good idea? Why now? And why keep it secret from Sheather, the task force and ASIO?

Here we enter shadowlands.

There is no primary archival evidence about what went on between Special Branch officers Krawczyk, Helson and Watson and Richard Seary on 28 March 1978 between 4.15 pm and 6.45 pm, save that they met at Special Branch headquarters to discuss the possibility of Seary joining the Ananda Marga and attempting to gain inside information and then feed it back to the detectives. In short, to function in much the same way as the two ASIO agents who have been working within the sect since late 1977. This meeting is so clouded by competing recollections it is not even clear how Seary has come to be at Special Branch in the first place. Was he asked? Did he offer?

Even some seven years later, during the extensive inquiry held under Section 475 of the *Crimes Act* into the convictions (based significantly on Seary's evidence) of Timothy Edward Anderson, Paul Shawn Alister and Ross Anthony Dunn, the reasons remain opaque. During the course of that inquiry in 1984–85, all that sharp-eyed Commissioner James Wood can prise out of Krawczyk is that 'by the time of the meeting he was aware of Seary's earlier contact with the police, but he was unable to recall how it was that the meeting came about'.[3] Likewise Detective Helson 'could not recall the circumstances in which the meeting came about'.[4]

Detective Watson is completely uninformative, stating that he 'had not heard of Seary before the meeting'.[5] As to Seary's reasons for getting into bed with Special Branch — the Section 475 inquiry lists at least half a dozen contradictory motives. Seary confessed to friends, or in writing, that he was brought on board: one, because he had wasted police time with the Hare Krishna accusations and thus was bullied into infiltrating the Margiis; two, because they thought he was the Hilton bomber; three, because he understood Sanskrit (which he didn't); four, because he was half crazy like the Margiis and could worm his way into the sect — and so on and so forth.[6] Yet none of these explanations, or those to come, are backed up by evidence. Furthermore, all of this speculation comes in retrospect, and is tied irrevocably to the miscarriage of justice cases that are yet to occur.

What if we go back to the day in question, forget what is to come and try to slip into their skins?

28 March 1978

It's 43 days since the Hilton bombing.

For the likes of Detective Norm Sheather and the Hilton task force, it can't seem like much time at all for a major case, but this cannot be the feeling of Special Branch Detectives Krawczyk, Helson and Watson, who have doggedly been on the trail of the Ananda Marga for almost a year. They have been at the frontline of the attacks on and threats against Indian nationals since the previous winter and have put in mind- and bum-numbing hours of surveillance. They too have borne the brunt of the failure to protect CHOGRM and are under attack by elements of the press who hold them up to ridicule, or worse, accuse them of blackmail, conspiracy and murder. Then there was the bomb found at the Indian High Commission in Canberra. And what do they have on their prime suspects? Nothing. Nothing but the bland denials issued by the sect with smooth regularity. Circumstantially it all seems to point to an inner cell within the Ananda Marga, hidden deep within an oblivious rank and file membership. The fact is there is nothing concrete to hang onto despite the hours they have spent watching and listening.

What about the bright young boys and girls over at ASIO? What about the two informants they have had inside the sect since late the year before? Where is their intelligence? Apart from tiny tidbits, they seem to be completely incapable of producing solid leads. I suppose it might occur to Special Branch during that early evening in late March, as Richard Seary faces them across the desk, that Norm and his handsomely resourced Hilton task force don't seem to be faring much better than the cloak and dagger ASIO contingent either. Why wait for them to fuck up? Why not strike out on your own?

Presumably the members of Special Branch believed they could change the course of the investigation and perhaps become the heroes of the day.

It's easy to imagine either Krawczyk, Helson or Watson being intensely frustrated by the lack of traction within the investigation. If I shared their suspicions about the sect I might feel as if I were being mocked. 'Looky, another bomb. First the Hilton, now Canberra. What are you going to do?' It's fascinating to note how intimate these detectives are with the fresh terror of this newly discovered bomb, with its potential to rip through walls and flesh, and how mouthwateringly tempting the circumstantial evidence surrounding it is. It is Krawczyk's name on both the original reports relaying details about the components of the High Commission bomb, and on the report:

> ... concerning a description of a male and female suspects [sic] relative to the bomb incident at the Indian High Commission ... located on the 25th, March, 1978. Also is [sic] a photo-fit picture of the possible male suspect.[1]

He must have felt tantalisingly close. Yes, the description is general, yet the gender mix, the age, the brazenness of the actions — casually throwing a bag full of explosives over the back wall of an official compound — do bear a startling similarity to those Margii couples caught in other countries over the last few months.

If it were me, I can imagine feeling that things could be done better — that I could do things better. Remember, the Margiis say they have been infiltrated by ASIO, so it's possible that those operatives are horribly compromised and will never get anywhere. (In almost 20 years' time ASIO will commission and publish a declassified report to address some of these questions. In it they will admit that 'ASIO ran agents within the Ananda Marga. Most agents

28 **March** 1978

apparently provided only limited coverage of the sect.'²)

Why not recruit your own agent? It's a good time to start afresh. Why not Seary? He looks like a hippie, smells like a hippie, but behaves like a nark. He was happy enough to point the finger at the Hare Krishnas, who obviously accept him. Why not get him to take his suspicious mind into the Margiis? The more you think about it, it's the randomness and speed of Special Branch's choice that makes Seary kind of perfect. Anyone asking about him knows he's been loosely allied with the Hare Krishnas for years, drifted around, done this or that, done time, had and got over a drug problem, had a tricky childhood. He's bright, the right age — just the sort of person the Margiis might like. What's more, he's clearly up for it. Whether motivated by adventure, a bit of cash or just because going undercover for the police to help solve a big crime sounds like huge amounts of fun — he jumps on board.

And why would you tell too many people about it if you were Special Branch? Why tell ASIO if they never give you any information and treat you like second-rate coppers? Why tell Sheather and his team? They're only likely to be annoyed. Let's face it, on 28 March 1978 who knows what Seary will or will not discover? Why upset the applecart at this stage? Easy does it, wait and see what happens. Why not 'let him have a run and see how he goes'?³ How bad can the consequences be?

Krawczyk, Watson and Helson are not completely secretive about Seary's recruitment. They inform their boss, Deputy Commissioner Perrin, the officer in charge of Special Branch at the time of the Hilton inquiry, and he has no particular objection.[4] The detectives then make a basic perusal of Seary's fingerprint record and get an oral clearance from ASIO 'that it had no adverse information in relation to him', but do not inform them that Seary is being run as an agent.[5]

That's about it. He is immediately sent into the field. His mission: to infiltrate the Ananda Marga in order to determine whether they were involved in the Hilton bombing.

It's hard to say whether this complete lack of guidance and training is a hindrance or a virtue. Does it make him a good or bad spy? More or less credible as a witness? If the detectives from Special Branch genuinely believe that the violent inner circle of the Margiis both here and abroad are responsible not just for the Hilton but the wave of violent acts claimed in the name of UPRF, they are sending a man without the slightest notion of spycraft into what is effectively a terrorist organisation. Alternatively, perhaps, they believe that sending in someone with fresh eyes will reveal the Margiis are innocent.

It's tricky to clarify from the material available in the archive. Things get murky from this point. Seary's

28 March 1978

narrative, his every footfall and utterance become so caught up with the Anderson, Alister and Dunn story, with blowing up white supremacists, false arrests, verbals, and on and on which will consume the entire investigation, it's hard to pick one's way backwards through the dark thicket of patchy and ambiguous information. Once Seary enters the Hilton story, everything he says and does becomes the focus of multiple secondary sources that will proliferate like fungi. These start emerging from 1979 onwards and divide into three arenas:

A. Analysis — in the form of books, films, articles — that unwaveringly supports Alister, Anderson and Dunn in their miscarriage of justice case and regards Seary as a liar and/or a police agent provocateur.

B. Reportage that takes Seary and the police at their word and believes the trio of Margiis are guilty as charged, ignoring all the oddities of the case.

C. All those trials and inquiries dedicated to determining whether A or B or something in between is the truth.

Each of these explores in depth the events surrounding the arrest of the three young men on 15 and 16 June 1978. Other details that bob up that are not relevant to the issues surrounding Anderson, Alister and Dunn are simply discarded. Yet within this detritus are many revelations.

As far as Anderson, Alister and Dunn and their

supporters are concerned, everything that issues from the mouth of Richard Seary from 16 February onwards is a fantasy — fuelled by either Special Branch's incompetence or, more malevolently, by specific design.

Making events even harder to navigate during this period is that certain agencies have, to use a euphemism, ceased to communicate effectively with each other. For a month or so both the Hilton task force and ASIO are kept away from the clandestine meetings between Seary and his Special Branch handlers. The two principal reasons Krawczyk, Watson and Helson later give for this are strangely contradictory. First, they say they didn't want to pass on information emanating from Seary too early because, if they could not absolutely substantiate it, they would be made to look foolish.[6] Second, because they were afraid that their rivals in ASIO would steal Seary once they figured out how valuable he was.[7] It may seem childish but it's also very human. At the time I think these Special Branch detectives were at their wits' end.

It is also possible they are compelled to take this sort of risk because, once again, Sarkar's case is coming up for review — this time by the Patna High Court. All the police must be conscious of how things played out the last two times Sarkar's appeals failed. Perhaps Special Branch just want to try something different, to have one last audacious fling at the case, to attempt to claw back some authority. Who knows, had things gone differently, maybe they could have solved the case and been hailed for thinking outside the box. Of course this is not to be and this 'concern ... that if Seary [is] identified or intelligence linked to him, he might be lost to Special Branch' will have cataclysmic consequences for all involved. In a massive understatement in the findings of the Section 475 inquiry, Justice James Wood will note that while 'this attitude [is] understandable, [it is] not conducive to the most effective operation of police/intelligence investigations in this country'.[8]

The one advantage of the siege mentalities of ASIO, the Hilton task force and Special Branch (although ASIO and the task force do continue to share some information) during the initial running of Seary in April and May is that they can hardly be accused of colluding. Indeed, one of the few ways to penetrate the fog surrounding what might have occurred is to try and identify points of concurrence in the information gathered during this period from independent sources, many of them outside the Hilton archive in New South Wales State Records.

For me the most startling point is this: the information Seary provides to Special Branch, in the form of tape-recorded debriefings with detectives (principally Krawczyk) before 30 May 1978, and the information he gives after 30 May, seems to emerge from two parallel and distinct universes. Before 30 May,

Seary's information is all about Kapil Arn and our friend Abhiik Kumar. After 30 May it's all Anderson, Alister and Dunn. Given that he will 'shop' these three on 15 June, he has a two-week window to make their acquaintance. In regard to Anderson and Dunn, Seary only meets them properly between 11 and 13 June. In the Section 475 inquiry, Seary will say of Anderson, 'I hardly knew [him] at all.'[9]

Another critical point is that until 30 May certain elements of Seary's intelligence about the Ananda Marga can be corroborated by information gathered independently by the other investigative agencies. After 30 May, almost none can.

So reconstructing the separate investigative strands up until 30 May, what do we know that is beyond dispute?

28 March 1978

A new wave
of terror

Two days after Special Branch recruit Seary, Norm Sheather receives information (most likely from ASIO) that despite an upcoming conference in Katmandu about Sarkar's imminent appeal, Abhiik Kumar decides to stay in Australia and to send someone else in his stead.[1] This is unusual — the globe-trotting Kumar rarely remains in one place for long and it is rarer still for him to delegate another Margii to take his place. Kumar sends Mathew Donald Meighan (probably the same person as David Mathew Meighan), whom we met through the parents of Timothy Jones, who is still languishing in a Bangkok jail. For five years Meighan acted as go-between for Mum, Dad and their estranged Margii son.

Does this delegation indicate something is afoot in Australia? Sheather and his team stay on their investigative trajectory, keeping the focus on the movements of the Margii leadership, Kumar in particular, and on the most recent bomb found at the Indian High Commission. Sheather contacts his international police colleagues for precise forensic information from the bomb attacks (actual or thwarted) carried out by real or phantom Margiis. Perhaps these bombs share similar construction.

This latest bomb in Canberra has not only unleashed a burst of possibly misguided action in Special Branch, it has also re-energised Sheather and the Hilton task force with the sense that a new wave of terror against Indian nationals is inevitable. The same report from 'a confidential source concerning the sect Ananda Marga' that details Kumar's decision not to travel to Katmandu for the conference on 30 March states that:

> It is thought by the source that the activities of Ananda Marga have increased prior to SARKAR's … appeal. At that stage the demonstration on 22 March 1978 and the abortive bomb attack at the Indian high commission, Canberra, on 25 March 1978, were given as examples. In regard of the latter incidents no evidence is available to connect same to the sect Ananda Marga … Information to date indicates that Sarkar's case comes before the Patna Court on 3rd April 1978.[2]

The international meeting of the Ananda Marga leaders in Katmandu is scheduled to conclude the same day — presumably with decisions to be made about what to do if the appeal does not proceed. It's the first time Abhiik Kumar will not be at an international Ananda Marga leadership meeting in India that coincides with one of Sarkar's key court dates.

Perhaps Kumar's absence gives Sarkar the good luck he needs. On 3 April the Patna High Court grants the supreme leader of the Margiis the right to appeal his conviction of multiple murder.

One can imagine it's a great time to join the sect if you're planning to enter it as a covert operative. The membership, who have fought for Sarkar's release for seven years, are euphoric. Two days later, on 5 April, Richard Seary travels to the Balmain home of Kapil Arn to begin the first of four introductory sessions into the beliefs and practices of the Ananda Marga, which will take place over a month. In addition to the usual fare about mediation, yoga and Ananda Marga philosophy, there is much excited talk about Sarkar's appeal.

A few days later Seary has his first debrief with Krawczyk. This meeting is not recorded but at the same time Seary doesn't actually have anything much to report. Special Branch in a fit of hilarity assigns Seary the code name M Ghandi [sic] and they start to make meticulous records of the modest financial transactions that pass between agent and handler —

$10 received on 13/4/78, $30 on 19/4/78 — 'receipt signed by Krawczyk and Ghandi'. Ghandi is his Special Branch moniker for financial book keeping; Seary's Ananda Marga appellation is Virata.[3]

Underneath the hope and the excitement that novitiate Seary observes among the membership about Baba's appeal, Sheather and the task force are picking up grumblings from other sources that troubles lie ahead. In Australia and abroad the Margiis make increasing assertions about the Bangkok Three having been set up by the Thai police. The trial of Margii John William Duff, accused of attempted kidnapping and assault of the military, naval and air advisor to the Indian High Commission Colonel Singh and his wife the year before, is set to commence in Canberra in early May. This case is also regarded by the sect as made up of lies and slander — yet another travesty of justice and another case of persecution without substance.

On 9 April, in the lead-up to Duff's trial, a bomb is found outside the Brisbane apartment of a relative of Colonel Singh.[4] On 13 April the sect issues a press release:

> ... calling on the Federal government to make a full investigation into the recent incidents involving employees, relatives and property of the Indian high commission suggesting that they [are] involved [in] a campaign directed to discrediting

the Ananda Marga and to prejudicing the appeal of PR Sarkar.[5]

Around the same time Seary joins the sect, Sheather receives further intelligence from the Danish, US and Thai police about Ananda Marga activities, including the identification of a potential new major player in the sect based in the Philippines. But more of that in a moment. What's important to observe is that Sheather and the task force continue to be open to non–Ananda Marga leads.

In April the Commonwealth Police send a longish report to Norm about a Ms EMD, an allegedly 'militant politically active communist … capable of involvement in such a bombing incident [like the Hilton]'.[6] The information comes from an informant referred to only as C.283. This intelligence is rich with the allure of an international espionage thriller — a Portuguese-born female terrorist trained in 'bomb construction knowledge' by an unknown South African while they shared a flat in Bronte, near Bondi Beach. Read closely, it all seems unlikely to amount to much. The informant seems both vague and self-important. He tells Assistant Commissioner JD Davies that, 'he would ring my number again at 11 am (29 March) to check the result of inquiries. If positive we should "go softly" as he has an "in" with her and may be able to help.' The informant never calls back.[7]

Special Branch also continues to receive other leads. In early April, Special Branch officer Watson writes a report about a Mrs Grace N, who accuses her de facto husband, Anthony (not the former Mr N) of being the bomber. He was attending a six-month 'explosives course in Melbourne' at the time and would ring her every night except 'for a five day lapse about the time of the Hilton bombing, [when] there were no calls'. Furthermore, after the bombing, Anthony would laugh and joke about the people who were killed in the Hilton explosion and warn her to expect a visit from the police. He had a preoccupation with death and regularly sent money to the IRA. Mrs N, however, emerges as a problematic witness; it seems the reason she makes this statement is because a detective has questioned her about almost burning down her house 'when she attempted to burn holes in [Anthony's] clothing so he couldn't wear it again'. She had also been charged previously with 'malicious wounding when she attacked [him] as a result of a domestic dispute'.[8]

*

Seary's second and third forays to the introductory Margii lectures, like the first, result in no information and despite the fact that Seary and Krawczyk meet on 12 and 19 April to debrief after each of the sessions, these meetings are also not recorded.

In late April Seary starts to get innovative. He skips his fourth introductory meeting and instead goes the following night to meet with Kapil alone. The debrief of this meeting *is* recorded by detectives Krawczyk and Watson. According to Seary, he's inveigling his way into Kapil's heart by:

> ... basically making myself out to be a bad piece of work ... and saying things we did in the Hares. The time about how the two Hares had killed themselves in New Zealand when the bomb they made exploded ... also I told [him] how we had an idea of blowing up the Homebush meatworks ... when I told him about being involved with the bombing Homebush Abbs he said I'll just tell that to some friends of mine who are quite radical and said to be with the VSS. I said — what's the VSS. He said, oh well in English you can call it the Volunteer Social Services.

Seary goes on to paint a picture of the VSS as the radical arm of the Margiis, responsible for the murder of the six defecting Margiis in 1971 — the crime for which Sarkar was imprisoned. The VSS believes the Indian CBI is allied to the KGB and that anyone connected to them — Indian government officials, diplomats, and the like — is fair game. These radicals:

… kill people they regard as *rakass* or demons and they think they are doing an honourable act by killing them, they also regard policeman [sic] as legitimate targets. At least they do in India and what goes on in India goes here too. And you can see by the way they address or talk about Commonwealth Police … they'd be in bliss if that policeman died in that bombing.[9]

Seary asks what he should do 'if it comes to the point of me to actually knock someone off what's my position then to knock a Margii off or stop someone else getting hurt?' Seary is told to 'ring them to alert them before it happens'. Later, Seary adds, 'I had to take a vow of secrecy last night to death' and, 'The other groups in the Margiis treat the VSS like a joke. They actually don't like them, they think they are too heavy …'[10]

It's not clear from the transcript whether Kapil is actually providing this dark thumbnail sketch of the VSS or whether Seary is regurgitating material he has gleaned from other sources like newspapers or even, I suppose, from Special Branch. All Kapil is quoted as saying directly is that he'd like Seary to meet some people — that 'there are a lot of things in the pipeline at the moment going on and these people would like to talk to you and see you'.[11] Kapil at no point suggests he endorses such radicals or their violent courses of action. Given that Seary's initiation into the sect is to occur a few weeks hence, it's just as possible Kapil is attempting to determine whether he is a police informant.

In years to come crusaders for Anderson, Alister and Dunn such as Tom Molomby, the author of *Spies, Bombs and the Path of Bliss*, will scoff at the idea that such material would be revealed to someone this new to the organisation.[12] Nevertheless, like it or not, Seary does have bona fides that make him credible to the Margiis in a way another agent may not. He was a Hare, he'd been in jail at various times, and the (albeit) isolated acts of violence that he retails to Kapil did occur, which well may have made him seem even more authentic.[13] The Hilton task force also knows that Kapil Arn is a senior member of the sect and close to the leadership, particularly Abhiik Kumar, so if anyone did have contacts to an inner radical cell, it would be him.

The fact is that these allegations about the sect are extremely common. The papers frequently publish stories about them and they accord perfectly with what police around the world, including Australia's police, believe to be true. At the very least they are the claims UPRF have been making very publicly for over nine months. I can also think of a few reasons why Kapil may tell a new member rumours about what happens to those who defect from the sect — it's a good way to measure someone's allegiance. I assume you'd learn a great deal from how they reacted to such gruesome material. Maybe it's a test.

It's clear too that Seary is revelling in his role — he tells Krawczyk he'd like to say that he had a pistol licence to give his role as a hothead more weight, and also requests a listening device.[14] Finally he asks what his position is if he is 'asked to drop a parcel off at such and such a point and the parcel contains bom-bombs [sic] you know'.[15] Which in all honesty seems a fair enough question under the circumstances. The first two requests are denied — the listening device rather tragically, as it might have avoided the fracas that is to come. In regard to the latter, the advice is to call his handler.

Seary's initiation is to take place at the Ananda Marga headquarters in Newtown the following Sunday. That night, presumably to seal the deal, Seary heads off with Kapil Arn and another Margii called Ainjile Morrison to undertake a spray-painting and postering campaign in Ultimo. The three of them happily spray up 'Fight for Justice, Meditate for Peace, Join Ananda Marga now' and the Prout slogan, 'Prout, the only way out'. Mid-slogan Kapil is arrested for defacing property, spray can in hand, by the local police. Seary has the good fortune to further ingratiate himself as a keen foot soldier by bailing the older man out of jail.[16]

Although a contact briefing is held between

Special Branch and Seary on 2 May,[17] the next tape recording does not occur until the 7th. Matters appear to have progressed rapidly between Seary and the Margiis. Seary reports he has attended many meetings, been initiated into the sect the day before and been invited to a retreat. Ainjile has told Seary that there is to be a 'complete full new campaign against the Commonwealth Police — starting with posters and then other things'. Even more exciting are the conversations with Kapil who, subsequent to his arrest, starts to tell Seary 'about his other exploits with the spray can' and then about the 'coming revolution'. Kapil tells him that part of the training was 'self-defence and firearm practice and things like that'. But of all the things Seary reports, most notable is his reference to the Acharya, the Ananda Marga leader Abhiik Kumar, wanting to put Seary into the Volunteer Social Service and directing him to see Paul Alister, the leader of VSS, about joining up.[18] Reading these transcripts carefully, they don't seem implausible (a later accusation against them). Once again Kapil Arn hasn't uttered a single word that characterises him as a violent activist, nor one who condones such behaviour. All he actually talks about are his 'exploits with a spray can'. As for the talk of the coming revolution, there is much corroborating evidence for this — most emanating from the Ananda Marga itself.

The Margiis' May 1978 newsletter (published

by the public relations department of Ananda Marga, Pracaraka Samgha) confirms Kapil's claim to Seary that there is 'much in the pipeline'. The newsletter opens with a detailed overview of Baba's court case in Patna and how well it appears to be going:

> On 16 April [Baba] *said,* 'This year will be a very good year for all of us. You know when I was arrested Ananda Marga work was only in five countries. When I came in jail it spread in more than 87 countries. *Had I been outside it won't have been in so many countries.* But my physical presence is also necessary — so it is very near. The enemies tried their level best to suppress the fact by implicating in false cases, harassing, torturing etc., but they could not do anything. AM will remain forever.'[19]

Other coming actions outlined in the newsletter include the start of the 'FREE THE BANGKOK 3' campaign. A detailed catalogue of the deficiencies of the case is laid out for members. Much is made of attempts by the Australian Commonwealth Police to squeeze information from the three about the Hilton bombing as well ('the most serious case of harassment by the Australian Commonwealth Police').[20] There is a lengthy piece from Timothy Jones himself. His eloquent dissection of his visit from members of

Sheather's task force demonstrates the sect's perception of the Australian police at the time:

> It certainly seems probable that the Aust. Police are pressurizing the Thai prosecution into building the case into an anti=Australian [sic] government move. This would serve their purpose nicely, since in a police state such as this, conviction is likely. All three of us have been asked by Thai/Aust. investigators/F.B.I about the Hilton incident — they were evidently trying to make connections.[21]

In the same vein, the May newsletter also contains a lengthy discourse about Pranava's case, which is thoroughly critiqued as an act of pure police fabrication and harassment. Non-Margiis know Pranava as John William Duff, currently on trial in Canberra for the kidnap and assault of Colonel Singh and his wife. The newsletter is full of instructions on what actions members can take to voice their concerns about the various cases. If Baba is freed (as it is fervently hoped in mid-May), Margiis are encouraged to participate in a range of celebratory activities that publicise the joyous news. With regard to the Duff case, they should lobby local members of parliament, organise poster campaigns, participate in demonstrations and so on. To convey the tone and spirit of these instructions, the front page of the newsletter ends with the headline 'Live Fight and Die for your Ideology'.[22] So yes, Seary quoting Kapil saying there is much in the 'pipeline' in Ananda Marga-land in early May is perfectly accurate.

*

In the second week of May Sheather receives bomb diagrams found in the possession of a Margii in London, as well as news of an improvised explosive device (IED) planted in an Air India office in Kuala Lumpur that went off without casualties in November 1977.[23]

These incidents cannot be obviously connected to each other, nor to those at the Hilton, the High Commission in Canberra or the latest bomb in Brisbane. The London diagrams, allegedly found by the London Metropolitan Police in the possession of Ananda Marga member Catalina Rivera Cabanatan, are fascinating. Done in a style reminiscent of a classic children's book, there are illustrations showing how to make a door handle bomb, a homemade hand grenade, a 'walk trap' (wire, safety pin, heavy firing pin, detonator and TNT) and a 'nipple time bomb'.[24]

I suppose niggling at the back of everyone's mind, from the detectives at Special Branch to Sheather and his team, ASIO, the Australian Government — and no doubt the leadership of the Ananda Marga — is the question: what if Sarkar is unsuccessful in this appeal? Legally there aren't too many other options. What will happen then?

By 15 May, the date of the third tape-recorded debrief, Richard Seary's rapid momentum in securing a place in the sect appears to have continued. He has been given the opportunity to go to two Margii camps the following weekend. One of them is to be a VSS camp to be run by Alister. He's been told by some unnamed member (who has participated before) that there is to be arms training — he is asked to bring along a machete or a rifle.[25]

Seary also tells Krawczyk and Helson that the night before he'd been at a sect meeting at which Kapil Arn's wife was extremely agitated about her husband's imminent court appearance following his arrest in Ultimo. As Seary tells it, the Acharya (Abhiik Kumar) explained to her, 'I already told him an alternative thing to do.' In response Kapil's upset wife turns to Kumar and says, 'Did you tell him to blow it up too?' As befits a religious leader, the Acharya does not rise to the bait and replies evenly, 'You said that, not me.'[26]

Krawczyk, long acquainted with suggestive hints that lead nowhere about Margiis and bombs, starts to get more specific in his questions to Seary. What's happening with the two radicals that Kapil Arn said he was going to introduce him to? Seary whines that he hasn't had much of a chance to see Kapil on his own. He adds that Kapil is very close to the Acharya Kumar and there is tension between Kumar and Alister — something to do with Alister having failed acharya training.

While none of this amounts to much more than banter, what makes it interesting is that someone else (possibly ASIO or Interpol) is also watching Kumar closely that night. About the same time Detective Krawczyk and Helson are recording Seary, a report (its author's name redacted) is sent over to Sheather and the task force. Dated 15 May 1978 and titled 'Information Received From [Redacted] Re. Brandon Alias Hoffman Alias Alexander', it says:

> At 3 pm this date information received from [blacked out] that person using the name of Michael Luke Brandon, using Passport No. P.075549 departed Sydney International Airport on Thai International Airlines Flight no. 982, 11.20am on 15/5/78 for Bangkok via Singapore. Passport endorsed one month holiday. Previous information has been obtained by this enquiry that Jon Hoffman, alias Jason Holman Alexander, changed his name by deed poll to Michael Luke Brandon.[27]

So Abhiik Kumar has yet another new name and a brand new passport. He has slipped out of the country undetected: 'enquiries at the Customs Branch at Sydney Airport revealed that there was no currency search of Brandon and he did not receive any extra scrutiny or enquiries when he departed'.[28] Crafty bastard!

The following day the trial of Margii John William (Pranava) Duff in Canberra comes to an abrupt halt when the jury is discharged after 12 days, after inadmissible evidence is given. A new trial is ordered to commence with a new jury on 24 July.[29]

Two days later, on 18 May, Sydney is hit by another bomb blast. At 7.40 pm 'a bomb blast shattered a plate glass window at the New South Wales Police Headquarters in College St'.[30] The bomb, while not large and resulting in no injuries, is alarming — the devices seem to be turning up with disturbing regularity. The police investigators take the debris to be examined and compared to the bomb fragments from the Hilton and the bomb from the Indian High Commission.

What does Norm Sheather make of this devilry? Not much — he's on leave, as will be nastily reported in the paper in a few days' time. Not only has he been kept out of the loop by the clandestine actions of his colleagues in Special Branch, he is also being mocked and derided in public.

At the very moment Richard Seary heads off to his first Volunteer Social Services camp (and alleged arms training) in Ashton Park, Mosman (around the back of Taronga Zoo, where the new car park is), Sheather is being hectored like an errant schoolboy. In response to the bombing at police headquarters, the *Sun-Herald* adopts the tone of an aggrieved headmaster:

> Three months later, the Hilton inquiry looks like being a sad, lost cause ... There is still little hope of finding the Hilton murderers ... Three months after the blast that killed two council workmen and a policeman there is little hope the $100,000 reward will be claimed.

It's Norm who is pushed forward as the author of this sad state of affairs. Not only is he, 'the officer in charge', on leave that week, it seems his second in command, Detective Sergeant Bruce Jackson, is also 'off for four days'. The *Sun-Herald* spent *two days* (their italics) making phone calls that fail to discover who is heading the investigation in their absence. What a far cry it is, the Sunday tabloid declaims, from the mighty hundredfold of detectives (actually 58) who began the team. A number that dropped to 70 after a fortnight, then to 37 by mid-March and now only constitutes a mere handful. The article pits the monumental, but in its view pointless, effort of interviewing '1500 people ranging from religious groups to political activists and plain cranks ... to produce only three strong leads'.

The reporter, Roger Franklin, then sets out the tragic narrative arcs of rising and falling action, the hopes of promising leads — like the Mr Whippy ice-cream van, and box-carrying, Piggy Muldoon–hating Penny from New Zealand — which are irrevocably dashed. As is the latest sliver of hope that came in the form of a strip of super-8 film sent anonymously to the police. Unlike Zapruder's history-defining piece of celluloid, this is simply a dead end. On examination it reveals a man carrying a brown box towards the bin outside the Hilton — a man who turns out to be a local shopkeeper getting rid of some rubbish.[31]

It's amazing how little this reporter is able to glean about what is really going on in the investigation, and how closely the reduced task force is holding its cards to its chest. The 'leads' the article refers to are so far down the priorities list for Norm and his investigative team they appear laughable. Still, it must grate that things do suddenly appear to be going a wee bit pear-shaped. Having Abhiik Kumar throw on another pantomime mask and slip out of Australia as Michael Brandon must stick in the craw a bit, as must all those bloody bombs. If Norm's mood is bleak, it is hard to imagine what it's going to be like when he finds out a few weeks later that Seary has been recruited as an operative to gather information about his case.

'A full-scale terrorist war'

Seary has his fourth tape-recorded debrief with Krawczyk and Helson on 24 May, immediately after his attendance at the VSS and related Margii camps. It's a doozy. Given that he's been immersed with Margiis on camp sites for days on end, it isn't surprising that he's chummed up with a few of them and picked up some chatter. In brief, Seary claims he has heard that if Baba is not released during the current appeal process, there will be 'a full-scale terrorist war coming about the middle of June'. This attack will be coordinated by the head of the Volunteer Social Services, who is coming to Australia from Manila. Seary relates the information that Abhiik has gone to India to await the outcome of the trial and to confer with Baba. He then details the unarmed combat training he received at the VSS camp and the war games he saw; conversations with Margiis about the existence of caches of weapons; the existence of a VSS uniform; and the existence of the Universal Proutist Revolutionary Federation. Heady stuff indeed, to be lambasted in years to come as far-fetched nonsense.[1]

And yet, and yet ... there is corroboration for much of this. Not only is Seary's account of the postering and of Kapil's arrest of 30 April supported by independent local area command 'police observations',[2] we know that the camps were held and that Seary attended them. ASIO was undertaking its own surveillance. We know that Abhiik has indeed left the country. There is independent corroboration of Seary's acharya in Manila, the head of the VSS, who is allegedly to lead the violent uprising of Margiis should Sarkar not be released.

A telex to the Hilton task force from COMPOL or Interpol with information supplied by Hong Kong's Special Branch states 'we can confirm Acharya Japananda is global secretary of volunteers social service, whose headquarters is in Manila'. Like Kumar, he is a man of many names and dangerous (or unlucky) friends:

> ... a list of AM members supplied by Hong Kong Special Branch has the following entry — Japanand [sic] Avahoot aka Nimay Chandra

son of Nand Lai Rai Choudry ... We note that a Mani Rai Choudhury ... travelled with Timothy Jones from Bangkok to Katmandu in January this year. Choudhury transited Bangkok from Manila, in company of Victoria Mary Shepherd ... Transliterations of Indian names are complex and it is probably that Choudhury/Choudry are the same name. Choudhury however is a very common name.[3]

Like Abhiik Kumar, Acharya or Avadhut Japananda has been travelling in the company of long-term Ananda Marga members immediately prior to their arrests in Bangkok and Manila. It must be concerning to Special Branch and the Hilton task force to imagine such a man entering Australia.

Even with corroboration, it is true that Seary's list of Margii activities is, as James Wood will come to describe it, 'startling'.[4] However, when one looks at the lengthy transcript itself, these 'facts' emerge fairly vaguely and are issued with all manner of qualifications. To be honest it reads to me like someone struggling to fathom the nature of the people around him and unsure of what to make of what he has heard, rather than just spouting allegations in order to stitch them up. On 24 May Seary comes across as particularly circumspect. When asked by Krawczyk (referred to phonetically as C in the transcript) whether he thinks the Margiis are held together by the imprisonment of Baba or by something else, Seary replies:

> S. It appears to be — it appears to be the cause to which they're cohering around.
>
> C. So, with the release of Baba.
>
> S. No, there's nothing I could truthfully — I mean I have my own feelings but there is nothing I could truthfully say that I've heard in specific reference to it.[5]

Krawczyk asks him what these feelings are.

> S. Well my feelings are that they are an extremely dedicated, very very dangerous, fanatical religious group. They believe their leader is God and so anything they do in defence of him is justifiable. They believe they're the new saviours of mankind … they believe in the wholesale destruction of our present day society and replace it with Prout.

This is pretty strong beer but also pretty true — Margiis do believe Baba is a god and they do believe that Prout should replace both capitalism and communism as the third force. But it is also immediately tempered by the answer Seary gives when Krawczyk asks, 'Do you feel they could be capable of carrying out some of their ideologies?'

Seary replies, 'Well, they are a very strange, very mixed breed.'[6] He tells his handler how a lot of the Margii ideas are very good, such as their social service activities (disaster relief, soup kitchens and such). It's their rigidity and extremism that he thinks will prevent them from gaining popular support. Having to believe that the leader is a god (as opposed to a guru) and members burning themselves to death to protest Baba's imprisonment are not exactly the ideology of peace and love that attracts most Westerners to Eastern religions. Even if Seary's testimony is a pack of lies, he surely makes a good point when he observes that self-immolation reveals 'the mentality of the people you're dealing with. You know, if a person is prepared to burn himself to death you know than [sic] to die in a gunfight is nothing.'[7] Despite this assertion he seems reluctant to paint them all with one brush.

As to whether his compatriots at the VSS camp were of that persuasion, Seary talks at length about a 'very nice chap', a school principal and single father he met there who didn't strike him as the type to blindly follow orders. But he believes followers are kept in the dark about the inner workings of the sect. Seary guesstimates that maybe two-thirds might carry out such acts — 'especially the women whom I've found to be more fanatical than the men' — and a third probably wouldn't. All through the debrief he repeats general suspicions but punctuates his answers about what he has heard with the phrase 'no specific mention' and provides no concrete evidence pointing to violent tendencies in any particular sect member. Asked again if he's yet met the 'two radicals':

> Seary. No, I haven't and whether they are operating as Universal Proutist Revolutionaries Front which is a separate deal with all the Margiis but it is controlled by Baba but they are the very extremist wing.
>
> J.[8] Very extremist?
>
> Seary. Yes and the only thing that I've heard was that they do exist in this country.
>
> J. How many do you know?
>
> Seary. I don't know. I've got no idea how many.[9]

Seary likewise has nothing specific to say about Narada (aka Alister aka O'Callaghan, who was convicted of throwing the pig's head in 1977 and who will be arrested on 15 June), who heads the VSS in Australia, but doesn't seem to care for him much. He delights in telling Special Branch how the 'nice chap' he met at the camp tells Narada to shove something up his arse when disagreeing with a command he has issued. Of his original Margii contact, Kapil, he has nothing much to say.[10]

Special Branch, despite their issues with ASIO, do make an effort to immediately pass some of this concerning information on to other investigative departments, although it is done rather informally and on a somewhat ad hoc basis. Under oath, years later, Special Branch officers will reiterate their uncertainty about what Seary was saying into a tape recorder in those small rooms. They must have wondered whether it was all nonsense. But what if it is true and they react too soon and lose the critical piece of intelligence that blows the case open? What if ASIO marches in and just takes over Seary themselves? They want to keep their source close — deep down, the intelligence they are getting from him does seem pretty authentic. However, some time after the 24 May revelations, 'some material [is] communicated informally between desk officers, and also between senior officers of Special Branch, ASIO and COMPOL'.[11] A 'document' is presented and a meeting 'to discuss possible threats to Indian personnel and establishments in Australia'[12] is convened. At all times Seary is referred to only as an informant, not as connected to Special Branch.

The only thing that Seary seems to be absolutely certain of in the entire 26 pages of the 24 May transcript is that Abhiik Kumar is the man in charge of everything, the 'all over commander, the commandant ...[who] would know everything that's going on'.[13] He does add, though, that the man in Manila who runs VSS worldwide does have seniority in some things. If the man in Manila decreed that the VSS had to take action, Abhiik would have to comply.

'Abique [sic] would be definitely told what was going on but the VSS is worked as a separate unit and the guy who is in charge of the VSS is an 'avid hoot [sic] which is higher up than simply a acharia [sic] like Abique [sic]'.[14] Variant spellings aside, this information reflects exactly the complex layers of hierarchy in the sect — an acharya (a teacher, learned person or sect leader) is not as powerful as an avadhut (a mystic or saint).

Five days later, in Seary's fifth tape-recorded debrief on 29 May, we learn that Seary has suddenly reconnected with Kapil Arn. After apparent weeks of limited contact and Kapil's busy schedule, suddenly they are bosom chums. Like a pining schoolgirl, Seary finds himself miraculously waiting for a taxi with this intriguing man, who doesn't ignore him but instead lavishes attention on him. They start with small talk about firecrackers and the Queen's birthday, and Kapil begins wittering on about how much he likes firecrackers and rockets and rocketry. He'd designed and built a two-stage rocket. He and his friends had tried to blow up a bridge. 'They used plastic tubing which they filled with black powder and they had fuses and they lit it and there was a God almighty bang and nothing happened.' Seary seems to become giddy with this sudden rush of intimacy and when Kapil quips in reaction to his failed explosion, 'Next time I should use amatol,' Seary gushes to Krawczyk, 'I would think that anyone who knows of amatol would know about explosives because amatol is an explosive and quite a powerful one and it wouldn't be sort of common knowledge.'[15]

Standing side by side on a cold late-May day, Seary says Kapil holds out his hand and points at some 'little burn-like scars'. Seary asks him how he got them, adding, 'Not blowing up the bridge?'

'Oh no, this is much more recent,' says Kapil, 'I was very lucky ... I could have blown my hand off.' Then he adds, 'I had an accident with a detonator.'[16]

Krawczyk seems to become quite giddy himself. He's all over this. He asks Seary, 'Now, in your opinion, you've dealt with detonators and that before — would that be similar — the injuries he had on his hand?'

Instantly Seary reverts to the head prefect mode he'd adopted when apprising Detective Ireland of his suspicions about the Hare Krishnas in February:

> It would depend on the size of the det. If it was a small priming detonator, it would have left those

marks, if it had been an electric det. standard charge size, it would have blown his whole hand off, unless it had gone off when he wasn't in actual contact with it. If he was holding it and it was a normal det. it would have blown his hand off.

Seary then starts speculating. He'd seen similar wounds in Lightning Ridge, and if Kapil knows rocketry then he must know bomb making ... In all this excitement Seary does seem to glean that something is afoot.[17]

> Seary: [Kapil] seems rather interested at this stage to tell me of his exploits and wants me to come around and do things with me ... it would appear that it involves explosives ... I definitely get the feeling that he's priming me for something.
>
> Krawczyk: He's planning you for something?
>
> Seary: Yes, he's priming me.
>
> Krawczyk: Priming you for something?
>
> Seary: He wants to see how eager I am to support him, that's my feeling.
>
> Krawczyk: That's my feeling, seriously?

Seary: Seriously, that's my feeling. You know he knows my background as far as explosives are concerned, he knows my background and I've told you about my police involvements and things like that and arrests, and I think he's impressed. I think he would probably like me to join his cliché [sic].[18]

Seary intuits that:

> ... my feeling is that Kapila [sic] could be involved with a group that the average Margii doesn't know about who is [in] collusion with or being told what to do by Abhiik, who's in direct contact with Baba in India, and as such, their terrorist wing goes through that sort of function from Baba to Abhiik to Kapila to Kapila's friends ... I would say if this United Revolutionary Proutist Front exists, then he is most definitely a member.

Seary detects complicated divisions in the sect and doesn't believe that Alister and the Volunteer Social Service know about it. 'No, they might act under a different set of circumstances. You know they could be doing their own little terrorist trips.' Kapil worked with Abhiik, Alister with the man in the Philippines.[19]

The Margii leader in the Philippines must be feeling the pressure. That week US-born sect members

Victoria Shepherd and Stephen Dyer are sentenced to 17 years in a Manila prison for the stabbing and attempted murder of the Indian diplomat on 7 February.[20]

It's about here, at the close of 29 May 1978, that I slam into a wall. After this everything seems to become unstable, incoherent, illogical. Here we have been, over the course of months and months, pursuing the threads that have drawn us through the labyrinth. Through the eyes of Norm and the team after the Hilton bombing, our monster has never really changed, has he? That tall turbaned man at the airport: Abhiik Kumar, aka, aka, etc., etc. — now waiting for his god to be released or not from prison in India. He's the one we've been sniffing around. He's the one we think may be good for it, him and his inner sanctum of like-minded souls ensconced in Prout or a cell within that cell. Just as Seary describes it. But wait — we don't have any evidence quite yet, do we? But golly it feels like you can taste it.

Then, just like that, everything goes dark. It's like a tanker splits in two, flooding the ocean with dark viscous waves of impenetrable oil, coating everything in their path, killing everything. What to make of what comes next in the historical record? It's as if Tom Stoppard starts writing the narrative, doing his cute and clever things with familiar Shakespearean storylines — what if Rosencrantz and Guildenstern take centre stage? What if Shakespeare falls in love? Let's turn the box upside down and shake hard. Think of how funny it will be. How disconcerting. Innovative. Brilliant.

What else to make of the fact that bit players like Anderson, Alister and Dunn suddenly hijack the plot? Within two weeks — and for decades to come — they are the Margiis you know. The sect members you defend or hunt down; the stars of the show.

I mean it's kind of odd, don't you think, that Richard Seary, who has been buddying up to Abhiik and Kapil and the 'nice chap' he met at the VSS camp all through April and May, is suddenly exclusively in the company of Anderson, Dunn and Alister and intimately embroiled in their intrigues. He appears only to have properly met the first two in June — in Anderson's case possibly on 13 June — and although he had met Alister earlier, he still barely knew him and reportedly disliked him.

Also odd is the fact that the targets completely change. In June we do a complete shift from a universe in which Margiis allegedly attack and threaten Indian nationals (shopkeepers, flight attendants, children, high commissioners) in India, Thailand, Manila, Sweden, the USA, the UK, Denmark, Germany, Australia and so on, to Margiis attacking ... Nazis.

June 1978

The events of June 1978 get so completely chaotic and impossible to corroborate that one has to proceed with care. Let's dip our feet in and wade through the muck for a moment and see what we can feel squelching between our toes.

For the first ten days in June there is no contact between Richard Seary and his Special Branch handlers. It is possible they are attempting to gain some independent corroboration for Seary's unnerving allegations of a potential 'all-out terrorist war' should Baba fail to win his appeal. Despite their reluctance to share unsubstantiated claims, the 24 May debriefing has stirred the pot. The information moves from one desk to another and, despite the rivalry, ends up at ASIO on 8 June. It is more than likely that Sheather and the Hilton task force are apprised of the intelligence, as it is clear that a 26-page 'debrief of a "usually reliable"

New South Wales police informant who had penetrated Ananda Marga' is passed from the New South Wales police to the Commonwealth Police and thence to ASIO.[1] They are sufficiently alarmed to rapidly convene a meeting of the Protective Services Coordination Centre the next day, and the names of the Manila-based global secretary for the VSS, Acharya Japananda aka Japananda Avadhut aka Nimay Chandra, are placed on international airport watchlists. Someone — or a few someones — in these organisations decides next to bring the pot to the boil and make these suspicions public. Why not go to the press and see if they can shake someone from the tree?

Meanwhile, when Seary and Krawczyk sit down on 10 June for their sixth tape-recorded debrief, Seary introduces him to our new Nazi villain — the rightwing white supremacist Robert Cameron, the head of the Australian faction of the National Alliance. For reasons that are not entirely coherent, the Ananda Marga have decided to target this organisation with demonstrations, poster campaigns and letters to newspapers. Causing some kind of a fracas outside the organisation's headquarters will bring the police out to protect the National Alliance, thus publicly demonstrating that the police are siding with racists:

> … sort of protecting them and so they hope to get political gain out of that. Also, they said if

there was any bombings or things of the National Alliance, then they could use that as political things again, saying that it was being used by the police and people like the National Alliance to frame the Margiis.²

It seems monumentally convoluted, and Special Branch doesn't appear to be much impressed. It accompanies bluster that Seary claims to have heard in relation to the Bangkok Three. The Margiis believe that the Commonwealth Police sent to interview the three, Inspectors Hull and Sharp, in fact set them up, and 'they are going to do something about' it. This is not profoundly different from what is explicitly stated in the Ananda Marga newsletter for May. More bravado allegedly comes from Alister when he describes to Seary what the VSS will do if Baba is not released. He apparently details a 'grand plan' that entails breaking Baba out of jail in India and then spiriting him into Australia via its poorly protected northern coastline. After that there's more talk of the all-out war that will erupt here, there and everywhere against all who continue to support the incarceration of Baba the god — this includes the Commonwealth Police, the Indian CBI, ASIO and Special Branch.³

It pays to remember that these are groups of very young men and women, not much more than teenagers, who are alleged to be spouting the rhetoric above.

A bunch of social revolutionaries who feel aggrieved that the one they worship has been locked up. If you add this to Seary's own tendency to embroider and embellish, who's to say these conversations didn't take place? But the subject matter is completely new. Why the focus on Cameron and his skinhead mates? Note also this startling new indiscretion. Alister is apparently running off at the mouth.

Krawczyk is not so impressed with all this big generalised talk and doesn't pass the information on.

What do I make of this seismic shift in tone and content from Seary? There are many theories. James Wood speculates in the Section 475 inquiry that perhaps by late May Seary wanted out. He had applied for and been accepted into Sydney University to study psychology and anthropology (non-degree courses) in early June.[4] Things were heating up and he had other (safer) options for expanding the mind and thus may have been exaggerating certain things.[5] Yes, it is absolutely true that nasty Robert Cameron and his racist organisation abruptly become the focus of Margii ire in June; letters are written, demonstrations are held. But why? Whose directive was this? Kapil's? Instructions Kumar left? Or is the organisation going rogue? Are people veering off on their own paths while the leader is away? Is the lack of discretion reported by Seary stuff he is making up? Or is it because someone like Kapil is on to him and directing others to trip him up?

There is one possible insight Seary supplies in the 10 June debrief. He is asked:

> In relation to the Hilton, there was a demonstration at the airport and then the bombing at the Hilton, now do you feel that they would do, all in the same category, go to that extent with this National Alliance?

Seary replies:

> I think so, ah, if it does happen it will certainly be the modus operandi for the group, the demonstration for their political purposes then their follow up using the follow up to say that it was done to frame them, which they kill two birds with one stone they get more political mileage out of it plus their objective done. Ah, it is a political exercise this thing and I think, yes, they are quite capable of [it] and I think it's quite feasible that they will do a follow up, and even to the extent of psyching up of some of their lesser members perhaps a bit of violence which would take the blame off those in authority and they could say it wasn't really one of their members at all.[6]

Seary adds, a minute later, that while he's not exactly sure if Kapil Arn would be in a position to authorise a violent action, he is absolutely positive that the Acharya (Abhiik) Kumar, despite being overseas, would be the one to green-light it. 'Any violence, activities done in the name of Ananda Marga anywhere in the world, he has to sanction. So any activities which they have done anywhere in the world, he is privy to it.'[7]

I wonder sometimes whether the rising fractiousness within the Australian Margiis begins to mirror exactly that going on between the various investigative agencies. If so, what is about to occur over the next five days is an epic and unavoidable collision in which everyone shares the blame.

There is no more direct evidence of how utterly at cross-purposes the separate investigative organisations have become by early to mid-June than the calculated leak (fuelled by Seary's 24 May revelations) to the newspapers on 11 June. It is clear that ASIO and possibly Sheather's team are responsible for the information that appears in the *Sun-Herald*. The headline shrieks:

> SECURITY MEN SURE THEY KNOW
> HILTON HOTEL BOMBERS: Security chiefs
> believe they know the identities of the terrorists
> responsible for the Sydney Hilton bomb outrage.

With a refreshing lack of equivocation it seems the 'security chiefs' know the bombers to be a young man

June 1978

and a young woman, both members of the religious sect Ananda Marga. The young woman is currently in Australia but the man is overseas. It seems obvious that anyone within the sect would imagine they are referring to Abhiik Kumar. The 'security experts' quoted go on to declare that while they 'have no doubt who the bombers are', they have 'no real evidence against them'. These two bombers are radical members of the sect who also follow the Proutist movement and do not represent the majority of sect members.[8]

What are they trying to achieve with this leak? To unnerve this suspected female bomber? To encourage a reasonable sect member to break ranks? To send a message to Kumar in India that they are on to him? To rattle his chain?

Whether by design or coincidence, in mid-June Ananda Marga members seem agitated, or at least intent on increasing the number of their public demonstrations and actions. In addition, the focus of the sect feels split and chaotic. Also at this time there is an abrupt change of tack and the focus on protesting against the National Alliance is put on hold in favour of organising demonstrations and actions in support of fellow Margii John William Duff, on trial in Canberra. It is through these latter actions that Ross Dunn is thrust forward as a significant character in Seary's confessions. By 12 and 15 June, in the seventh and eighth tape-recorded debriefs, according to Seary the focus of the Margiis is a variety of actions to be staged in Canberra to support Duff. None of the activities Seary is to be involved in have particularly clear goals — lock picking, flag tampering — and it's not exactly clear who Dunn is, besides, allegedly, a member of or leader of Prout. Seary describes a frantic amount of activity and meetings in this four-day period that feels directionless.

This rush of alleged Margii actions in Sydney, none as yet demonstrably violent, are played out for real, with demonstrable violence, across the ocean when on 14 June, 25-year-old Swiss-born Elizabeth Weniger, wrapped in saffron robes, strolls down to Rizal Park in Manila. She sits down and begins to pray. Witnesses watch as she then pours petrol over herself and strikes 'a match, turning herself into a human torch'. As this horrific image, a protest against Stephen Dyer's and Victoria Shepherd's convictions, is seared into the retinas of the onlookers, they recall Elizabeth chanting rhythmic prayers, then collapsing 'crying "Baba", [the] name of the Ananda Marga God'.[9]

The madness of the day

So finally we arrive at 15 June, a day on which no one can agree on anything. It's simply impossible to determine the absolute truth of this day and night. All the events that are known are perfectly ambiguous. Like an eternal conundrum or an ouroborus, the 'evidence' seems to reflect the testimony of whoever is making the argument — before flipping over and reflecting the exact opposite — leading one back to start all over again trying to winnow out who did what to whom. Something happened. Someone lied. Seary? The police? Anderson, Alister and Dunn? All of them?

One thing's for certain, the events of the day destroy any chance for Sheather's team to proceed coherently with the Hilton investigation as it is. He, like everyone else, will be compelled to follow a completely new path, swept along by the monumental force of what occurs. After the deluge, there will be nuggets to dig out that will eventually lead us back to our quarry, but for now — enter the madness of the day.

It begins normally enough this Thursday. Well, normal within the framework of the Special Branch running their man in the Ananda Marga. That morning Seary and Krawczyk sit down face to face for their eighth tape-recorded debrief. It's full of inconclusive conversations and descriptions of meetings with Anderson, Alister and Dunn, with whom he has suddenly been spending more time. There's talk of actions planned for Canberra — something involving a flagpole — and renewed interest in action against Robert Cameron. According to Seary, Anderson has asked him to locate the neo-fascist's home address. Other than that, there's mention that Seary has offered to stand in for Alister at the following night's Ananda Marga soup patrol.[1]

Having once again unburdened himself to his confessor, Seary wanders back to the Ananda Marga. And then …?

If you're the accused Margiis, at some point that afternoon Seary, Alister and Dunn, with Anderson's knowledge and approval, decide to drive out to Robert Cameron's home in Yagoona (about 45 minutes' drive from the centre of Sydney) after 11 pm with the purpose of daubing the exterior of his house with anti-racist slogans.

The madness of the day

If you're Seary and the police, at some point on Thursday afternoon Anderson, Alister and Dunn decide that, with Anderson's approval and Seary's assistance as driver, Alister and Dunn will travel to Yagoona with the intent of blowing up the home of Robert Cameron and everyone inside it. After the blast they will phone Anderson at the sect's headquarters and he will issue statements to the press claiming the murder in the name of UPRF.

It's easy to be sucked into the minutiae of these competing versions and to marvel at the complete incompatibility of the two accounts. God, it occupied journalists and commentators for years. Details about Anderson sleeping in an office at No. 9 Queen Street, Newtown, and not No. 5 where he lived, either because he had to leave for work early the next day and did not want to wake his son, or as proof he was waiting to send press releases claiming responsibility for the bombing. Or about Anderson sitting in the car with them all on nearby Carillon Avenue and getting out at the corner prior to the trek to Yagoona — either because Anderson is just finishing a chat to his mate Paul about the Margii soup patrol before Alister, Seary and Dunn embark on their anti-racist campaign, or giving the trio their final instructions on the operation to blow up the Nazi bastard.

This day, so picked apart and interrogated through two trials, two appeals (one to the High Court), an inquest and an inquiry, can never be seen afresh. Questions as to what was most plausible, probable or likely lose their currency under the suspicious gaze of the warring parties. Everything can be attacked, everything is questioned. Depending on whose side you're on, whatever is coming out of the other party's mouth is just pure invention and gobbledygook. For the accused, the position is that Seary basically conjures up this conspiracy to murder Cameron in order to frame the trio and then makes it real by stealing a car and bringing a bomb with him on the harmless sign-painting jaunt. Anderson, Alister and Dunn will propose that Seary, in order to get out of his suffocating relationship with Special Branch, invents this ludicrous tale, tips off the police and supplies the evidence — the bomb, the letters to the press — himself. The police, while *not* colluding at the outset, will then fabricate evidence and confessions to support the convictions of the three.

For Seary, after ten weeks in the sect, six as an initiated member, that Thursday afternoon he is suddenly thrust into the centre. He has been selected to drive these conspirators to the scene of their intended crime. In Seary's version, Anderson, Alister, Dunn and Seary meet on a university oval in order to discuss a violent action at the home of Robert Cameron; in Anderson, Alister and Dunn's version, they meet with Seary on the university oval because one of them wants to hire it for a soccer match. You can go on about this stuff ad nauseam. It's a bit like listening to two aggrieved lovers reiterate each other's imagined betrayals — part of you doesn't want to get involved, as some of it comes across as petty and irritating. Except, of course, in this case the stakes are much higher than a broken relationship. For Anderson, Alister, Dunn, and even Seary, the consequences of the day are devastating.

There is a single piece of independent intelligence from ASIO that day, from one of their agents within the sect. It too is maddeningly elusive. Their informant had detected that something was up within the Ananda Marga that afternoon. So concerned was the agent he contacted his superiors to communicate a warning that, 'Something funny was going on, something he couldn't understand.'[2]

These are the few agreed upon facts:

At 5.15 pm on the fateful day, Richard Seary rings Detective Krawczyk and says he has to meet him urgently. They meet. Seary blurts out that he has just come from a meeting in which Anderson, Alister and Dunn have outlined their plot to murder Cameron and that furthermore they don't care who dies in the explosion — family, pets, small children. Even more alarming is that all this is to take place that very night, in a matter of hours. Seary declares he has been ordered to obtain a car and to pick up the Margii men at 11 pm in Carillon Avenue, alongside Sydney

University, and then drive them to Cameron's home. This is to take place in less than six hours.

I have to ask: if you were Detective Krawczyk, how would you respond to this kind of information? Seary is your agent, your recruit, you're not exactly sure of the value of all his intelligence but you think some of it is pretty good. You think that members of the sect are involved with terrorist bomb threats. You know that some of the international members have been caught carrying out similar activities. True, the Nazi target is a wild card, a variation on the theme of targeting Indian nationals that you have come to expect. What do you do? What if the threat, however unusual, is true?

You do things by the book. You go to see your boss.

Krawczyk shuttles Seary to police headquarters to see Inspector Perrin, the head of Special Branch. While Seary's existence is known to Perrin, they have never met. The three men sit down. Krawczyk starts talking. The conversation is recorded. Alas it will be the last one that is for the next 24 hours.[3]

K: This is Inspector Perrin. This is Richard Seary.
Now tell the inspector what you told me earlier.

S: There is going to be a bombing in Sydney tonight. The Margiis are going to blow up the fellow Cameron from the National Alliance.

The madness of the day

Perrin is like a hound dog, sniffing quizzically, and starts barking out a series of questions at Seary: when, where, what and who. Seary doesn't blink in the face of this barrage. Instead he elaborates on the plot:

> Well it was decided to bomb Cameron's home and kill him and anyone in it. I was told to get a car and meet Narada [Alister] and Vishvamitra [Dunn] at 11 o'clock at Carillion Avenue near the uni gates, then we would go to a house, I wasn't told where, and pick up a device and then we were to go to 16 Gregory Street [Yagoona]. I was told I had to drive past the house and pull up near a reservoir and the other two would walk back and put the bomb in the house. After the bomb had gone off we were to ring Govinda [Anderson] at Newtown. Narada is to ring the number which is 5-- 2174 and say is that 5-- 2177 and Govinda will say 'No you have the wrong number.' Govinda will then know that the job has been done and will issue press and radio releases in the name of The One World Revolutionary Army, claiming responsibility for the job.[4]

Perrin doesn't even attempt to hide his scepticism:[5]

> Perrin: Are you sure this is right? It seems incredible that anyone would consider blowing

up a man and his family simply because he is the leader of a political organisation like the National Alliance, it's only got a few members.⁶

Again Seary doesn't flinch. They are going to do it and he has to get a car and pick them up.
'What if [you don't] get the car?' Perrin retorts.
'They would do it without me,' says Seary.
What Perrin can't get his head around is why the hell this perplexing man is so willing to assist the police.

> Perrin: Now I want to get this straight. You are prepared to borrow a friend's car and drive it and pick up these men and then a bomb and take it to Gregory Street. Why?⁷

To which Seary makes the heroically civic answer, 'Well, I think these people have to be stopped from doing this.' Perrin isn't persuaded and keeps up his interrogation. What will happen if the police intercept the car en route?
Seary answers, 'I feel sure Narada will detonate the bomb. They say you have to be willing to die for your cause.'
'Are you prepared to die?' demands Perrin.
'I don't want to die, no. I just hope the police know how to handle the situation,' Seary replies.

The madness of the day

Perrin tries to get some kind of bead on this situation. Will these men be armed? Which route will they take to Gregory Street? Seary says he has no idea. He imagines it will depend on where they collect the bomb. Perrin seems particularly annoyed that Seary seems so certain of the plot to kill Cameron in a few hours' time but so utterly vague on specifics of the bomb's whereabouts.

Perrin: You have no idea where that is?

Seary: No, I haven't been told.

Perrin: Do you have any idea at all?

Suddenly, Seary might: 'I think, but it's only a guess, that it would be Kapil's place in Balmain.'[8]
Poor Inspector Perrin. Now Krawczyk has 'delegated up', he has to deal with this poisoned chalice. It's now Thursday night, mere hours away from the execution of this supposed plot to blow up a household of people deep in the suburban sticks. How would it reflect on him if he let his doubts take root and he did nothing? Would he be derided like the hapless Superintendent Reginald Douglas,[9] who sent the directive not to check the bins outside the Hilton for bombs? Imagine being that guy, the one that failed to act. While the public can probably be counted on to

have little sympathy for the neo-Nazi being blown up, they're not going to feel the same way about the man's wife and kids, are they?

Perrin is trapped. He can only go forward and act, no matter how unconvinced he may feel. Harder to explain is the series of procedural oversights that follow this decision. Seary is sent off unaccompanied to borrow a friend's car. He is not fitted with a listening device. They don't procure a car for him and fit it with a listening device. Allegedly all they say is something along the lines of, 'We will have you under surveillance once you arrive to pick up the men in Carillon Avenue.'[10] Maybe Inspector Perrin is reluctant to go all out until he can actually have the police eyeball the suspects together at 11 pm. Maybe it's the lateness of the hour, the lack of time to scramble expert teams to handle a threat such as this, that leads to mistakes. There is so much to do. As soon as Richard Seary completes his tale of imminent terror, Perrin has to assemble three sets of police to cover the operation. Naturally in the spirit of 'delegating up', Perrin first informs his bosses, Police Commissioner Wood and Superintendent Black.[11] Next he has to locate some cops. Thursday evening on a frigid night in Sydney 1978 — senior expert police such as the Special Weapons and Operations Squad aren't exactly standing in a room downstairs ready to vault into action. Some are at home, some are at the pub. Miraculously, they are rounded up swiftly, brought in and briefed.

The briefing prepared by Special Branch at CIB underlines the belief that this operation is critically linked to the ongoing investigation into the Hilton bombing: 'All the persons [who are to be picked up by Seary] are members of the Ananda Marga sect and at this stage it is suspected that two of them, namely, O'Callaghan [Alister] and Dunn, would have vital information concerning the Hilton bomb inquiry.'[12] Independently of Seary, Special Branch have their suspicions about these two individuals. Alister has been arrested in the past for attacks against Indian nationals and he is associated with VSS. Dunn is believed to be part of Prout, and while they can't yet prove it, they believe Prout members to be involved in the bombing.

It is pointed out that the sect members are constantly involved in physical, possibly military, training, they are known to carry daggers, and at least one member has a degree in Mining Engineering and is an expert in explosives. The final point in the Special Branch briefing that night literally drops from the sky and reunites us with our old comrade Abhiik Kumar, who once again has an unerring capacity to arrive in or depart countries immediately before or after bombings or attempted bombings.

Sect leader Michael Luke BRANDON (number of alias) currently overseas and informant in Bangkok, Thailand states that he has made approaches for the purchase of explosives and also RADIO CONTROLLED TIME DEVICES. Sect Leader due to arrive in Australia 8.35am on Thailands flight on Friday 16 June 1978. [13]

In 11 hours' time.

Imagine how on edge you'd be if you were a member of either police squad. You'd be thinking about the Hilton. Thinking about zealots and the potential horror of the whole thing going badly. After all, this is a likely scenario from what Seary is suggesting — that if the Margiis think the cops are going to stop the car, Alister will set the bomb off. Perrin and Helson of Special Branch bring the squad up to speed on what they know of the sect. It can hardly instil confidence in the Weapons Squad to discover that Margiis believe their god is on trial, that they occasionally set themselves on fire, or that almost ten of them have been arrested around the globe for terrorist acts. Add to this that the whole enterprise is going to take place in Yagoona, a graveyard-quiet suburb of fibro houses on quarter-acre blocks, and that the target is the leader of the Australian wing of the National Alliance, and this must make the whole operation seem even more peculiar and disturbing.

A lot has been said about New South Wales police officers over the years — some of it by me in a documentary called *The Inquisition* — about the endemic

The madness of the day

corruption, the blue walls of silence and the like, but on an operation like this one cannot fault their courage. In short, they are instructed to set off for Yagoona after Seary has collected the Margiis in Newtown, and to apprehend them in the act — or immediately prior to the act. To enter a scene without hesitation in which all six of them could be blown sky high.

Simultaneously Perrin mobilises the Observation Squad to cover the Margii headquarters in Queen Street, Newtown, which is just around the corner from Carillon Avenue, the site of the intended pick-up. A mix of Special Branch detectives, including Krawczyk and Observation Squad police, seven in total, are dispatched to Newtown to observe the rendezvous.

It is among all this frenzy that Seary leaves police headquarters, around 9 pm, via the basement.[14] He walks out into the cold, wet night of a Sydney winter and all is lost.

Yagoona

Between 9 pm and 11 pm all Seary needs to do is borrow a friend's car. Perhaps that's why the police don't accompany him — how hard can that be? Perrin, on the other hand, has to ensure the smooth coordination of almost 20 police officers at separate locations: Newtown, Yagoona and CIB headquarters. Perhaps it is no surprise that Seary is left utterly unsupervised over the next few hours.

Things start to go wrong immediately. Seary can't find anyone who'll lend him a car. After wandering around for 90 minutes he finally decides to nick one from Foveaux Street, Surry Hills. He hotwires an HT Holden and drives towards Sydney Uni.

By the time Dunn, in the back, Alister, up front, and Seary, driving, set off for 16 Gregory Street, there is a large blue denim bag in the car containing all the components to make a good size bomb. In it sit ten sticks of gelignite, batteries, a timer and a detonator. Seary and seven policemen will swear under oath that Dunn arrives at the car in Carillon Avenue with the bag — or carrying something that looks 'bag-like'. The trio of Margiis will counter that Seary pulls up to collect them with the bag containing the bomb already in the back seat. Dunn and Alister will swear that they had no idea the bag contained a bomb until Seary tells them about it just before their arrival at Yagoona. Anderson will assert he had absolutely no idea about a bomb until the police turn up to arrest him later that night.

Let these differences lie for now. Next there is a kind of comedic aside when Seary realises he has managed to steal a car with an empty tank — there is a little physical farce as the men locate a back lane and struggle to break open the petrol cap, then locate a service station and fill up in order to make the getaway car functional. After this, alone in the dark, zooming towards their destination, a bomb nestled on the back seat and followed discreetly by the Observation Squad, there are versions of what is or is not said. Supposed confessions and accusations. Misunderstandings and conflict. None of it is recorded. All of it is hearsay.

Down Parramatta Road then sweeping up the mighty Hume Highway and then we're at Yagoona. Seary misses the turn-off to Gregory Street and takes the next left at Horton Street that runs alongside

Bass Hill Public School. The Special Weapons and Operations Squad swoop in behind the Margiis' car. Detective Summerfield, driving the lead car, forces the Holden off the road into the front yard of a modest weatherboard on Horton Street.[1]

At that moment these two worlds that have orbited each other uneasily for so many months smash together in a collision of noise and light. Three slight, bearded young men are dragged from a car and across the road, handcuffed and made to lie down on the pavement in front of the school.

Then the Army bomb disposal unit arrives, with a Captain Stevenson[2] in full uniform warning the detectives to stay away as the bomb might be set. The Army officers invade the car and dismantle the unprimed bomb. This, too, with all its gleaming components, is spread out in front of the school.

The Margiis on one side, the police on the other, are incomprehensible to each other. Nothing captures this better than the police photographs taken that night. There are three action shots of each of the sect members being escorted away from the scene by separate sets of policemen. The police are all huge. Tall, handsome men in suits and matching dark raincoats, three with those glossy Tom Selleck moustaches so popular in the '70s. Their expressions are a mix of triumph and relief. In their tatty street clothes, Alister and Dunn look tiny beside them, their hands behind their backs. In these frozen tableaux, Alister looks stunned and Dunn, childlike and bereft. Even Seary, who is likewise shackled and aware of what is to occur, wears an expression of intense anxiety.[3] One of the things that strikes me is how effortlessly Seary looks like he's one of them, a Margii through and through, a true believer.

Everyone would have been so scared, though, wouldn't they? While the bomb they retrieve from the back seat is unarmed, 'each of the components was operational and there was a continuity of the electrical circuit'. All one had to do to get it up and running would be to 'place the leg wires and the detonator on the positive and negative terminals of the batteries'. If approximately 12 to 15 sticks of gelignite can obliterate the back of a steel garbage truck, eviscerate two men and shatter glass 16 storeys high, 10 sticks would have destroyed the car, its occupants and anyone within 15 feet of it. This would have included the occupants of the house six or so feet from where the car came to rest. Whoever brought the bomb was playing an extraordinarily high stakes game.[4]

Making things even more surreal is that neither Robert Cameron, nor his dog, wife or kiddies actually live at 16 Gregory Street, Yagoona. He'd moved out of the area a year earlier. Seary had plucked the address from an old telephone directory. Had either scheme succeeded, the residents of 16 Gregory Street might have woken on Friday morning to find their home daubed with inexplicable slogans like 'Prout hates racists' — or they mightn't have woken up at all.

Not long after the drama at Yagoona, the Observation Squad, padded out with additional detectives, pours into the Ananda Marga's Newtown HQ, ascending to the office and hoovering up — or, as the Margiis claim, planting — evidence.

Here the plot both thickens and twists. We have a new bit player who will dominate the show for years to come. In 1978 I doubt anyone would make much of the inclusion of Detective Roger Rogerson in the crack team assembled for the raid on the Margiis that night. At the time he's a lauded and decorated officer, known to bring cases in. Of course by 1986 his reputation is such that you may as well have hired Attila the Hun or Vlad the Impaler if you were going to put question marks over the integrity of the operation that night. His presence at the Margii residence becomes one of those immovable obstacles that blocks out the light. In view of his various alleged and proven transgressions in the coming decades — murder, green-lighting criminals, fabricating evidence — it's difficult to be certain about anything he's involved with. If you're guilty of some things are you guilty of everything? Does it automatically follow that all he touches is infected with the same dark traits?

It's not as if he's the only one running the show.

Krawczyk and Helson, who had been at the Horton Street scene, are directed by Inspector Perrin to return to the Newtown police station and meet up with Rogerson. After a conference, the three of them, along with another three detectives, head to Queen Street and find a Margii guard outside. The police force the front door open. They ask for Anderson and locate him on the top floor, lying on his back, his eyes open.[5] He is arrested and taken to CIB headquarters.

Here's the problem: according to the police, the arrested sect members are refreshingly forthcoming both at Yagoona and at Queen Street and then at CIB headquarters. They don't seem to be able to shut up, not only about their involvement in the crime, but also their lack of remorse. Immediately after being cautioned, Anderson supposedly tells Rogerson, in front of Detectives Howard, Krawczyk and Helson:

'I don't intend to say a lot. I will say this. It will not stop here. What was going to happen tonight was the only justice that Cameron and his kind deserve. You will suffer the consequence for this.'[6]

The problem is that no one has thought to turn on a tape recorder. It is possible that in fact they have decided deliberately *not* to turn on a tape recorder. Thus all the 'conversations' are dutifully recorded in police notebooks. Hence these kinds of confessions were called 'verbals'. In short they could be incriminating, unverifiable statements fabricated by corrupt police.

It's a spectacularly stupid decision. Even if Anderson, Alister and Dunn did utter every word they were accused of saying that night, it can't ever be proved, can it? Think what you like about Rogerson, but I've spent a great deal of time with Detective Krawczyk's meticulous records and reading transcripts of his interviews with Seary. He does things transparently and without equivocation. While some of the Seary debrief tapes are mislabelled, which fuels a variety of attacks from the Margiis, Krawczyk did think to record them. I find it hard to believe he would have thought that simply jotting notes down during interrogations was a good idea.

What these verbals do is create doubt. Enough doubt, along with other doubtful circumstances such as the lack of surveillance when Seary collected the Margiis in Carillon Avenue, and questions over Seary's credibility, to free these three men in seven years' time.

While there are disturbing problems in the 'evidence' (as there will be for Anderson's trial in 1989), after reading everything available I also stand by what James Wood says in the conclusion to the 1984–85 Section 475 inquiry:

> In these circumstances, I have no alternative other than to express the conclusion that, while strong suspicion attached to the petitioners [Anderson, Alister and Dunn] in relation to the counts on

which they stood indicted and were convicted, a doubt remains as to their guilt.[7]

Did Seary bring a bomb of devastating power to a suburban street, all in order to frame the sect members, escape his relationship with Special Branch and be free to go to university? If this was Seary's intention it utterly failed. In his own way he will be shackled to this act for the rest of his life. In August 1991 he goes so far as to make a serious complaint about ASIO failing to bring forward their agents inside the sect, who he alleges could have corroborated his claims about Margii violence.[8]

As recently as 1999, Seary unsuccessfully sues Tom Molomby, a staunch supporter of Anderson, Alister and Dunn, for defamation[9] over his book *Spies, Bombs and the Path of Bliss* published 13 years earlier.[10] In the book Molomby alleges that Seary is a liar and a perjurer and that it is possible he is the Hilton bomber himself. So if Seary invented all his allegations about the Ananda Marga and brought the bomb to Yagoona just to get away from the sect and Special Branch, it didn't work out very well.

There is a third possible interpretation of what happened the night of the arrests at Yagoona, an interpretation beyond the versions presented by Richard Seary and the police on the one hand and the Margiis and their supporters on the other. An interpretation

I toy with in idle hours, which can't be proved: that Anderson, Dunn and Alister are set up by Abhiik Kumar. That the Australasian leader of the sect is so rattled by the allegations against him in the *Sun-Herald* on 11 June that he sends Seary, of whom he is suspicious, and the others, two of whom he dislikes (Alister, who Seary alleges in his Special Branch tapes Abhiik can't bear, and Anderson, whom Abhiik has had a documented spat with the day before the Hilton bombing), so they can get caught and thus divert police attention away from himself and other higher-up Margiis like Kapil Arn who are suspected of the Hilton bombing and other acts of international violence.

While it's just a theory based on pure speculation, it's not without merit. For example, by 16 June all the attention on Kumar seems to cease. I can find nothing in the police archives as to whether or not he arrives, as expected, on the 8.35 am flight from Thailand. He doesn't. The fact is, after these extraordinary arrests in Yagoona and Newtown, it seems that the entire gaze of the New South Wales police — Special Branch included — is upon these three Margiis and no others. If one asks the age-old question 'Who benefits?' with regard to the Yagoona arrests, the answer is Abhiik Kumar.

For example, one of the items collected the night of the 15 June arrests is a tape recording entitled 'Fight Against the Demon', narrated by 'Abhiik

Kumara [sic]'.[11] This recording was located at the VSS headquarters in Burwood, raided simultaneously with the Margii headquarters in Newtown. While the subsequent police transcription of the tape is littered with spelling mistakes, its message is clear: sect members are not supposed to sit idly by while the 'demons' deny the human and legal rights of their leader, Baba. They are expected to vigorously oppose those who oppress the sect. It is not enough to fight darkness with 'light' nor to imagine that simple good works will realign the balance. A member must actively fight and struggle with the demons, 'avoidance of that struggle is pure hypocrisy … it is a useless life. You might as well be dead':

> It's clear Baba does not believe that humanity is fighting sufficiently, that's why he is telling us to be vigorously active. So life is conflict … Baba said that even the apposles [sic] of peace were not allowed to work peacefully. Consider … Jesus how he was crucified or how many times they tried to kill Baba consider Baba's condition now, in jail. Are we to be at the mercy of these demons that would kill him if they could? Are we to sit idle, relying on fate, consider if it is possible for this true devity [sic] not to fight the demons, for the true spiritualists, not to be also social revolutionary.

Kumar goes on to reiterate how the charges that have been brought by the Indian Government against Baba are outrageous and unsubstantiated. They are a violation of his human rights. Something has to be done.

> I have said before that the meek shall inherit the earth. They'll do that, but they'll only inherit the earth when they are ready to fight for it, to live for it, to fight for it, to die for it and they will have to fight against these demons, against those self seeking opportunists who are presently controlling this entire planet and the destiny of the entire human race.

He then recounts an instance of one of Baba's miracles, and concludes his long impassioned speech with:

> You may be many things, but first and foremost you are a spiritualist, and on the social plane that means you are a revolutionary ... Those of you who have eyes to see, then see his [Baba's] physical condition now, those of you who have ears and can hear, then hear this *varney* [phonetic from the tape]. Hear this message and hear it right, hear it correctly and then do something, do something ...[12]

It's hard to interpret this as anything other than a call to physical activism against the enemies of the sect. While perhaps not explicitly inciting violence by sect members, it certainly could be argued that certain individuals listening to such a speech could take it to mean exactly that. It does seem to indicate that Kumar, rather than his foot soldiers, should be the one to watch. If violence, or the threat of violence, is thought to be committed by sect members, it makes complete sense that it is Kumar who would have authorised it.

Despite this, the police, under Inspector Perrin of Special Branch, seem completely uninterested in looking at suspects higher up in the Margii hierarchy, and appear content with the trio they have captured. Again it's worth remembering that Seary only met Dunn and Anderson a few days immediately before 15 June, and that the Hilton task force never seemed to regard them as major players. It was Kumar they were watching.

Not any more.

To make matters worse, Richard Seary seems to be intent on shredding his remaining credibility.

By the time morning dawns on 16 June, the members of Ananda Marga must be aware not only of the arrests of Paul Alister, the head of Volunteer Social Services, Ross Dunn, possibly a leader of Prout, and Tim Anderson, the Ananda Marga public relations officer, but also that Richard Seary is a police informant. He has nothing to lose now. He has no reason to feel he can't unburden himself completely to the police. But he does not.

Despite Special Branch mentioning the possibility that Alister and Dunn have knowledge of the Hilton bombing in their 15 June debrief to police prior to the Yagoona arrests, Seary hasn't contributed anything concrete to support this. In his eight taped debriefings with Special Branch up to the morning of the 15th, he makes the odd veiled allusion, but nothing he says is even vaguely conclusive. Nor does Seary make any mention of the Hilton bombing in his official interview on 16 June after the trio's arrest. He diligently relates all the information regarding the alleged plot to blow up Mr Cameron and his family, and that's it.

Then abruptly Norm Sheather steps back into view in the archive. The last time he captured our attention he was being lambasted in the papers for being the absent leader of a doomed investigation. Now he thrusts himself forward, propelled perhaps by the rush of emotions he must feel in reaction to the arrest of the three Margiis.

Is Norm appalled, enraged or uplifted by the news of the arrests? Of the involvement of one Richard Seary, who is working as a Special Branch agent? It's difficult to know precisely when this information is made known to the head of the Hilton task force. It's possible Norm is brought into the loop at the time of the 24 May revelations about an 'all-out war', but it's hard to say. He's clearly been sidelined and nowhere does his name appear in the heady, frantic preparations for the 15 June Yagoona and Newtown operations. It's rather a pity that Roger Rogerson and not Norm Sheather met with Krawczyk and Helson at Newtown police station before bouncing off to arrest Anderson. Perhaps Sheather would have remembered to push the button on the tape recorder. A pity, too, that Norm wasn't involved in the briefings of the Observation and Special Weapons squads — he may have been more apt to point out the need to be meticulous in collecting corroborating evidence when dealing with a complex, secretive sect highly skilled at plausible deniability.

At any rate, Inspector Perrin doesn't seem to have called him. Maybe he thought that Detective Inspector Sheather was too important to haul away from dinner at the family home. Maybe Perrin decided that the recruitment of Seary was his call and that he would take all the blame or all the glory.

The result is that Norm Sheather does not reappear in the archive until 22 June. It is, however, clear that he has taken the initiative to place himself back in the fray. In 1985, Sheather tells James Wood, 'Well, I believed that in view of [Seary's involvement] with the three gentlemen presently before this inquiry that you would expect something to be known about the Hilton Hotel bombing and I interviewed him to see what information he could convey to me that would assist me in the inquiry.'[13]

On 22 June Seary participates in a three and a half hour interview with Detective Inspector Sheather, the faithful Detective Sergeant Jackson and Inspector Perrin, who, after all, is the one who initially approved Seary's recruitment. At the outset of the interview it is made clear to Seary that inquiries are being made about the Hilton bombing in relation to the Yagoona 'incident'. He is then given his record of interview from the night of 16 June, asked to read over it and whether he has anything to add.

He does.

Seven long days after Yagoona, Seary, startlingly, produces the mother lode.

'Have you ever seen what this stuff can do?'

It turns out Seary hasn't just omitted a few bits and pieces. He has omitted the extraordinary revelation that on the way to bomb Cameron, Alister and Dunn made it pretty bloody clear — basically confessing to him — that they had also bombed the Hilton. Apparently they blurted all this out with little prompting:

> Seary: Dunn was doing something with the explosives in the backseat and I told him to be careful. He replied that it was alright. I asked him if he had had any experience with explosives and he replied that he would rather not say. Narada then said 'It is OK because Virata (myself) [Seary's Margii name] was a member of V.S.S. and

was OK.' I said to Visvamitra [sic], 'Have you ever seen what this stuff can do?' He replied, 'Sure I have seen what twelve sticks can do' I said, 'How do you mean' He answered, 'Well, the Hilton' At this point Narada said, 'Don't think about that just be sure that you have the timer and fuses OK we don't want any mistakes this time.'[1]

In response to this astonishing pronouncement, Sheather and Perrin seem thunderstruck and reduced to the most banal kind of police-speak.

> Sheather: Much of the information you have given us during the interview is not contained in that interview conducted between Detective Sergeant Jackson and yourself at the Criminal Investigation Branch on Friday the 16th June. Can you give me a reason for that?
>
> Seary: I was under a lot of strain and I thought at the time that I had given a satisfactory answer to the questions asked by Mister Jackson at that stage.[2]

Years later it is revealed in court that Seary felt that Norm Sheather particularly disliked him. Personally, I'm surprised Norm is able to contain himself and doesn't reach across the table and throttle him then and there. First the procedural problems on the night of the arrests and now this cataclysmic admission, made — preposterously — six days after the first exhaustive interview.

Then there's more ...

Towards the end of the interview on 22 June (around 11.50 pm), Seary says he's tired and asks if he can finish the interview at a later date. Sheather agrees and picks up the trail on 26 June 1978, ten days after the first interview regarding the Yagoona incident.

At this interview Seary is even more garrulous. He remembers talk of egg timers, of how the Hilton gelignite had been wrapped like a packet of fish and chips in newspaper[3] and, even more startling, that prior to the trip to Yagoona, Anderson had been gabbing on about Dunn previously having put together a bomb in the street. Furthermore, Seary asserts that 'They [Anderson, Alister and Dunn] were always speaking of bombing jobs in plural and were always making references to a previous bombing where mistakes had been made, by Visvamitra [sic; Dunn] in the timing devices.'[4]

Seary is now beginning to revise things he has already told Krawczyk in the eight recorded debriefs.

Over the next month Seary's version of what was admitted by the trio in relation to the Hilton blooms with detail, depth and breadth. He keeps feeding new intelligence to Inspector Perrin, much to the intense annoyance of both Sheather and Detective Krawczyk. Finally Sheather hauls him back in for yet a further interview on 17 July 1978. Now Seary states that in the car Alister told him:

> ... that he Govinda [Anderson], Vismametra [sic; Dunn] and a friend whom he did not name had placed an explosive at the Hilton. Narada said that on the afternoon of the 12th he had walked through the crowds outside the Hilton in order to, as he put it, check out the place. After checking he said 'I signalled to Visamitra [sic] and he came up from the chocolate shop. Visamitra placed into the rubbish bin the device.[5]

Seary is either oblivious to the ramifications of what he has just said or utterly committed to pretending he can't see what the big deal is. Sheather has to restrain himself:

> Sheather: Do you agree that at no stage during our previous two interviews did you give any information that would identify any person as placing the explosive device in the garbage can outside the Hilton Hotel on the 13th February, 1978 or on the 12th of that month?[6]

'Have you ever seen what this stuff can do?'

This is followed by a tiny bit of dancing around by Seary when he implies that he alluded to this when he reported the conversation with Dunn about the effects of 12 sticks of gelignite.

Norm doesn't buy this and replies, 'Do you agree that that alone does not identify the person responsible for placing the device in the garbage bin in front of the Hilton Hotel?'[7]

To which Seary makes the extraordinary statement that:

> Seary: I realise that now and I am sorry that I made the mistake of trying to assess your evidence for you but I didn't want to be the one who directly put Visamitra [sic] in prison for this offence.[8]

Norm gazes at Seary — he's sorry he didn't mean to be assessing the evidence for them; he didn't want to be the one to put Dunn away. Who does this bedraggled, scraggly bearded, self-aggrandising man think he is? Miss Marple? Inspector Poirot? Norm must be hurtled back to that day four short months ago when Seary sat across from him spinning unsubstantiated concoctions about the Hare Krishnas. What if this is more of the same? Could he just be making it up? The horror of this thought must stab Norm in the stomach. Seary does have the earmarks of a pleaser — the information that has tumbled out of his mouth post Yagoona is like a spreading infection growing more florid with each interview. It puts one in mind of those unhinged souls who were so eager to confess to the Hilton bombing. Why, why, why did Special Branch recruit and run Richard Seary? And then why withhold that information from the task force? But Norm Sheather knows the answer to that: he would have said it was an idiotic idea doomed to failure.

Yet for all the animosity and irritation, there has to be something deep within, not just Norm Sheather, but all of the team, that longs for what Seary says to be true. That finally they have the evidence they have been seeking, that their suspicions are vindicated, the case is wrapped up. That those fatherless children of the Hilton bombing victims can grow old knowing the identity of the murderers and knowing their punishment. Some of the information from Seary in the tape-recorded Special Branch debriefs before Yagoona is pretty solid, it can be corroborated. Of course there is no mention of the Hilton in them. Sheather and the team listen hard to Seary's increasing list of excuses as to the unfathomable delays in telling them about the Hilton confession.

He didn't have a phone. He was tired and didn't want to unduly prolong the first interview. The police were inept and should have arrested everyone at Carillon Avenue and thus endangered everyone by waiting

'Have you ever seen what this stuff can do?'

till Yagoona. The Weapons Squad were mean to him and hurt him yanking him out of the stolen car. My favourite? That Detective Jackson didn't ask him the right questions during the first interview on 16 June. He wanted to protect Ross Dunn, of whom he had grown fond, and felt that he was being used by the Ananda Marga. The information was 'harassed' out of him by Detective Krawczyk. That he wanted Anderson, Alister and Dunn to confess first, as it was better if this came from them and not him. He wasn't sure if they had been telling him the truth or winding him up. He did not 'particularly like Detective Inspector Sheather' and thus only gave him the relevant information that would lead him to ask the correct questions.[9]

Does Norm feel the hope ebbing away as the excuses pile up like logs on a funeral pyre? The shaky foundations of Seary's Hilton bombing accusations simply liquefy under the weight of them. Of course we know they gain no traction from this point on — I mean yes they are brought up again and again and again but because they are so flimsy they never make it to court.

When in 1985 James Wood comes to decipher the often inexplicable and contradictory evidence, even he admits, 'It is impossible to reach any conclusion in relation to the accuracy and worth of the intelligence provided by Seary.'[10] I can't imagine that this statement gave him much comfort, particularly as those following the case were hoping for unequivocal conclusions. Wood added a caveat, saying perhaps one could start to determine accuracy and worth of Seary's information but:

> This would require a careful consideration and evaluation of such independently acquired information as did become available to the inquiry, and of material which may or may not exist in the hands of intelligence and police agencies other than the New South Wales Special Branch. This was neither practical, nor did it seem profitable.[11]

What Wood seems to be itching to say is that if you look closely enough, you can start to tease out the good from the bad. It's obvious that the excuses for delaying the 'confessions' after the Yagoona arrests, and indeed the incremental embellishment of them, border on the 'unintelligible and preposterous'. Wood responds drily to Seary's claim that it was sympathy for Dunn that kept him silent in the first interview: 'Why should he entertain sympathy or concern for Dunn, when if the facts were as he suggested, Dunn was an active participant in a horrifying crime in 1978, and was setting out in June 1978 to murder a family of five?'[12]

What happens is that these inconsistencies, like 'verbal' confessions, like the presence of Rogerson,

'Have you ever seen what this stuff can do?'

create doubt. And we know what that does to a legal case. Despite all this, James Wood, perhaps thinking back on poor Sheather's scuttled Hilton investigation, makes a bit of a play at being detective himself. Summing up the whole sorry saga he asks:

> Were the Petitioners and Police carefully manoeuvred into position by Seary, and the extrinsic facts skilfully manipulated by him, so that a well forged circumstantial case might appear? Alternatively, did the events transpire in the general way that Seary described, leaving him in a position where, convinced of the Petitioners' guilt yet fearful that the Crown case may not be watertight, he was prepared to embellish and fill in the areas where he suspected problems might arise?[13]

But as Wood concludes, 'Although I incline to the latter view, I am satisfied that the first alternative cannot be excluded.'[14]

To be honest, I incline to the latter view myself, as I imagine Norm Sheather may have done seven years earlier. There is much to support what Seary alleges prior to Yagoona, and after that night he is gilding the lily or improvising wildly to try to ensure the charges will stick. Given his investment in the case, he wants to be seen as the hero of the day and helpfully fills in the gaps. I don't imagine thinking this way brings much solace to Sheather at the time, faced as he is with a disintegrating investigation. It's only a few months ago that he was going after the big game — communicating with a dozen international police agencies all intent on the same target: the upper echelons of the Ananda Marga, those within the rarefied and closed sanctum of leaders who receive direct orders from the imprisoned Baba, from whom all things within Ananda Marga and Prout emanate. The sect members who they believe have waged a campaign of terror for over a year. Instead of telexes from Interpol, Norm Sheather is stuck getting unverifiable nonsense from Seary.

Then, as if to hammer home all the failures of the investigation and underscore the unlikelihood of this crime ever being solved, the man at the middle of it all, the living god that is Mr PR (Baba) Sarkar, imprisoned in India for seven years for the murder of six treacherous Margiis, is found not guilty and is to be released.

'Have you ever seen what this stuff can do?'

July 1978

On 4 July 1978 the Patna High Court in Eastern India overturns Sarkar's murder conviction. For sect members the court decision could not be sweeter or more complete. Sarkar's four co-defendants, also accused of assassinating the six sect defectors in 1970, are likewise cleared. The ruling from the High Court is that the Indian Government failed to prove the murder charges beyond reasonable doubt, and that they had relied too heavily on the testimony of a single witness, 'Mr Marhwanand Awadhoot [sic]', who 'had been proved totally unreliable'.[1]

An addendum to the report in the *Sydney Morning Herald* adds that the 'Australian president of Ananda Marga, Mr Mark Dimelow, said last night that the sect's members in Australia were jubilant over the acquittal of their leader.'[2] I'm not sure how jubilant Tim Anderson, Ross Dunn and Paul Alister are, sitting in their prison cells as this news trickles down to them. While their guilt or innocence over the 'Yagoona incident' is still to be determined, either way, the timing's appalling. If they are found guilty and the aim was to propel the release of their leader, then they have been caught in a terrorist act that has turned out to be utterly pointless. If they are innocent, then they have begun a parallel journey of unjust incarceration that coincides neatly with Baba's exoneration. These three men will not enjoy the fruits of the sect's victory, which marks the apex not only of their united international efforts to free Baba, but of the sect's phenomenal growth and global spread through the 1970s, which has been so tied up with the campaign to free its leader.

What of Norm Sheather and his small band of brothers from New South Wales police, Special Branch and COMPOL? How do they react? Are they relieved that there is little chance of an 'all-out war' now Baba is free? Perhaps the feeling is that even if Richard Seary is a little strange, maybe these Yagoona arrests will pan out and provide the critical information needed to solve the Hilton bombing. Maybe it is time to let go and move on. Things may not be wrapped up as tightly as one might hope, but surely it's enough to assuage the hunger of the press and the public, who clamour for closure. It might even appease the young truth-seekers and defenders of civil liberties who have long argued that the sect has been ruthlessly

July 1978

persecuted. After all, the Indian Government, who the Ananda Marga has accused of masterminding a vast global conspiracy to discredit them, has not interfered in the Indian court system and Baba is free to go. One can hardly find fault in that. What they or the press make of the Yagoona arrests is harder to discern at first. Most are quiet in the face of what appears to be overwhelmingly damning evidence against the Margiis.

It's July 1978. What happens next? I'm going to tell you two things. The first you can forget about till later on, and the second I'll interrogate throughout this chapter. The first thing that happens will remain totally hidden for the next three years, although rumours will start to circulate about it from about this time on. What happens is that on 11 July, five days after Baba's successful appeal, someone rents a student locker at the University of New South Wales Roundhouse in the name of Melton.[3] On that day, or some time between then and 16 May the following year, someone places within it a black vinyl carry bag. The bag is discovered but not opened in September 1980, when New South Wales Uni handyman Mr Harry Harvy Lees pries the locker open after the fee has not been paid.[4]

Our diligent handyman ferries the unopened bag off to lost property.[5] When this bag is finally opened a year later, in 1981, it is found to contain, not so much a smoking gun, but a steaming DIY bomb. While we will return to the long list of the bag's contents at a later date — one packet of strip solder, one clock arm, one yellow towel and so on — what should lodge in your mind for the moment is the 52 individual sticks of gelignite wrapped in a copy of the *Sydney Morning Herald* dated 11 February 1978, a day and a bit before the Hilton bombing.[6]

The second thing that happens is, if not strange, certainly intriguing. If you are examining the Hilton Bombing Records, as I have been, it looks like the main investigative trajectory of the Hilton task force comes to an abrupt halt. Yes, of course, there are reams of material regarding the trial and appeals of Anderson, Alister and Dunn, and the inquest, and on for the next 18 years, but almost nothing other than that. If you *do not* wish to follow the narrative line that accuses Anderson, Alister and Dunn (or, later, that just accuses Anderson) — or, conversely, exonerates them — and instead want to follow the trail of Abhiik Kumar and the like, as I do — there are literally no more pieces of paper for the rest of the year. While some important archives pertaining to Kumar exist from 1979 on, my folders for primary police sources, August through to December 1978, are completely empty.

Before invoking yet another cockamamie conspiracy theory, consider these things. While it is absolutely clear that the arrest of the three young Margiis at Yagoona, along with their purported confessions about the Hilton via Seary, have thrown Sheather's investigation into a death spin from which it will not recover, it does provoke questions. Why would Norm Sheather, who had been so willing for so long to keep an open mind about suspects other than members of the Ananda Marga, as well as focusing on the sect's elite, stop so abruptly? It is obvious in those interviews with Seary that Sheather is both incredulous about the Hilton 'confessions' and dubious that they are substantial enough to result in convictions. Furthermore, none of these three were Norm Sheather's quarry. Would he and all the team who had pored over the intelligence from Interpol and ASIO and Special Branch, inching ever closer to the Margii elite for months, watching them swoop around the world, checking in with Baba in India then swooping out again, just drop the whole thing because three local minions had been arrested? Did they simply decide to abandon the investigative focus on Abhiik Kumar aka Jon Hoffman aka Jason Holman Alexander aka Mark Randall aka Stephen James Manly aka David Hart aka Michael Brandon?

Something else is going on.

Looking at the Hilton records, it seems that immediately after Yagoona on 15 June Norm et al push themselves back from their desks with a sigh à la *Babe* that says 'That'll do', but this is not what happens at all. It is true that both Norm Sheather and the Hilton task force begin to wind up, however it also marks the launch of an extraordinary last stand of the investigation, the ramifications of which resonate powerfully in modern Australia. We just have to look elsewhere for our information.

The principal sources I gleaned to piece together what occurred over the next six months are twofold: the super-public, being the daily newspapers, and the super-secret, being the federal Cabinet papers that began to be released under the 30-year rule in 2008. Peppered throughout are other primary archives I located from a range of sources that appeared over the last few decades — declassified ASIO reports and detritus from the ongoing trials. This is the story they relate.

Let's return to the article that appeared in the *Sun-Herald* on 11 June, just before the Yagoona arrests on 15 June. This is the article that seemed intentionally planted, that stated the investigators knew the identity of the bombers — a young woman and a young man, both sect members, the latter currently in India, which is where Abhiik Kumar is. What becomes clear in a matter of weeks is that the article is not the only act of official provocation around this time. On 13 June Kumar's latest passport, in the name of Michael Brandon, is cancelled by the federal government,[7] meaning that the police are in a position to detain him for questioning when he gets off that flight from Thailand on the morning of 16 June.

Except he's not on that flight. He does not return

to Australia. Instead, they have Anderson, Alister and Dunn in custody because the day before Kumar is due, Seary has launched a massive police operation based on the sudden and totally unexpected news that three sect members are heading off that very night to blow up a Nazi. Pretty weird timing. You couldn't imagine a better orchestrated bait and switch, could you? Amazing coincidence.

Anyway …

Baba is released and after celebrations in India, the no doubt relieved and euphoric Kumar, using his Brandon passport, finally boards a flight to Sydney, which touches down on 9 August 1978. He is immediately detained. We know about this from the Ananda Marga themselves.

> The spiritual leader of the Ananda Marga sect in Australia was detained by Commonwealth Police at Sydney Airport last night on his return from India, an official from the sect said. Commonwealth Police refused to comment on whether 28 year old Mr Jason Alexander, known as Acarya [sic] Abhiik Kumar in the sect, had been detained. However, the president of the sect in Australia, Mr Mark Dimellow [sic], said he had seen Mr Alexander led away from the Customs area by two plainclothes detectives. Mr Dimellow said he had spoken to Mr Alexander briefly.

Mr Alexander had said he had been arrested and his passport confiscated. Mr Alexander left Australia 10 weeks ago to work on a book in India and meet the sect's leader, Baba, who was recently released from an Indian jail.[8]

The cancellation of Kumar's Brandon passport on 13 June comes on orders from high up within the federal government. A top secret report on the Ananda Marga is in the process of being compiled, in consultation with the Department of Prime Minister and Cabinet, the Department of Foreign Affairs, the Department of Immigration and Ethnic Affairs, and the departments of Attorney-General's, Education, Administrative Services and Treasury, as well as ASIO and the Commonwealth Police. When the report is finally presented to Cabinet later in the year, it is startlingly clear that none of these parties believe that the Yagoona Three are anything but foot soldiers like John William Duff, presently before the courts on assault and attempted kidnapping charges, and that they intend to pursue Abhiik Kumar with everything they can collectively throw at him.[9]

The process of cancelling the Michael Brandon passport — no small legal feat — is set in motion in the wake of the Hilton bombing and the international acts of violence associated with the Margiis (Bangkok, London, Manila). Andrew Peacock, the Minister for

Foreign Affairs, convened a Passports Working Group whose task was to consider all applications for passports by Australian Ananda Marga members. Norm Sheather and the ever-present Detective Sergeant Bruce Jackson are invited to Canberra to participate in the group. By June the members of this collective believe they have sufficient grounds to provide a legal basis for the minister to cancel Brandon's passport. The Passports Working Group 'took into consideration criminal evidence supplied by COMPOL which indicated while in Bangkok, he was engaged in conspiratorial conduct in relation to arranging the illegal purchase of explosives and that he also sought to obtain false Canadian or British passports'.[10]

In brief, the Working Group feel they have compelling evidence linking Abhiik Kumar to the explosives found on the Bangkok Three just after the Hilton, and this is enough to revoke his passport.

There is a certain degree of practical genius as well as symbolic power in stopping the globetrotting spiritual leader in his tracks and forcing him to stay put in Sydney under the watchful eye of the authorities. Much is made of the fact that while Brandon is a naturalised Australian citizen, this is very recent (he only became a citizen in early 1977, probably because of the impending travel ban on foreign Margiis) and he is US born and raised. It is clear that part of the intention behind the cancellation of the passport is to sway the hearts and minds of the public. As part of this orchestrated attack on the sect's elite, the Department of Foreign Affairs issues a statement to the press the day after Kumar's detention which makes clear that this man is an undesirable Australian — indeed they question whether he deserves the right to be a citizen:

> A spokesman for the Foreign Affairs Department said last night that the Federal government was no longer willing to require of a foreign government the protection and assistance for Mr Brandon normally afforded an Australian citizen.[11]

This all makes sense and it's a good PR move to characterise him as an unsavoury type yet offer up no details about what he's actually done, instead leaving it to the public to imagine his evil deeds. In the same vein, and on virtually the same day, the Thai Government suddenly announces that they are to release the three Ananda Marga members imprisoned in Bangkok — the Australians Jones and Spark and the American Sarah Child. This decision is clearly made in consultation with the Australian Government. The news appears in an article attached to the one about Kumar's loss of his passport and rights as an Australian citizen: *Thailand to Free Ananda Marga Trio. No Passport for Sect Leader*. The Thais have no problem being utterly clear about their motives for freeing the trio:

July 1978

'Thailand decided today to release [the three members of the Ananda Marga sect] because the government feared terrorist reprisals if a court sentenced them to long jail terms.'[12]

In order to ameliorate the process and presumably save face, the Thai authorities offer Jones, Spark and Child a Faustian pact of sorts — they can go free but only if they change their pleas of not guilty to 'Having possessed 1.25 kg of plastic explosives, to guilty, in exchange for light sentences.'[13] So light, in fact, that they will be out the following Tuesday, having served six months. After that they are to be deported back to their countries of origin — Jones and Spark to Australia, where they haven't set foot for almost five years, and Child to an 'unspecified destination'. Selling a small part of their souls in order to take the deal doesn't faze them a bit. On the contrary, they argue that if they didn't switch their pleas as requested, their lawyers said they could be liable for sentences of up to 20 years. They also claim that, 'We pleaded guilty after the offer was made to us, as we saw we had no chance of a fair trial in Thailand,'[14] which seems a bit rich given the Thais have just given them a golden ticket and released them.

Overall, Spark and Jones are remarkably untouched — possibly even emboldened — by the entire experience. In addition to maintaining their innocence, despite their guilty pleas, they declare to journalists, 'Outside prison we can act. We know people in Australia are hostile to Ananda Marga but that's only because they don't know the truth. We aim to change that.'[15] For Timothy Jones, the whole thing has given him an opportunity to renew his vows, announcing that 'he would dedicate the rest of his life to Ananda Marga'. For Caroline Spark, 25, of Canberra, it was all a bit like a holiday or spiritual spa: 'I leave prison with some reluctance. Where else could I spend nine hours a day in meditation as I have been doing?'[16]

One element of this abrupt offer of liberty that jars is the statement from the Australian embassy officials, who 'assured the two Australians that there were no plans for charges to be brought against them in Australia relating to the events in Thailand'.[17] Why are they being so nice? Is it another attempt to try and get them to turn against Abhiik Kumar or each other? The threats haven't worked so maybe their thinking is 'let's give them something to be grateful for and see if that works'.

I thought this might be the case at first but then realised this was not the *raison d'etre*. Given the soaring bleats of devotion issuing from the mouths of Spark and Jones post release, and their distinct lack of gratitude to either the Thai or Australian authorities, it's impossible to imagine the cops, who'd made various attempts to get them to cooperate throughout their

July 1978

incarceration, thinking these two would ever be good for turning. The secret Cabinet paper makes clear that what they want, as in the case of Kumar, is to keep them close and to keep them in one place. As soon as the ardent pair are deported to Australia, their passports are also cancelled.

What the Australian authorities want is to curtail the freewheeling gallivanting that these particular Margiis have engaged in for years. They want Kumar, Jones and Spark, who they suspect of dark and criminal deeds, to stand still so that they can watch them. They want to assert their control and make it clear to these cult members who has the power. The days of flitting in and out of countries and slipping on new names and identities are over. You will stay where we put you.

If some of this seems a tad familiar in contemporary Australia — the cancellation of passports, the aggressive assertion of federal government authority over individuals who are regarded as suspicious but not actually charged with anything — that's because it's possible that what we are witnessing is not so much the birth of Fortress Australia as its conception. Scholars and sceptics alike have claimed that the Hilton bombing brought in widespread and sweeping changes to the security agencies in Australia. By the end of 1978, the Marks inquiry (instigated by Fraser immediately after the bombing) will lead to the formation of the

Australian Federal Police; the following year increased powers of surveillance are given to ASIO, and paramilitary SWAT-style units are created in state police services, as is the domestic Special Air Service (SAS) in the Australian Defence Force. Crisis Policy centres are established with the authority to take control of parts of the country in times of emergency.[18]

There is no question that after the bombing Australia implemented a much more rigid and systemised process of determining who was to be kept within our borders and who was to be kept out.

That said, the situation is a lot more complicated than first meets the eye. It is very easy, as we have seen, to simply caricature a government as a bunch of civil liberty stomping fascists intent on eroding individual rights simply because they're fascists and that's what fascists do. Usually things are more nuanced and human. The bringing to heel of Abhiik Kumar in August 1978 is born as much out of exasperation as out of genuine fear.

Evidence in years to come will bear out that none of these entities — ASIO, COMPOL, the federal government, the police — have any doubt that this man is responsible for the Hilton bombing and other atrocities here and abroad. They are frightened of him and want to convict him. Yet despite their collective might, all their authority and money and organisational clout, they have severely underestimated their target.

July 1978

I'm sure if I was a physicist I could name the tendency or principle associated with bringing a highly volatile and mobile element to stasis which in turn causes it to erupt catastrophically. When it is revealed on 9 August that Michael Brandon's passport has been cancelled, the outrage from the membership of the Australian Ananda Marga on behalf of their spiritual leader is immediate, vocal and deeply disturbing. The actions it unleashes completely outweigh reactions to the arrests of Anderson, Alister and Dunn eight weeks earlier.

Exactly what the Australian authorities think is going to happen next is impossible to know. It could be a wait-and-see scenario. Perhaps the embedded ASIO agents were hoping that the free Baba euphoria would loosen lips, although one imagines Seary's exposure as an informant would make this less likely.

What they aren't expecting is an assault on federal parliament.

A hardline policy

On Wednesday afternoon, 16 August 1978, about 24 hours after the annual budget speech, the cut and thrust of Question Time in the House of Representatives is just concluding. The House is jam-packed with politicians bickering, joking and flirting. As things start to wind up, Prime Minister Fraser pulls his lanky length upward and starts to lead his entourage across the chamber towards the exit. At that moment a young man in the public gallery leaps to his feet screaming 'Free Michael Brandon',[1] and hurls something at the members below. The pollies jerk their heads up in fright as they are showered in reams of paper. It seems a little comical now, to have been so frightened by a rain of Ananda Marga leaflets, but one of the things Malcolm Fraser told me (when he'd done chastising me for looking into the bombing at all) was that this protester could have been throwing hand grenades.

'Really?' you say. 'Really?' Yes. Back in those innocent times no one is searched or questioned or prevented from entering the public gallery of Parliament. There are no walk-through metal detectors or wands or wary security guards on alert. What is even more extraordinary is that when the screaming protester, Margii Roger Thompson of Newtown,[2] is hauled away by the attendant, there isn't even a law to charge him under. In 1978 the parliamentary privilege that allows Australian politicians to say and, to some extent do, whatever they bloody well want within that chamber also extends to members of the public in the gallery. Strictly speaking the attendant who hauls away the ranting Thompson doesn't even have the right to remove him. Under the laws of the day, he is able to scream and shout and throw things to his heart's content. He is simply representing the sect and acting on his right to legitimately protest against the police persecution of the Australian Ananda Marga leader.

Three weeks later, parliament goes into another panic when an aide sees a shoe box left in a toilet off King's Hall. The aide prises off the lid, spies Ananda Marga leaflets inside and decides that it's probably a bomb. The building is evacuated.

This incident, according to the papers, 'spotlights the lack of security surrounding all federal parliamentarians, from the Prime Minister down'.[3]

Then it happens again:

For the second time in six weeks, the Chamber of the House of Representatives was showered yesterday with leaflets from the Ananda Marga. Just after question time a woman stood up in the gallery, shouted 'return Michael Brandon's passport' and threw hundreds of leaflets into the chamber.

This time the Commonwealth Police haul the woman away and question her for two hours. But as before, there is no law to charge her under, so she is released. The papers report that this second incident is once again motivated by the sect's anger at 'Michael Brandon, head of the Ananda Marga in Australia [having] his passport confiscated on August 9 after his return to Australia from a visit to India.' The difference this time, however, is that the shouting and leaflet-throwing woman 'hardly raised a ripple in the House', with Speaker Sir Billy Snedden choosing simply to ignore her, while several members are reported as letting out a collective groan.[4] While this could be evidence of how quickly Aussie politicians toughen up in the face of danger, it's possible that many of them have inside information that's girding their loins ... Something secret.

At the very moment the impassioned sect member is demanding the return of her beloved leader's passport, a group of men are sitting in a room in the very

A hardline policy

same building finalising Submission No. 2520. This submission is the final Cabinet Minutes of the Intelligence and Security Committee, who have formulated Australia's very first Policy and Organisation in Relation to Counter Terrorism. These blokes aren't mucking about, and missy up in the gallery is lucky she wasn't lobbing grenades, given that the Committee has just agreed that:

(a) Australia adopt a 'hardline' policy in dealing with terrorist incidents, that is: —
   (i) the police and, where it is appropriate to authorise their employment, elements of the Defence Force, be instructed to take firm action against the terrorists and obtain their surrender;
   (ii) if tactical negotiations aimed at surrender fail and in particular if violent action by the terrorists (for example, killing or injuring hostages or major property damage) is anticipated, action to be taken to subdue the terrorists by force; and
   (iii) the timing and manner of such forceful action and the tactics applied to facilitate its success be, in the final balance, subject to the principle of minimising the risk of the loss of innocent life; and

(b) only in particular circumstances and as the ultimate alternative, when all options available under sub paragraph 1 (a) above have been considered and found unacceptable, would the possibility of concessions (other than minor concessions such as food and medical supplies) be considered by Ministers in consultation with the Prime Minister.[5]

So there you have it: no more Mr Nice Guy stuff. The gloves are off and while this document, which will remain secret for the next 30 years, makes it clear that this new policy is not to be published, it does encourage the Australian Government to issue statements 'emphasising Australian opposition to any attempt by terrorist organisations to achieve their aim by terrorist acts, and the Australian Government's intention, if any such attempt were made within its jurisdiction, to take all appropriate action to counter it'.[6]

However, it is all very well to hammer out this kind of manifesto within the cool wood-panelled rooms of parliament when you imagine your foe is some kind of faceless gun-toting thug. It's quite another to keep the hard line when faced with the burning flesh of a pretty young heiress.

The immolation of
Lynette Phillips

While the bureaucrats are busy writing policy and scrambling to review the laws surrounding parliamentary privilege in order to criminalise future disruptions of federal parliament, a 25-year-old Australian member of Prout, Lynette Phillips, travelling on a British passport, disembarks from the cross-Channel ferry at Folkestone on 26 September 1978.[1] Accompanying the dark-haired Lynette are two women, a Brazilian and a Swede, also members of Prout. They are stopped by Customs and their bags are searched. Contained in their luggage is material on self-immolation, and in Lynette's shoulder bag is a statement that reads: 'Lynette Phillips (Santi) Proutist Universal Citizen ... Lover of humanity ... Self Immolated in London on September 26th, 1978.'[2]

How do the British authorities react?

They decide to make it someone else's problem. The Brazilian and the Swede are dragged into security for immediate deportation back to Ostend, from whence they came. Lynette, despite her disturbing threats, is given permission to stay in Britain for two months. While this seems utterly absurd, particularly given that the three English Margiis — Shaw, Waring and Kidd — are in jail about to face trial for attempted murder in London in a month's time, within hours it's clear the authorities are still passing the buck. As soon as Lynette walks through passport control into the diesel fumes of an autumnal English day and heads for London, the British Home Office alerts Scotland Yard. The police then tail her all the way to Parliament Square, arrest her, then escort her back to the ferry and deport her to Belgium. There is an unnerving and faintly ridiculous photograph that immortalises the moment at Parliament House with Lynette, head bowed and swathed in pale baggy robes and matching skull-cap, standing beside her captor in shiny uniform and helmet — a cowed serf next to a cartoon bobby.[3]

The Brits will claim that this is all done with the full knowledge of the staff at Australia House. The London police state that they contacted 'authorities' at Australia House and requested a passport photograph of 'Miss Phillips' in order to 'aid them in recognising her if she attempted to carry out her plans to set herself alight'.[4]

The immolation of Lynette Phillips

Within a week the staff at Australia House will deny they were ever contacted by the British police, and will say that they didn't know Lynette had been deported until two days later, on 28 September.

Arriving in Belgium, Lynette, the daughter of mining millionairess Millie Phillips and her ex-husband, businessman Harold Phillips,[5] is undaunted. With unwavering intent she travels to yet another capital of international significance — this time, Geneva.

When Lynette arrives in the Swiss city on 2 October, her frantic parents, who were eventually informed of her deportation, have been fruitlessly looking for her for days. So too are members of the Ananda Marga in London and Sweden, who claim that she contacted them on 27 September after her expulsion from London and will not, despite their protestations, be dissuaded from her quest. They do not attempt to contact her parents.[6]

As night approaches in Geneva, Lynette, en route to the Palais des Nations, the United Nations building, stops at a service station and buys a can of petrol. She locates a pay phone and calls a number of news agency offices within the Palais 'asking them to send photographers as something would shortly be happening in the Palais des Nations. It would be "spectacular".'[7]

Lynette, reportedly an introverted girl, privately educated, who dropped out of Medicine and craved attention, isn't wrong about that.

Lynette sits down on the lawn out the front of the UN and calmly places placards of heavy paper on the grass: 'Prouts Universal — Prout (progressive utilization theory) ... a flaming torch in the dark night of exploitation ... UNO holds the lives of billions but delegates prefer luxurious lives to their human responsibilities ... Baba Nam Kevalam [The word of the Father is truth].' She takes off her shoes and places them and her handbag neatly on the grass and pours the petrol over herself and sets herself alight. The Margiis have another martyr. Lynette is number eight.[8]

Amazingly, all the photographers standing in front of her outside the main entrance to the Palais don't do a thing but just snap away. The following day's papers are full of 'photos of the woman sitting cross-legged, hands on knees in a yoga position in the middle of intense flames'.[9] I don't know whether to write this off simply as 'it was the '70s' or whether it's an example of hardline journalism to unflinchingly record the brutal truth, but it's a scene that is hard to digest. The spectators must have been aware of what was about to occur. How many ways are there to interpret the petrol, the robes, the expression of joy on sweet Lynette's face? The photograph that adorns the front page of *The Age* of her burning — her arms slightly raised, her skin already black with her skull beginning to show — leaves little to the imagination.[10]

The immolation of Lynette Phillips

Of all these burnt Margiis, Lynette is the only one I can get any intimate sense of. Her short biography is one of ongoing heartbreak and despair, like some luckless character in a Greek tragedy. Intensively sensitive as a child, Lynette Phillips so wanted God that, she later wrote, she cried 'tears night after night wanting to know that reality'.[11] This rich girl from a good Jewish family may in fact have been reeling from the unpleasant separation of her extremely successful parents just after she turned six. From that point on she remains conflicted, her loyalties painfully split between them. By the time she starts high school, first at SCEGGS, a private girls' school, and then at North Sydney Girls High, a selective state school, teachers regard her as a 'lovely' and 'gifted' girl who is also 'very frightened'.[12]

By her final year of high school in 1971, her father is so perturbed by her mental fragility he takes her to see a psychologist. The assessment in part reads, 'Lyn is still well aware that you and Mrs Phillips are in a contest about her. She is unable to commit herself to either side of this conflict because the penalties for doing so would be enormous.' The psychologist added that in his view Lynette 'would exploit the situation to her own disadvantage'.[13]

Therapy does not help. The following year she drops out of Medicine at the University of New South Wales after only a few months and starts to travel, unravel and take drugs. There are three patchy years of rattling back and forth between Asia and Sydney until eventually, in 1975, she winds up with a faith healer in the Philippines. This leads on to vegetarianism, which leads her to the Margiis. She joins the Australian Ananda Marga in 1975 and, interestingly, unlike our friend Timothy Jones, continues to see her parents on a regular basis. In fact she frequently has her Margii comrades over for extended stays at Mum or Dad's well-appointed homes. Her parents are understandably relieved that at least she's off drugs and appears to have some purpose. Lynette is taken with the social services agenda of the religion, as are her parents. However, it will be said that even within the sect she remains troubled. Another sect member, Bruce Dyer, will tell a reporter some months after her death that she could not find her niche and 'she did not have a special skill to offer'.[14]

You have to wonder what kind of special skill one needs to shine in a religion like this. I wouldn't have thought yoga, meditating a lot, doling out soup or collecting money for disaster victims would have been such a stretch for someone who was capable of becoming a doctor. This statement reads to me like someone trying to play down her unstable personality. The fact is, Lynette appears to be a perfect candidate for a cult — passionate, fragile, single-minded, fanatical, devoted and rich.

By September 1977 her mother, Millie, worried

again, offers to pay for Lynette to go to a clinic in Switzerland and sends her off with a clutch of credit cards. Lynette appears to love the idea, but it's a ruse. She disappears after a few weeks and goes on a spending spree across Europe. Millie cancels the credit cards. At the start of the New Year, Lynette, still in Europe, goes on an Ananda Marga women's retreat which she describes in long letters to each parent as giving her peace, serenity and the strength she craves.[15]

By late February, after the Hilton bombing, her horizons once again begin to darken and churn. She finds out that a Margii friend of hers, a German girl, Erica, has burnt herself to death, and she writes to her father Harold, 'It was quite a shock to hear the news.' Apart from being quite spaced out about her future, she was completely calm and normal, 'emanating a peacefulness and positivity seldom experienced before'. She then adds a disturbing postscript, which must constrict her father's heart — 'but for me the burning is going to take too much time. Five minutes of petrol flame would be too easy for me and of no use to anyone.'[16] A few days later, coinciding with the Margii arrests in Bangkok and Manila, she writes that while she believes that the members of Ananda Marga and Prout are perfectly harmless, she also believes 'some troublemakers were sheltering under Prout's umbrella'.[17]

Despite, or because of, her consternation, she joins Prout. In April, Lynette attempts to visit Sarkar in prison and flies into Calcutta airport. The Indians don't like the look of her and deport her. It's at this stage that her father, a British citizen, arranges for her to get a UK passport and she travels to London and scores a transcribing job at the BBC. A Mrs Sheila Barton says of Lynette's time there, 'She seemed an ordinary, pleasant girl and talked about how she'd like to help people.'[18] By June 1978 she travels to Copenhagen, to the world headquarters of Prout, and works for both them and Ananda Marga. She keeps writing to Millie and Harold, sending them epic 20-page sagas and ringing them every few weeks. In a letter to her dad in July she says she finds the work for Prout 'boring' and 'mundane'.[19] Harold suggests they meet up and Lynette agrees so he books his ticket to fly to Europe on 9 August.

It is here that things become so hopelessly sad. Could her death have been prevented if she and her father had met? But fate conspires against them. Some time in July, Lynette goes to visit a training camp for Ananda Marga nuns deep in the cool dark forests of Sweden. She is smitten both by the location — an exquisite tiny village near a limpid lake — and by the Margii who runs the training. He is so taken with her, he offers to train her as a nun for free, instead of having to pay the going rate, an offer which is very 'unusual'. In a letter to Harold she makes it clear she has considered such a vocation before and now may be

The immolation of Lynette Phillips

the time to undertake the months of gruelling practice involving 'intensive meditation, study and discipline (4 am rise, cold washes etc.)'.[20]

Then silence. In early August Harold calls Prout's Copenhagen office in anticipation of his arrival on 9 August, only to be told that Lynette has left to begin her training as a Margii nun and will not be back for months. He cancels his flight. A few days later he gets a letter from his daughter telling him she has indeed taken the plunge to become a nun.[21]

Whatever happens next unhinges her sufficiently to set herself on fire in nine weeks' time. It's difficult to track her movements. Despite the fact the training is meant to take three to nine months, she apparently leaves Sweden and the training camp a few weeks later accompanied by a middle-aged Brazilian woman, the same one who will be deported from Britain on 26 September and who will also eventually self-immolate.[22]

What has Lynette's tragic trajectory and suicide got to do with Michael Brandon and his confiscated passport?

'Campaigns of violence and intimidation'

Lynette's self-immolation in Geneva hits the British papers on 3 October and the grisly photograph of her on fire is published in Australia the next day. Two things propel her death into critical local significance by 12 October. The first is an almighty diplomatic stoush between Britain and Australia over the circumstances of Lynette's deportation from the UK, and the second is that a Mr Peter Henry of Sydney (who has gone into hiding), a member of Ananda Marga (and Prout), sends an unambiguous threat to Canberra that he will self-immolate within days unless Michael Brandon's passport is immediately returned, among other demands.[1]

Once again one is flung into the vortex of

accusations and counter-accusations that swirl cyclonically each time an act of violence, in this case self-inflicted violence, is attributed to the sect. The world organisational secretary for Proutist Universal (Acharya Tadbahvananda), based at Prout's headquarters in Copenhagen — a 'stately home in the wealthy suburb of Rungsted', where Lynette had worked — states that, 'We do not encourage or appreciate such activities' and denies 'that the act of self-immolation is discussed openly in the Prout movement'. Tadbahvananda adds that had he known what she was going to do, he would have 'forced her not to do it [and now] she has thrown her life away needlessly'.

Journalist Ian Frykberg, reporting this conversation, immediately offers an opposite account, stating that another Copenhagen Prout member, Mr Richard Gay, said that, 'He and Miss Phillips had discussed self-immolation and the seven members of the movement who had already committed the act.'[2] Frykberg also confirms that there are clear connections between Prout HQ and the 'two Prout training centres in Australia'. While the Acharya is busy denying he had any idea of Lynette's desperate quest to suicide, he also feels it important to note that there are 10 Prout trainees at each centre in Australia and 'we are very happy with our membership in Australia — it is growing all the time'.

Gary Coyle, the secretary of the Sydney office

of Prout, admits he was totally aware of Lynette's intention and on 29 September, a few days before her death, had received her 'typed self-immolation proclamation' and forwarded copies of it to Australian newspapers that day, but they did not run it. Other Australian Ananda Marga members Ainjile Morrison and Bruce Dyer also admit they knew of Lynette's plan after they were contacted by Lynette's mother Millie on 1 October. They went to Millie's home and attempted to call 'all the Ananda Marga places in Europe they thought she might be'. They spoke to the London leader, Barry Green, who hadn't seen her and was 'very opposed to her plan'.[3] Contradictions abound as to who knew of her intention to set herself alight — and indeed, who supported it.

Further confusing things is her motive. Given that Sarkar is now free, her protest makes no immediate sense. It's Frykberg who makes the possible connection the following day. The Acharya in Copenhagen avows Prout's non-violence policy and asserts that, unlike the Ananda Marga, it is not a religion but a political movement: 'Prout is against religion because it demarcates society. The movement's aim is to give the political power in the world to moralists.'

The Acharya also reiterates that he was unaware of and did not appreciate Lynette's self-immolation, but adds, Frykberg notes, in the 'next breath', 'we of course understand the thoughts that must have driven her to do it'. Acharya Tadbahvananda, who Frykberg describes as 'the man in charge', then goes on to talk about how many members have been 'framed' in recent cases where violence has been alleged, 'particularly Australia'. Frykberg points out that 'even in Copenhagen the recent events in Australia alleging Ananda Marga involvement are well known'. The 'man in charge' asserts 'opponents are using Australia to squash the sect by getting the Australian Government to ban it, and then hoping that other governments will follow'.[4] Which could imply that Lynette's act of annihilation in Geneva is a protest against the 'framing' of Duff and of the Yagoona Three, as well as Michael Brandon's cancelled passport.

It will emerge that immediately prior to her death Lynette had written long (unsent) obsessive letters to sect members in Australia detailing her compulsion to self-immolate. These seem to suggest a potential link, but one she herself wants to obscure. She writes that her act 'grew from a burning desire, an inner need to do something to help stop the criminality of our exploited lives ... [and] it was inspired by the sacrifice of seven others for the same cause',[5] and she also stresses that her plan has been devised in secret. As far as her father, Harold, is concerned, this is an outright lie she has concocted in order to protect the sect both here and abroad. He and his estranged wife believe Lynette, mentally vulnerable, has been brainwashed by

Prout and manipulated into the act. He believes that the fact that all her letters were posted to Sydney after her death 'indicates a military-style conspiracy and that someone was with her [in Geneva] all the time to remove her diary after she died and post it off to the sect office in Sweden'.[6]

The sect in Australia certainly sends out a volley of mixed messages. Sydney Margii spokesperson Ainjile Morrison says it is tragic that people regard Lynette as a 'programmed zombie, brainwashed into this act. It was an act of genuine sacrifice which she herself planned. She was rational about it. Buddhist monks self-immolated during the Vietnam War and no one said they were programmed. Can't you see the nobility of dying for your ideals?'[7]

Local Ananda Marga member Bruce Dyer is likewise intent on lamenting, not endorsing, her death, but then praising her actions. Dyer states that the Ananda Marga 'regard her as a very great person' and 'we regard her letters like the relics of a saint'. The Australian Proutists also regard her as 'almost a saint' with local Prout member Craig Walter asserting that 'her death was a tragedy, but it was a great sacrifice. She was Australia's first spiritual soldier.'[8]

Whether ordained by Prout or not, Lynette's 'spectacular' suicide certainly grabs the attention of the Australian Government. First, Lynette's no doubt heartbroken father, Harold, arrives in London to lodge a protest against the British Government, which he says 'shares responsibility for his daughter's death because it deported her knowing she was going to burn herself to death'.⁹ The Australian High Commission keeps to its story that it was not informed of the deportation, and Scotland Yard keeps to theirs — that the Aussies were aware all along. I have to say I find this a bit convoluted — it can't have been all that complex to detain the obsessed young woman intent on self-harm under the *Mental Health Act* and, at the very least, as her father points out, 'to inform her parents'.

Andrew Peacock, the Minister for Foreign Affairs, flies into this diplomatic fracas when he arrives in London the next day on a 'routine visit'. He is asked to intervene as 'Mr Phillips [continues to demand] the British Government [...] hold an official inquiry into how his daughter — who had a prepared, signed statement on her intended self-immolation when she was arrested — was allowed to leave Britain'.¹⁰

Simultaneously, all hell is breaking loose back in Australia. Ananda Marga member Peter Henry demands the return of Brandon's passport, the issuing of a visa to Donju Gista, an Indian member of the sect living in America, and the cessation of the 'persecution of the Ananda Marga sect by the Australian Government' or 'he would burn himself to death next Tuesday'.¹¹

I reckon this would be a great test to set all

Acting Ministers for Foreign Affairs to assess their mettle while the boss is overseas. What do you do? Call his bluff? Sweat him out? Play hardball? Beg him to reconsider? Poor Ian Sinclair, acting in Andrew Peacock's position, attempts all of these at once. First he makes the conciliatory statement 'that he was willing to re-examine the issues which led to an Ananda Marga member threatening to burn himself to death'. He immediately counters this by stating (in keeping with the new counter-terrorism policy) that 'no government could act under duress of threats of the kind or take any decision while a threat remained'.[12] That's all well and good, but Sinclair and his colleagues must have little doubt, given the recent horror of Lynette's actions, that the threat is real. Sinclair hastily organises a meeting with Henry's wife, Cetana, and two members of Ananda Marga in an attempt to avert catastrophe. It is of little apparent value, despite Sinclair's reported offers to urgently re-examine the matters of both the visa and the passport, and to discuss them with Mr Henry if he would contact his Canberra office to arrange a meeting.

In response, 'Mrs Cetana Henry stated after meeting Mr Sinclair she was certain her husband would go through with his threat [adding] the meeting had not resulted in any "real" action.'[13]

Let's take stock as Mr Sinclair and his government colleagues surely do at this moment. Since Abhiik

Kumar discovered on 9 August that his Michael Brandon passport had been cancelled, the Ananda Marga has disrupted Australian federal parliament twice, requiring the creation of new legislation; the daughter of some prominent wealthy Australians has burnt herself to death on the steps of the United Nations; and now a local sect member is threatening to do the same next Tuesday. There have been accompanying demonstrations, letters to newspapers, and lots of articles claiming that there are up to 80 000 members of Prout around the globe. The Australian Prout centres in Sydney and Perth have only opened recently yet already boast up to 20 trainees. Unlike their Swedish counterparts, who went out of their way to denounce Lynette's suicide, the Ananda Marga in Australia doesn't even bother to distance itself from Peter Henry's threat. Margii spokesperson Ainjile Morrison tells the press that Peter Henry is 'a rational and sincere person and his fire-suicide threat must be taken seriously'.[14]

Myself, I'd be scared shitless. If the membership is willing to make these kinds of extreme gestures, what aren't they capable of? What's next? The government must be wondering how far can this go. Will it start with Mr Henry setting himself on fire on the steps of Parliament House, then extend to a pair of like-minded Margiis in Sydney or Melbourne? Perhaps they will do it in threes or fours. Maybe start lobbing bombs. Why would any rational person imagine this kind of activism/madness was going to stop? Does Mr Sinclair urgently call Mr Peacock in London? Is there a war council in Canberra? Is Malcolm Fraser called in? All these things occur.

Evidence that the Australian Government regards this as the start of a potential third wave of violence from sect members is found in another confidential Cabinet paper, written in early October. The paper, prepared by Attorney-General Peter Durack, seeks:

> ... authority for legislation to deal with disorderly conduct in Parliament House such [as] has recently occurred in the House of Representatives galleries and to give proper protection to officers enforcing order in the public galleries and other parts of the Parliament building to which the public have access.[15]

Among those consulted are 'officers of the Senate, the House of Representatives, the Department of the Prime Minister and Cabinet and the Department of Administrative Services'. You can hear the panic in the prose. Under the title 'URGENCY', the Cabinet paper declares 'the matter is urgent because of the second incident by members of the Ananda Marga sect in the House of Representatives. Further attempts to disrupt Parliament can be expected if action is not taken urgently.'[16]

There are a lot of 'urgents' in that paragraph. Yet one can detect the government sliding rapidly away from its non-negotiable counter-terrorism policy, circulated a little over three weeks earlier. This is clear when Mr Peter Henry announces on 17 October that he is not going to burn himself to death after all. Appeals from his family, sect members, the Anglican Archbishop of Melbourne and — critically — the actions of the Acting Minister for Foreign Affairs, have given him pause. Peter Henry, reportedly looking 'tanned and relaxed', fronts a press conference with his wife and baby daughter. He announces breezily, 'I think the publicity of the past week about my actions has achieved my aim and Mr Sinclair ... has agreed to reconsider the decision over Michael Brandon's passport.'[17]

Clearly if you make the right sort of terrifying threats, despite the newly hewn counter-terrorism policy, you can still negotiate aggressively and successfully with the authorities.

What is so impressive throughout all this threatened violence over the passport is that the owner of it, Michael Brandon (aka Kumar), has not uttered a single word the entire time. Of course he doesn't need to — it's perfectly obvious there is no lack of minions to throw things, scream, protest or burn in the quest to get his passport back. Why lift a finger when you can just watch your brethren do it all for you?

A new phenomenon

By late October the government is not just on the back foot but scrambling for solutions. They convene another consultation group made up of all the same departments and organisations that had gathered in the immediate aftermath of the Hilton bombing. This time the tone is completely reactive. The agenda is to summarise clearly the events involving all members of the Ananda Marga sect to date, and to decide if the strategies in place — immigration restrictions, suspension of recognition of and assistance to Ananda Marga, protective measures for Indian establishments in Australia — are sufficient given recent events. The question is then raised 'whether further measures should be taken in the light of the continued harassment of the government'. The question next to this is a more worrisome one: 'Whether the further measures might provoke increased harassment and violence against the government and other authorities and establishments, and, if so, should this weigh against further measures?'[1]

Like the paper on counter-terrorism, this document, finalised by November and marked 'secret', will remain classified for 30 years. The threat assessment from ASIO, COMPOL and the Department of Foreign affairs is stark and unambiguous. It is reiterated that starting in August 1977, Ananda Marga members in Australia and throughout the world mounted a campaign of violent harassment of Indian nationals in order to achieve the release of their imprisoned leader, Sarkar; 'the campaign assumed world wide proportions, ceasing after Sarkar's release on bail in August 1978'.[2] Now they believe it is beginning again.

The ASIO summary is as follows:

> Currently, members in Australia are undertaking a campaign to secure the return of Ananda Marga's Australasian spiritual director's (ML Brandon) passport. To date, the campaign has not been violent, although threats of the use of violence have been made. The Ananda Marga Australasian sector stands out from Ananda Marga activity world-wide because of the apparent preparedness of its members to become involved in violence.[3]

The report warns that should this current campaign fail to secure the return of Brandon's passport, 'further incidents, some of which may be violent, will occur. There are indications that senior Ananda Marga members have decided on a possible long-term campaign for revolution in Australia.' On the positive side, 'Ananda Marga's capacity to enter into such a campaign is limited and it is not yet possible to determine the extent of support for revolutionary action within the sect'.[4]

Limited capacity or not, the Ananda Marga in Australia has to be dealt with. It's becoming terrifyingly clear that any legislation the government enacts, or any restriction it imposes on the sect, could create a horrific backlash of violence. Collating all the evidence from ASIO, Special Branch, Sheather's task force, COMPOL and Interpol over the last few years, it is manifest that, outside India, Australia's Margiis have been involved with more 'publicised acts of violence and harassment attributable to [sect] members than anywhere else'.[5] It's reasoned that this unenviable position is owing to Australia's more stringent measures against the organisation, which, in turn, led to increased retaliation. These facts twist into a Gordian knot that leaves the government flummoxed.

They carefully reconstruct the conundrum before them. While similar to what they faced in September 1977, months before the Hilton bombing, it is a problem they imagined would evaporate once the mighty

Sarkar was freed from his prison in Patna. How wrong they were. Indeed, what is becoming obvious is that:

> The application of restrictions has led to retaliation by Ananda Marga, a pattern which will probably repeat itself in the future. Australia therefore is presented with a new phenomenon, that of an organisation claiming to be spiritual and non-violent but harbouring militant fanatics determined to go to extraordinary lengths, including the use of violence, to achieve its ends, whatever they may be at any given time.[6]

In addition to this is the extraordinary admission that they are virtually powerless in the face of such extremism: 'The administrative, legal, and protective apparatus currently available to the government is not capable of dealing satisfactorily with the phenomenon, other than in a reactive way.'[7]

You can understand why they would want to keep documents like this secret for so long. It's hardly edifying for the public to see that their government is incapable of standing up to a deranged splinter group within a fringe cult adept at plausible deniability.

The way they characterise the situation in mid-November 1978 is that the 'basic problem is twofold': on the one hand there is 'how to deter individual fanatical members of the Ananda Marga from committing violent and unlawful acts to further the sect's cause', and on the other there is 'how to prevent the sect as an organisation from mounting campaigns of violence and intimidation. In either case, the hierarchy of Ananda Marga is able to dissociate itself, as an organisation, from unlawful acts.'[8]

The options available to the government are severely limited. The report outlines four potential courses of action and then underlines why each is imperfect. The first option could be to 'proscribe the organisation', that is, to ban it. It is immediately pointed out that no country in the world has done this and to enact such legislation in Australia would 'not only ... create legal difficulties ... it would be politically undesirable and might provoke demands that other organisations be proscribed (e.g. Croatian groups)'.[9]

The second option moots withdrawing all forms of government assistance and recognition, 'in addition to immigration and passport measures'. This would remove the Ananda Marga's recognition as a religious denomination, financial assistance to its schools and Commonwealth tax concessions. However, this is riddled with technical legal problems in the withdrawal of educational assistance and tax concessions. It would also require extremely complex complementary action from each state government.[10]

The third option is stunningly simple: 'to maintain the status quo, including the present restrictions'.

The drawbacks of this are also obvious — it maintains the current situation, which is regarded as untenable.[11]

A fourth idea is to give the Ananda Marga what they want — in effect, to give in to their demands. In brief the government would remove all current restrictions and allow the sect the rights and privileges accorded to similar organisations and their members. This is shot down instantly because 'at the present time this would bolster Ananda Marga's belief that their campaign of violence and harassment had been successful and encourage them to embark on other campaigns to force fresh concessions (e.g. the release of jailed members in Australia)'.

At the time of the report, these incarcerated members include Anderson, Alister and Dunn, along with Duff, who has just been sentenced to nine years' imprisonment by the Supreme Court of the ACT for 'unlawful acts against an Indian diplomat', and the 'relaxed and tanned' Mr Peter Henry who has been charged with creating a public mischief.[12]

Which of these four limited options to choose?

The decision is to go with number three and to maintain the status quo, despite its ramifications, and to enact a number of additional measures. These include the rather vague statement that 'some form of special legislation may be called for directed towards controlling acts of violence of the general nature of those in question'. Much clearer is the decision to keep completely silent at the present moment. The recommendation is that 'no statement be made by the government on Ananda Marga at present'. Instead, they will keep up to date with the situation and gather material for a public statement 'for use at an appropriate time'. If such a statement is to be made in the future, it will be jointly handled by the Prime Minister, the Minister for Foreign Affairs, the Minister for Immigration and Ethnic Affairs, and the Minister for Administrative Affairs. It is also suggested that such a statement could possibly be the 'forerunner of a long-term government programme to inform the public of the harmful side of the activities of the Ananda Marga'.[13]

Further measures include the suspension of any new government recognition and assistance (for example, for new Ananda Marga schools) and the continuing ban on 'non-Australian Ananda Marga adherents' entering Australia or being granted citizenship. It is suggested that ASIO and COMPOL 'increase their efforts to identify the potentially violent elements of Ananda Marga' and continue the 'appropriate protective measures ... for Indian establishments in Australia'. It is also agreed that 'the question of passports for Australian Ananda Marga members continue to be subject to advice from the Passports Working Group'.[14] This is the group who made the decision to seize Brandon's passport in the first place, which let's face it, led to a heap of trouble. What's their advice now?

Despite all the tough talk, it's hard to interpret what happens now as anything other than a complete backdown.

In less than a fortnight after the above report is tabled on 16 November 1978, the Michael Brandon passport is returned to its owner.

The *Sydney Morning Herald* seems fairly confident that this is the result of intimidation and fear of fiery suicides on the streets of Sydney:

> The Sydney leader of the Ananda Marga sect, Mr Michael Brandon, has been granted a restricted passport ... The cancellation [of his former passport] resulted in another member of the sect, Mr Peter Henry, threatening to burn himself to death.

The government, on the other hand, is a lot more evasive:

> A spokesman for the Minister for Foreign Affairs, Mr Peacock, said yesterday Mr Brandon had been granted a restricted passport last week. Although the government would not give any reasons for its decisions, he said Mr Brandon wanted a passport so he could carry out his pastoral duties ... The restricted passport only allows Mr Brandon to visit countries where he has duties to perform

on behalf of the Ananda Marga. These are New Zealand, Papua New Guinea, South East Asia, India and the South Pacific.[15]

The moment the passport is returned by a dragooned federal government, Abhiik Kumar, the number one suspect in the Hilton Hotel bombing and possible mastermind of other acts of terrorism both in Australia and abroad, hops on a plane to India. And then he's gone.

1979

Well, not quite completely gone ...

Like the end of any bad relationship, things will shudder on for a bit. Let's face it, if a bond is tight, no matter how dysfunctional, it's hard to let go. I may want to imagine Norm Sheather watching, stoic and steely-eyed, churning with emotion as his nemesis Abhiik Kumar boards the plane at Sydney airport for the final time and ascends into the heavens — however, things are rarely this cinematic.

While it might be obvious to Norm Sheather that things are over, there are players on both sides who continue to provoke and goad each other. It's not an easy break-up to watch or to track. After Kumar leaves Australia in late 1978 he becomes harder and harder to detect as the years roll by. That said, like all his appearances in the past, when he does pop his head up, it's always an astonishing, show-stopping performance.

For Norm Sheather, the arrest of the Yagoona Three, Seary's subsequent allegations and the confiscation of Kumar's Brandon passport coincide with the conclusion of the major Hilton operation around 'August, 1978'.[1] Eventually we will learn Norm's view on the matter but at the time it passes unreported.

From the start it's clear that Abhiik Kumar has no real desire to shift his base from Australia to destinations unknown. Despite the return of his passport and jaunt to India, he seems reluctant to slip away. He will claim in years to come that immediately prior to the reissuing of his restricted passport he was flown to Canberra — at the 'taxpayers' expense' and possibly at the behest of Malcolm Fraser — for a *tête à tête* with the Foreign Minister Andrew Peacock at Parliament House. After being chauffeured to this cosy meeting, Abhiik claims that Peacock did a deal with him: if he accepted a three-month restricted passport, then a six-month one would be issued and finally, presumably if he behaved, he'd be given a full passport.

Apparently motivating such reasonableness is a complaint Abhiik had filed with the Commonwealth Ombudsman about the original passport cancellation, citing relentless political persecution. He argued, 'Not many Australians with no criminal record and no charges or jail time pending have their passport revoked. The confiscation of my passport was an abuse of power that simply could not stand.'[2]

Fighting words. But Peacock and Fraser deny such a meeting ever took place.[3]

Playing the aggrieved party seems to come naturally to Kumar. Even on his restricted passport he is still determined both to wield his power and proclaim his injured status. By January 1979 he is abruptly back in Australia and in the headlines. Since their June 1978 arrests, Anderson, Alister and Dunn have repeatedly asked for visits from their spiritual advisor, Abhiik Kumar. This request is granted, but only if prison warders at Long Bay jail — citing security concerns — are allowed to observe the visits. The trio object vehemently and embark on a hunger strike in September 1978. By January this has stretched to four months and has Anderson and Alister in the prison hospital. Dunn too begins a fast but this has ended by the time the fracas hits the papers.[4]

The hunger strike sets the state Public Service Board, the Department of Corrective Services and the Long Bay prison officers at each other's throats. By mid-January 1979, the dispute ends up before a judge, Justice Dey, in a closed session as he attempts to weigh up the security concerns of the guards and the rights of the incarcerated men. An editorial in the *Sydney Morning Herald* points out:

> It must be remembered that the accused have not yet been tried, let alone found guilty. A prima

facie case has been made out against them on charges of conspiracy to murder [Cameron], and they will stand trial on February 19, more than five months after their committal. This is a long time to wait without the moral or spiritual support they seek.[5]

The editor does recognise that while the Ananda Marga may not evoke much on the public sympathy front, he does add that were the prisoners members of an 'orthodox religion', the refusal of visits from their minister would produce howls of protest.

What is so intriguing about this stand-off is how agitated the mere idea of Kumar makes the — presumably hard-nosed — prison guards of Long Bay jail. While Justice Dey is reported as being 'satisfied that the concern of the prison staff was genuinely held', and that 'the actions of the members of the sect have contributed to the attitude adopted by the prison officers', he nonetheless orders the guards to allow the sect leader into the jail at least on a trial basis. However, the guards simply refuse to accept Judge Dey's ruling. Instead, the Long Bay jail officers appeal to the full bench of the state Industrial Commission against the order. They really don't want Kumar in their jail. While the extremism of the hunger strike must be unsettling, what leaks out from behind the closed hearings is that what the officers are really afraid of is

1979

the 'anticipated brain-washing of one of the members' and 'the possible consequences of this'; that somehow Kumar will, during a visit, use his mind control on one or all of the trio and order them to attack.[6]

The editor of the *Sydney Morning Herald* asks exactly how the now stick-thin prisoners — two of them in wheelchairs — 'brainwashed' or not, are supposed to carry out these imagined assaults upon warders after Kumar has wandered through. 'Is the public to suppose that security is so weak at Long Bay that warders cannot live with the vague possibility of violence which may never appear?'[7]

Despite the scaredy-cat taunts from the *Herald*, I think what set the warders on edge was that they got intelligence about Kumar from their colleagues in the police force that painted a portrait of a man they would do well to be afraid of.

Whether those in charge are gun-shy because of the chaos over Kumar's passport, the spiritual leader of the Australasian Margiis is eventually allowed to enter the prison. It's possible the authorities also want to stamp out any behaviour that emulates tactics used by imprisoned ANC and IRA members around the globe that might characterise these incarcerated men as political prisoners.

The capitulation of the Long Bay prison staff to the visits is a short-lived victory for the sect leader. Kumar's three-month passport is set to expire in early March 1979 and there are claims that unnamed 'authorities' (Interpol? ASIO?) attempt to arrest him in Nepal around this time.[8] While evidence of this is sketchy, there are reports of him in Sydney throughout 1979. Detective Senior Constable Allan David Henderson says he speaks to Kumar in passing a number of times that year: on 19 February and twice between 9 July and 1 August 1979 during the court appearances of Alister, Anderson and Dunn.[9]

At the same time as this argy-bargy is going on about the human and spiritual rights of prisoners, the first anniversary of the Hilton bombing rolls by. It's a surprisingly muted event with a memorial gathering arranged by Sydney City Council workers remembering their dead. However, one voice rings out loud and clear up the coast in Newcastle. Detective Inspector Norm Sheather who, subsequent to his incredulous interviews with Seary in June and July 1978, has been virtually silent, makes the incendiary statement to the *Sydney Morning Herald* that the 'police knew who was responsible' for the Hilton bombing.

Norm Sheather, who is poised to take up his new duties as Detective Inspector of North-Eastern Police, a much calmer and quieter job than running the '100-man Hilton task force', goes on to make the assertion that 'he was confident the people responsible would eventually be charged'. He adds, 'We knew who did it from the first day after the bombing, but lack of evidence to stand up in court has prevented us from making arrests ... We know that three and possibly four individuals were involved ...' The article goes on to report that one of the biggest problems in obtaining evidence against the Hilton bombers was that no ingredients from the bomb were found. Sheather concludes by arguing, 'had we found even a small fragment we could have had something to work with in collecting evidence'.[10]

The effect of this provocative statement on Abhiik Kumar is unknown.

The next time the sect leader pops his head up, he is apparently in West Germany, where some time around late 1979 there are allegations of another attempt to arrest him. By 1980, after the conviction of his three comrades back in Sydney for conspiracy to murder Cameron, Kumar is still reportedly fighting for the renewal of his Australian passport and seeks asylum in Sweden. He will claim that under pressure from the Swedish Government the Australians do renew his passport, but again the evidence is flimsy and inconclusive.[11] From this point on I can find no indication that he ever returns to Australia.

From now on he will flit in and out of view. A ghost. But he'll turn up. He may have escaped Norm's clutches. He has not escaped mine.

The next time the spotlight finds this complex man scuttling through the archives will be during the

1982 Hilton coronial inquest, where his existence will be made known to a broad Australian audience for the first time.

What fascinates me about the years 1978–82 is how completely bifurcated the public knowledge of the sect, the bombing and the investigation are from the private experiences of those on the inside. On the first anniversary of the bombing, the name Abhiik Kumar means absolutely nothing to the Australian public. It sets off no clanging in anyone's chest, it raises no eyebrows, hearts don't quicken, journalists don't breathe in sharply when it appears in print. Yet to this point he has been ever-present in the archives — front and centre and, more to the point, the focus of the Hilton task force and Norm Sheather. How can someone so intrinsic to the case vanish so effortlessly?

Do all the parties, Special Branch, ASIO, the Commonwealth Police, the task force, the government, et al decide that near enough is good enough? Do they all sit down and think, fuck this bastard Kumar, what's the quickest way to get rid of him? Let's get him on a plane and out of the bloody country. Let's shut the gate, slam the door. We've locked up a few of them, we're probably never going to nail him — time to move on.

I ponder what my comrade Norm Sheather makes of all this. Is he happy to relinquish this beleaguered case, or does something continue to gnaw away at him?

The Hilton archives of 1979 provide a glimpse of a dramatic shift of perspective in the ongoing, if it can even be described as such, investigation of the Hilton bombing. Distinct from the muscular early days of positioning the case as part of a potential international inquiry that is open ended and forward thinking, things go abruptly into reverse. There is an unsigned, half-typed, half-hand-written dossier entitled *Notes & Criminal History of Ananda Marga*, which laboriously compiles and annotates every criminal act alleged or proven to be carried out by Ananda Marga around the world between March 1973 and February 1979 — a total of 69 events are listed.[12] Some of these are not such a big deal in and of themselves, such as No. 47, which lists the deportation of Lynette Phillips from India and Bangladesh, and others that are new, such as No. 54, describing the alleged attempt in February 1979 by three Ananda Marga members to hijack and destroy a USSR aeroplane between Oslo and Moscow, a plan which is thwarted when the hijackers are 'overpowered by passengers and Soviet security men' in Stockholm.[13]

Nonetheless, this document, which also includes tiny crabbed hand-written quotes from a variety of sect writings suggesting a propensity for violence among members, feels like an exercise in intense frustration. It's as if the author can't believe the case has hit such rocky shores and its chief antagonist has effectively jumped ship, and is thus compelled, like the Ancient

Mariner, to recite the past in all its minutiae. It also reads as if it is prepared for new eyes — perhaps as justification for what is perceived publicly as a failed case. There is something plaintive, if urgent, in the tone of the final paragraph of the 'Researchers Opinion' attached to the dossier. The unnamed writer states:

> I do not believe that the group will be eradicated or made peaceful until the circumstances which spawned the AM are conected [sic]. There must have been far more attacks on persons and organisations that they regard as lacking in 'moral spirit' than have been attributed to Ananda Marga. Most unattributed acts are still under investigation and research continues.[14]

Except research doesn't really continue. This is clear from the next document that emerges, the oddly titled *Resumé of the Hilton Hotel Bombing*, dated 24 October 1979, a kind of summing up of the investigation. Even odder is deciphering the purpose of the resumé.[15]

It is generated two months after the sentencing of Anderson, Alister and Dunn on 8 August 1979 to 16 years apiece for the conspiracy to murder Cameron (remember, no charges have been laid against them in relation to the Hilton bombing) and exudes the aura of a housekeeping exercise. It is a carefully typed summary that leads the reader through all the key points of the Hilton investigation. Again it is compulsive in its detail and yet it feels reductive. Weirdly, it eschews almost all mention of Abhiik Kumar, and focuses exclusively on the activities of Anderson, Alister and Dunn. One can sense the investigative narrative growing a new skin in which the Australasian spiritual leader is expunged from the record.

The résumé seems to finish, if not on a note of defeat, then certainly on a desire to pass on the now completely inert case to someone else. Points 42 and 43 in particular read as if they are addressed to cops from the future who might stumble accidentally upon the investigation after all the contemporary players are done and dusted:

> 42. The original copy of the running sheet and the index of the Hilton bomb inquiry are held at the Homicide Squad, Criminal Investigation Branch. All photographs and television films of the two demonstrations and of members of the Ananda Marga sect are held at Special Branch Office, Police Headquarters.
> 43. No date has yet been set for the hearing of the Inquest into the deaths of William Arthur FAVELL, Alex Raymond CARTER and Paul BIRMISTRIW [sic].[16]

Then out of nowhere a miracle occurs.

The locker and the gelignite

The discovery of the bomb kit in a university locker in April 1981 jolts the investigation back to life. As Mrs Patricia Elson, a clerk at the University of New South Wales Union goes about her orderly, if overdue, task of checking the contents and bags retrieved from the male lockers that had not been renewed on Tuesday 28 April 1981 between 2.45 and 3 pm,[1] let's rewind to when there were rumours circulating of gelignite being stored by the Ananda Marga in a university locker in 1978 and 1979.

The source of the information is one of the ASIO agents embedded within the Ananda Marga.

> In 1978 and 1979, ASIO received agent information that ... some explosives left over from the Hilton had been stored in a locker at Macquarie University, in Sydney.[2]

This was of sufficient merit to be passed on to the New South Wales police from ASIO, and in turn sparked a thorough, if ultimately fruitless, search of all the lockers at Macquarie University.[3]

Now, almost two years later, an unsuspecting Patricia Elson at the University of New South Wales is unzipping a black overnight bag 'in order to establish its ownership'. She has already examined a number of other abandoned bags, containing clothing and 'other student type stuff'. In this particular one she sees some oblong-shaped cards on top and underneath them an oily rag. She lifts this nasty thing up only to then encounter a 'dirty towel'. On lifting this away 'I saw sticks of gelignite taped together ... I knew the thing I saw in the bag was gelignite because it had the word gelignite on it.'[4]

Mrs Elson does not panic. She informs her superiors, who confirm the finding, evacuate the building and call the police. The discovery must seem like a kind of gift from a higher being to the New South Wales police, who you'd imagine had given up all hope that any new evidence about the Hilton would spring up. Yet there it is:

Six copper coloured detonators with yellow wire leads, three silver coloured metal detonators, a yellow towel, an orange table cloth, a plastic bag with the words 'Tandy Electronics' printed on it, two sets of battery terminals, two nine volt batteries which were taped together, three battery terminal leads, a roll of yellow fuse wires, a length of grey plastic covered wire, a roll of red plastic wire, a black and green clock arm, a metal breaker switch, a packet of metal contacts, a glass cutter with a blue and red coloured handle, a tube of metallic cement, a plastic ruler, two pairs of white woollen gloves, two University cards, an electoral card, an electoral roll card, a Sydney Technical College Card and an extract of a Birth Certificate on a plastic container.[5]

Each of these items will be scrutinised obsessively but it is the '52 sticks of AN gelignite [and the] copy of the *Sydney Morning Herald*, dated Saturday 11th February, 1978', which the first Detective Senior Sergeant on the scene notes 'was two days prior to the Hilton bombing', that provide all the thrills.[6]

Yet they are thrills designed to break hearts. The yield, or 'cache' as it will be referred to, promises many things and it appears at first to be the critical catalyst to reignite, if not solve, the virtually defunct Hilton investigation. But it will not deliver.

You certainly can't fault any of the police involved in the handling of the discovery, nor the subsequent investigation of the contents of the black vinyl bag. From meticulous witness statements, to photographs, to extensive reports on how items from the bag are transported and delivered for testing, no t's are left uncrossed, no i's undotted. The police seem to want to keep things calm and quiet and to go about matters in an orderly fashion — in short, to do things absolutely by the book so they hold up in court. Basically to do things completely differently from the police efforts in connection with Yagoona.

Despite all this care, the contents of the bag, with its apparent surface sheen of juicy evidentiary value, will yield up less and less the more closely it is examined. It seems impossible that you could unearth a more direct piece of evidence in an unsolved crime, like the murder weapon, for example, that turns out to be so utterly useless. For a start, there are no fingerprints on anything. Next, all the identification in the bag turns out not to be from some dimwit Margii who left their ID with the gelignite, but to have been stolen from a University of New South Wales student the year before — she had been attending (as it is referred to in the police report) a 'gay dance' at the Roundhouse when her bag was nicked.[7]

Next thing to cross off the list of possible excitements is the identity of who hired the locker in the first place. The University of New South Wales turns out to be much better at attention to detail than Special Branch, and they are able to produce the original receipt of the man who hired the locker on 11 July 1978. While this becomes the source of all manner of wild theories over the next decade, examining the police evidence it's hard to comprehend what all the fuss is about. The receipt for $6 is signed by an MJ Melton. The $6 indicates it's a new hire and not a renewal. A person can only hire a locker if they have a student card. While there were no New South Wales students known as MJ Melton there was one called JJ Melton — MJ are the initials of his father. Naturally enough the police hurry off to interview this young man.

John Jeffrey Melton is revealed to be a serving midshipman aboard HMAS *Melbourne*, which is stationed in Perth. Police are sent to Perth to interview him and it turns out that while he is indeed registered at the University of New South Wales, it is only through an associate course taken through the Royal Australian Naval College at Jervis Bay, 193 kilometres from the University of New South Wales Roundhouse where the discovery was made. He tells them he has never been to the University of New South Wales personally and that he never leased a locker.

Mmmm, think the police. The University of New South Wales staff are not only meticulous with their records but they are pretty adamant that they don't rent lockers without student ID. It doesn't have to be *their* university's student ID. Special Branch continue their investigations and reveal that 'NAME blacked out' thought that perhaps the locker had been hired using a student card he had been issued when he attended Wollongong University.

> On 5 January 1982 ... Police ascertained that in 1977 [name blacked out] attended Wollongong University as a student. He was also a drug addict at that time. [He] stated that in late 1977, he obtained some drugs from the Oxford Hotel, Wollongong, and used his Student identity Card as collateral for the purchase, as he did not have enough cash. The seller took the card and he has not seen it since. No further information is forthcoming as to whom obtained the Card at some later date. [8]

So what is the fuss about? It's about the fact that on 28 August 1989, JJ Melton, aged 29, hangs himself. This is a few months after Anderson's arrest and Pederick's confessions and a few months before either of their trials. It is suggested by Anderson's defence that this suicide is not a coincidence and that Melton was allegedly worried (although there are no witness statements substantiating this) about being called to give evidence. The thing is poor JJ Melton was never called as a witness for anything in the past (not the inquest in 1982, not the Section 475 inquiry in 1984–85). The Anderson defence omitted all mention of the 5 January 1982 police statement admitting previously being a drug addict and exchanging his student card for drugs in 1977. Nor did they mention that this indicated to police that whoever hired the locker had probably used a stolen identity card, which seems likely given that the locker contained other stolen student identification documents.

Look, I suppose it's possible that JJ Melton, who was at HMAS *Creswell* for the first six months of 1978, could have ended up in Sydney on his first shore leave and met a boy/girl who asked him to rent a locker in his (his dad's) name and he gave them the key before he got back on board for another long stint at sea. The thing is I doubt it.

Given that the physical contents of the locker seem to have at least a circumstantial link to the Hilton bombing, and that in early 1982 the New South Wales Government announces that there will be a coronial inquest into the deaths arising from the Hilton, New South Wales Special Branch are super keen to 'give evidence at the Inquest linking the Ananda Marga with the explosives found at the University of New South Wales'.[9] Special Branch want to use the intelligence gathered in 1978–79 by the ASIO agent embedded in the Ananda Marga about storing gelignite in a locker at Macquarie University. After some toing and froing ASIO refuses to allow this. First they argue they do not wish to compromise their still active agent, and second, such intelligence could be regarded as simply prejudicial hearsay and have no relevance to the inquest. ASIO's arguments seem reasonable, if maddening.

The inquest, 1982

So here we are in mid-1982 with the overdue Hilton bombing inquest about to begin and the discovery of a cache of gelignite and bomb paraphernalia that cannot be introduced into evidence. Whether this would have made a difference is anyone's guess, given that the inquest seems to be about everything but an investigation of the deaths of Alec Carter, William Favell and Paul Burmistriw who were blown apart by a bomb on 13 February 1978 outside the Hilton Hotel.

The coronial inquest is a chaotic circus combining the conspiracy allegations (ASIO et al planting the bomb), the miscarriage of justice allegations about Yagoona, and reams of material about Seary's unreliability as a witness. The transcripts are infused with anger, confusion and barbed asides from lawyers representing Seary, injured policeman Terry Griffiths, Dunn, Alister and Anderson.

It is only when one comes across Detective Inspector Norm Sheather's eloquent statement prepared for the inquest that the hysteria and shouting recedes and he returns us to the scene of the crime and the anguish of that night.

Sheather may have moved a long way (possibly down) from being at the head of Australia's largest homicide investigation to being the Detective Inspector of North-Eastern Police in 1979 and, in 1982, the Detective Inspector for Country Districts, but he is clear-eyed in his recollections and unflinching in accepting responsibility. Beat by bloody beat he takes the listener through the carnage he witnessed on arriving at the scene ('identification of the man FAVELL was only possible by the fingerprint of one finger-tip').[1] Sheather tells of his team of 58 expert detectives and of the thousands of interviews conducted over the six months he was in charge, and underlines that 'extensive investigations were carried out in all states of Australia and a number of overseas countries'. Despite all these monumental efforts, however, he admits 'no information was obtained which would be sufficient to identify the person or persons involved in causing the deaths of the three persons mentioned'.[2]

What he does not mention is the effect Seary's recruitment by Special Branch and the subsequent

Yagoona arrests on 15 June had upon his investigation. Instead he makes a mournful statement that 'there was extensive media coverage of this horrific incident and information was supplied to police concerning many possible suspects for this crime. All these avenues were thoroughly investigated, without success.'[3]

Sheather finishes with a kind of liturgy for the dead. He invokes the last minutes of each of the victims, carefully recounting the moments before their lives intersected with the bomb.

William Ebb, the garbage truck driver, saw 'Favell pick up the bin … he then turned his head and heard a deafening explosion. He saw a sheet of flame and glass shattering on both sides of the street.' As John Watson, another garbageman, passes Favell about to lift the bin outside the Hilton, en route to collect the one next to it, 'he heard the loud explosion and felt the blast that made him stumble'. Sergeant Arthur Hawtin was talking to Constable Burmistriw, 'when there was a blinding flash'; Senior Constable Terry Griffiths, 'looking south towards the garbage truck', hears 'a very loud explosion and immediately felt pain to his right foot and stomach. He can recall seeing what appeared to be long hair flying past his vision.' Colin Nicholls, a Hilton employee, saw Favell pick up the bin, hoist it to his shoulder and carry it to the back of the garbage truck, then empty it and 'immediately heard the loud explosion and saw an orange/yellow flash'. Norm

The inquest, 1982

keeps going through the testimony of each eyewitness. The prose is like an incantation. His investigation may have failed but he will not let those listening forget who was lost and what was torn apart.[4]

It's a tiny reprieve from the hysteria surrounding the Coroner's Court, some of it involving impromptu street theatre by sect members disrupting the proceedings, none of which could have given much comfort to the families of the dead. Then abruptly, just when you'd think things couldn't get much more bizarre, Abhiik Kumar makes his first public appearance in association with the Hilton bombing.

He doesn't appear in person, mind you, but he is conjured up spectacularly by the former Hilton night receptionist Manfred Von Gries, who witnessed the explosion from the Hilton escalator. Von Gries tells the coroner that while driving home after giving his witness statement to police the following morning, a heavily bearded man with thick glasses and a turban — yes, a turban — pulled up alongside him in a car containing three other people and threatened to kidnap his son if he continued to speak to the police.

'I had my passenger window down and I could see the driver's face toward me and scream out "When you go once more to the police, your son will be kidnapped."'

It then turns out he has identified this man, who spoke with a Texan accent, from surveillance photos given to him by police as none other than the spiritual leader of the Ananda Marga.[5] In court, Von Gries, rather theatrically is asked to put a circle around the turbaned head of the tall skinny man photographed by ASIO at the airport waiting with other members of the Ananda Marga for the arrival of the Indian Prime Minister Mr Desai, about 12 hours before the bombing.[6]

The papers scream out headlines such as 'Sect Leader Named in Link to Hilton Bombing'[7] and 'Witness Tells of Threat to Kidnap Son'[8] to an enraptured public who can add this to the heady mix of news flashes bursting from the inquest like 'Caller said ASIO linked to Bombing'[9] or 'Seary Denies Colouring his Story for Effect'.[10]

In a nutshell, the story Manfred Von Gries chronicles amounts to this: immediately before and after the bombing he saw a number of individuals loitering around the George Street entrance to the Hilton. The morning after the bombing he goes to the Campbell Street police station and, along with hundreds of others, gives his witness statement about the explosion and the individuals he had seen.[11] A Detective Sergeant Coco then shows him some photographs and Von Gries 'selected a photograph of a man standing side on ... as being similar to the man I saw in George St'.[12] The inference is that the man identified is a member of the Ananda Marga and the sect is somehow informed

The inquest, 1982

of this damning eyewitness account. Abhiik Kumar then mobilises a group of Margiis that very morning who all jump in a car and somehow track down Von Gries as he leaves the police station and (having already somehow found out he has a young son) make the kidnapping threat. Von Gries goes to the police the next day, after staying the night at the Hilton with his son for safety, and reports the threat. He is shown photographs but can't identify the bearded, turbaned man. Von Gries is then subject to ongoing harassment — abusive phone calls, car tampering, break-ins — for the next three or so years.

Here's the problem. Like so many allegations linking the Ananda Marga to the Hilton bombing, these too are besieged by contradictions and evidentiary problems. While no one denies Von Gries says he was threatened, no evidence exists as to whether the police ever recorded these threats in a statement at the time. Then it turns out that the abusive calls to him over the years may have been made by Hilton staff members. Next, and most problematic, Von Gries has only been shown the 12 February 1978 photographs of the Ananda Marga members at the airport, in which he identifies Abhiik Kumar as his verbal assailant, on 28 September 1982, the day before he gives evidence to the inquest. Even worse, the person who is then questioned about these particular photographs is Detective Senior Constable DA Henderson of Special Branch,[13] the same Special Branch that is being howled down at the inquest over their questionable recruitment of Seary. The lawyers have a field day dismantling the testimony of Von Gries, Henderson and Special Branch and highlighting the questionable four-year gap between the alleged threat and the identification.

In short, the allegations are worthless and, even if they could be substantiated, fairly pointless, as Abhiik Kumar is now 'living in Germany with other sect members' under the new name of David Hart.[14]

The coronial inquest topples into the sea a mere two weeks after it started. Once Seary reiterates his claims about Dunn's and Alister's confessions on the way to Yagoona, Coroner Norman Walsh states he is compelled to halt the inquest because there is 'a prima facie case for murder and conspiracy to murder against Alister and Dunn', and 'the evidence possibly disclosed' a conspiracy between the two and Anderson.[15]

Despite these bold pronouncements,[16] nothing comes of them. The New South Wales Attorney-General does not issue indictments and the matter is dropped.[17]

Yet beneath the shipwreck that is the inquest — a monumental waste of time and money that caused substantial pain for the victims and families of those murdered — something is happening deep underground. Simultaneous with the first public mention of Abhiik Kumar in connection with the Hilton bombing at the inquest, ASIO uncovers some startling intelligence. So what did ASIO find? This:

> In September 1982, an ASIO agent reported that the former spiritual director of Ananda Marga in Australia, 'Abhiik', had introduced a lecture [in an unnamed location but most plausibly West Germany] on bomb making and explosives by saying that he did not favour remote control devices because of their uncertainty. 'Abhiik' reportedly said that it had been a remote control device which had been placed outside the Hilton; that the Indian Prime Minister (Mr Desai) had passed the bomb twice, but on each occasion the remote control mechanism had failed.[18]

This extraordinary information, while potentially hearsay, does appear to unleash a kind of last hurrah from the original investigation teams. Special Branch and the New South Wales police decide they are going to have one more red-hot go at solving the crime, arresting the bastards and finding the evidence that will stand up in court.

To kick things off, our Detective Inspector Norm Sheather, who has been sent to patrol country pastures for a number of years, steps defiantly and proactively back into view.

May 1983

In May 1983, six months after the capsized inquest, the New South Wales police request a meeting with ASIO. They make it clear that they are seeking ASIO's assistance in 'considering whether information held by ASIO might be used to prosecute those persons indicted for the Hilton bombing'.[1] Up until this point the police and Special Branch believe they have only been given partial access to ASIO's intelligence. The Deputy Director-General of ASIO agrees that ASIO can reveal its holdings, but only on the condition that the police neither copy nor physically retain this information and, disappointingly, that none of the information is 'to be used in the police prosecution'.

On 7 or 8 June 1983 Norm Sheather reappears. He is representing the New South Wales police Hilton investigation team, and he and Inspector Young of Special Branch sit down with ASIO for a parley. ASIO warns the men that the material is sensitive and some of it could 'have resulted from attempts by the Ananda Marga to test the source, and could therefore be 100 per cent inaccurate'.[2] ASIO shows them 36 intelligence items relating to both the Hilton bombing and to Yagoona. Sheather realises immediately that many of these items have already been passed on to the New South Wales police orally between 1978 and 1981. What is new is 'a Margii's reported admission concerning the purchase of the explosives used in the bombing', and some talk about the police interviewing Margii members 'Citisvarupa' and 'Suvod' about the explosives.[3]

However, Norm remains unswayed. He looks at the information and it is clearly more of the same bits of tantalising, unverifiable chatter doomed to fail in court. He is damning in his assessment. He tells the ASIO officer at the meeting that he regards their material relating to the Hilton bombing 'overall, as having little probative value'.

ASIO seem somewhat taken aback and ask him if it would help the police 'if ASIO put the agent on the stand?' Sheather will not be moved, perhaps to him it sounds like Richard Seary all over again. His reply is that even with the full cooperation of an agent, this 'would not' secure a conviction.[4]

Unlike Sheather, Special Branch, ever hopeful, and feasibly smarting even more from the blows that have rained down on them since the revelations about Seary at the inquest, refuse to be so pessimistic. Instead they come up with a plan, which on the surface appears considered and quite brilliant. They will marry hard science to strong circumstantial intelligence and crack the thing wide open.

What they propose is this. With the help of Australia's best scientists, along with ASIO, they will conduct exhaustive comparative testing on every available bit of physical evidence taken from the series of bombings or attempted bombings, including the bits of wire and such recovered from the Hilton, that occurred throughout 1978.

The strength of the idea is that this time Special Branch recruits arm's length experts with distinguished and impossible-to-dispute credentials to lead the investigation.

The scientific team is headed by Dr Malcolm Hall of the Australian Federal Police Forensic Science Research Unit and Dr Hilton J Kobus from the Department of Chemistry at the Australian National University, Canberra. These men are invited to the Special Branch Ballistics Unit, Scientific and Technical Services, where they view 'a number of exhibits and other components of improvised explosive devices'. The purpose of the visit is to 'ascertain whether the exhibits were worthy of scientific comparison tests to establish similarities between bombing and attempted bombing incidents'.[5]

The scientists are asked to compare debris found at the Hilton bombing on 13 February 1978 — wires, battery pieces and sundry items (which you'll remember were difficult to identify definitively as part of a bomb and not simply refuse from the garbage truck) — with materials from the bomb found at the Indian High Commission on 25 March 1978, the bomb components from the police headquarters explosion on 18 May 1978, the bomb found in the back of the car with Alister, Dunn and Seary at Yagoona on 15 June 1978, and finally the contents of the University of New South Wales locker discovered on 28 April 1981 (but rented on 11 July 1978). It is the belief of Special Branch that 'all the bombs were partly made from components found in the cache at the University of New South Wales'.[6]

The good news is that Hall and Kobus are in agreement that there 'is an excellent chance of identifying similarities existing between the explosive devices'. The scientists go on to suggest a dizzying series of tests that they believe will yield results. Among the array of experiments, certain comparative tests will be carried out on the Hilton debris by a process of 'neutron activation analysis at the Atomic Energy Commission at Lucas Heights' and other 'analytical tests will also be carried out on the gelignite located at the University of New South Wales, and that recovered at Yagoona ... at the Analytical Laboratories, Lidcombe ...

arrangements are made with the Dangerous Goods Branch to have the explosives transported to the Laboratories'.[7]

The fervent desire is that these tests will provide some physical link to the 'information [that] has been received from a confidential source, which indicates that members of Ananda Marga, other than those already mentioned [i.e. not Anderson, Alister or Dunn], are involved with the various incidents shown in this report'.[8]

The moment the series of sophisticated experiments on the various bombs, exploded and unexploded, are approved and set in motion, disaster strikes.

Two days after the report requesting the tests is compiled, Special Branch issues a request to ASIO. They ask if Detectives Henderson and Helson could be allowed to examine all 'transcripts of technical surveillance carried out on Ananda Marga premises in Australia, one week prior to, and one week after' (a) the Hilton bombing, (b) the attempted bombing of the Indian High Commission, (c) the bombing of the New South Wales Police Headquarters, (d) the Yagoona incident, and (e) the discoveries of the explosives cache at the University of New South Wales.[9]

That doesn't seem a lot to ask, does it? Especially as ASIO seem to have been bending over backwards to cooperate a month earlier when they showed Sheather and Young their '36 items' of interest.

May 1983

But they don't cooperate. The request is flatly refused. The way ASIO puts it is: 'In regard to the police request for our technical product, our review found no relevant information, and, as unevaluated and unprocessed product obtained under ASIO's special powers should not be made available to people outside ASIO, it was an easy decision to deny that access.'[10]

Special Branch refuse to give up. However, once again, they fail to take note that the cautious Detective Inspector Sheather, as in the recruitment of Seary, is no longer beside them in this endeavour.

The tests will take over a year to complete and are carried out on every filament and fibre, every wire, every piece of gelignite, plus the batteries, the masking tape, the bags, the newspaper and the maroon balaclava found inside the blue bag at Yagoona. Dr Hall is particularly optimistic about what will be learnt from the detonators, which 'are important evidence linking four of the events'.[11] Testing takes place in Sydney, Melbourne and Adelaide at a range of institutions including the Australian Bomb Data Centre, the South Australian Forensic Science Centre, the University of Adelaide, the Australian Federal Police in Canberra along with the Atomic Energy Commission and the Analytical Laboratories in Sydney.

There are dozens of scientists involved, from Dr Kenneth Brown from the Department of Dentistry who is an expert in operating 'video-superimposition equipment',[12] to Lloyd Ernest Mulholland of the New South Wales Fingerprint Section and Dr Roger Shackleton of the Australian Bomb Data Centre.[13] The test methodologies involve, to name a few, a nanospectrometer (colour), a pyrolysis mass spectrometer, high performance liquid chromatography and microscopy neutron activation analysis.[14] There are detailed charts, columns and spreadsheets that align common items found at each site. Four of them have yellow wire, two have a similar printing defect on the gelignite labels, three have battery clips.[15] In short, it is impossible to question just how exhaustive the scientific analysis on these five bomb incidents is.

When the findings are collated and presented in October 1984 they are horribly ambivalent. Reading them it's hard to comprehend suggestions in the future that if they had been presented at either the Section 475 inquiry in 1984–85 or at Anderson's trial or appeal in 1989–90 the outcome of each would have been radically different. From the evidence I simply can't see how these assertions hold weight. For example:

Summary of the Results.

3.1 <u>Blue Tape :</u> The results show that the same type of blue tape occurred at both the Police Headquarters and the Yagoona scenes. However this is common insulation tape and there were no features on it that would make the pieces examined unusual.

3.2 Masking Tape : The examination showed clearly that the masking tape from the University of New South Wales and that from Yagoona was different and therefore could not have come from the same roll.

3.3. Electrical Wire (i) Detonator Wire. The yellow insulation on the detonator wire from all four scenes was the same colour and type ... However such wire is made in large quantities and the type of wire from the four scenes is likely to be fairly common. No features were found on the detonator wires that would make them unusual [16] ... (iii) the red wires from Yagoona and the Indian high Commission were clearly different ...[17]

This kind of measured analysis continues from Dr Kobus: 'It is not possible to form an opinion as to a common point of construction for the bombs from examination of fragments of material such as those reported.' Kobus concluded:

> Since there were no highly characteristic features to any of the items of similarity between the scenes and since there were many clear differences between other items from the various scenes, no

support can be given to the possibility of there being a common point of manufacture for the four bombs. From the results obtained in this report it is not possible to exclude the possibility that the bombs were manufactured independently of each other.[18]

Other separate comparative reports from scientists Ms AE Paraybyk, Mr RJ Lokan and Mr GB Smith, using different methodologies including microspectrophotometry, pyrolysis mass spectrometry and microscopy for physical detail, result in similar conclusions: 'the value of [the] similarity is limited ... the match ... is not strong associative evidence',[19] 'could have a common origin but the possibility of different sources cannot be excluded',[20] 'these results indicate that the red and black plastic wires in the Yagoona incident originated from a different source to [those] ... in the Indian High Commission incident'.[21]

Nonetheless, while the scientists from the South Australian Forensic Science Centre can find no strong evidence supporting a link between the bombs, nor evidence that the bombs from the Hilton, Indian High Commission, police headquarters and Yagoona were manufactured from components in the cache found at the University of New South Wales, John Harold Goulding from the Neutron Activation Analysis Section of the AFP is having more success.

May 1983

Goulding's focus is on identifying whether the trace elements of any of the grey or yellow detonator wire found at the various sites are similar. The virtue of the test is the principle that 'when two or more samples exhibit the same trace element profile it indicates that they were produced in the same synthetic batch. This holds whether the samples are copper wire, glass, paint or heroin.'[22] Goulding subjects the wires to the neutron activation analysis. He concludes that the components of the grey wires are too variable for comparison but finds that:

> The Yellow PVC insulated, single strand wire from the cache at the University of New South Wales, the Indian High Commission device, and the unit found at Yagoona, all exhibited the same trace elements [of Antimony, Arsenic, Cobalt, Gold, Iron, Mercury, Scandium, Selenium, Silver, and Zinc] in the same trace concentration.

Goulding concludes: 'experience has shown that these comparable trace element profiles can only occur when the samples had a common origin, i.e. the same ingot of refined copper'.[23]

It's something but it's not a whole lot. There are some similarities — the strongest being the matching printing fault on the gelignite wrappers from Yagoona and the cache from the University of New South

Wales, but there is little information provided on how big a batch of gelignite may have been affected by this manufacturing error. As Dr Hall himself admits after much of the testing has finished:

> From an evidentiary point of view, I would suggest that any lay person looking at the table would find some similarities that they might find significant, but at the same time there are some evident dissimilarities.[24]

It's hard to fathom how such *comme ci comme ca* results can transform into a kind of code breaking machine over the next decade. It's clear from the above that the comparisons are slight at best and even if *some* of the bombs can be tied together there is nothing tying the New South Wales Uni cache to the Hilton and, more importantly, nothing tying any individual to these bombs. Yet somehow the imagined value of these results grows as the years roll by. In 1993, Dr Hall himself approaches Roger Holdich, the Inspector-General of Intelligence and Security, and tells him explicitly that testing had thrown up 'significant similarities between the caches of explosives' and that in spite of this, the Wood Section 475 inquiry in 1984–85 had not sought to present this evidence in its findings. Holdich tries to get to the bottom of this assertion by interviewing Mark Tedeschi QC, who had been the crown prosecutor at Tim Anderson's trial in 1989. Dr Hall had also taken Tedeschi through the 'significant similarities', although a decision had been made not to present this evidence at Anderson's trial. Tedeschi's belief is that if the 1984–85 Section 475 inquiry (as to the guilt or innocence of the Yagoona Three) had used 'this material', it 'could very well have affected the outcome of the inquiry'.[25]

The truth is the original test results were not that strong in an evidentiary sense. All these statements suggesting that if only the results had been looked at closely by 'the proper authorities/at the inquiry/at the trial' they would have swayed the course of history do not seem to be correct.

So there you have it. The last red-hot go at getting to Abhiik comes to nothing.

So where does that leave us? Once the mayhem of the respective Pederick and Anderson trials ends with Anderson's successful appeal and Pederick's release, there's not a whole lot more that can be said. Kumar's appearances, like that of an ageing movie star, become rarer and rarer.

Sometimes I wonder if Norm Sheather, as he approached the end of his career and entered retirement, paid any attention to these infrequent turns of Abhiik Kumar on the public stage. Perhaps.

1989
and after

One thing I am pretty sure that Norm would have noticed is the fracas surrounding the abrupt arrest of Tim Anderson as the Hilton bomber in 1989 based on the accusations of convicted criminal Ray Denning. As mentioned earlier, what makes these slippery allegations stick is ex-Margii Evan Pederick's confession that he planted the bomb under orders from Anderson. While this confession, the subsequent police investigation and the prosecution case are riddled with inconsistencies, incoherencies and gigantic cock-ups, there remain a few things to clear up.

First, given the embarrassing revelations during the investigation and then at the trial that Pederick frequently got the basic facts completely wrong in his highly detailed account of attempting to blow up

Desai with a remote control device as he was greeted by Fraser outside the Hilton, there are nevertheless things in his confession that are bizarrely and inexplicably accurate. Things that might explain why, while the Queensland police who dealt with him first didn't take him seriously, the New South Wales police got so hot and bothered. Things it's hard to explain.

Pederick originally said he dumped the leftover gelignite from the Hilton in a locker at Macquarie University. While this is helpfully adjusted to become a locker at the University of New South Wales by the New South Wales police interviewing him in 1989 who 'jog' his memory — this in fact is the exact location that ASIO said they heard rumours about in 1978–79. Likewise his blather about using a remote control device that malfunctioned lines up beautifully with the 1982 ASIO intelligence that has Abhiik Kumar complaining about such devices. None of these things was in the public domain.

But the fact remains that most of what Pederick confessed (in obsessive detail) was proved to be inaccurate. The police and prosecution at the time made much of the lengthy passage of time between the bombing and the confession to explain such inconsistencies, but it wasn't really such a huge chunk of time, was it? Pederick said he was motivated to confess because of overwhelming guilt. You'd imagine, with that sort of blood on your hands, the events and your actions would still be seared indelibly in your brain a little over a decade afterwards.

Don't get me wrong. I can't comprehend how the case got to trial at all given the insanely shifting versions of who did what to whom, or how a jury found Anderson guilty on this slipshod mound of 'evidence'. It was a mess from start to finish. I do understand how Anderson won the appeal and I believe justice prevailed.

However, I also think that Pederick's confession differs from that of the mentally ill individuals who put up their hands for the crime during Sheather's tenure on the Hilton task force. Unlike those distracting confessions, full of madness and self-loathing, Pederick's confession has the hallmarks of someone who had access to inside information. Whether this 'information' was just wild gossip he had heard or whether some of it was true, it feels like a story borrowed second-hand from someone else. Like a Chinese whisper passed down the line.

The other thing that strikes you when you read Pederick's confession — something that was lost in the noise of outrage during Anderson's trial — was that he also named Abhiik Kumar as the mastermind behind the bomb.

Make of that what you will.

What is so peculiar about the saga of the Hilton bombing is that it produced two such spectacularly bizarre characters — Seary and Pederick — unknown to each other but of such astoundingly similar oddness and, let's face it, unreliability. The public finds each of them utterly unfathomable during their respective appearances (separated by over a decade) in the case. People seem unable to make head nor tail of what might be motivating them. Yet in the end each of them did display a certain consistency.

Seary maintained that while he was wrong about many things, particularly in relation to the supposed confessions about the Hilton bombing he claimed to have heard, what he reported to Special Branch about the Ananda Marga up to 15 June was the truth. In 1985 Seary told the media he was 'not a hundred per cent certain that Alister and Dunn did what they said they did … I'm a hundred per cent certain now that the Ananda Marga personnel and associates quite probably arranged and did the Hilton bombing'.[1] In Pederick's case, despite his attempt to appeal his sentence on the basis of Anderson's successful appeal discrediting his evidence, he has continued to assert that he planted the Hilton bomb.

The other thing that connects Seary and Pederick is an extraordinary document published in 1994 by the Office of the Inspector-General of Intelligence and Security. This report, titled *Complaint by Mr Richard John Seary against the Australian Security Intelligence Organisation: Final Report* is ASIO's first (and final public) paper on the Ananda Marga and the Hilton bombing. Authored by Roger Holdich, the Inspector-General of Intelligence and Security, it is, in essence, a highly detailed response to Richard Seary's accusations that ASIO had failed to produce evidence from its covert operatives within the sect that would have validated many of his allegations regarding the Ananda Marga. However, the report goes much further than simply rebutting Seary's complaints and offers some probing analysis about the case itself.

For example, at one point Holdich observes:

> It is interesting to note the differences between the accounts of Seary and Pederick. Whereas Seary implicated Alister, Dunn and Anderson in the bombing (with Anderson being a peripheral figure), Pederick has never formally accused Alister or Dunn. On the other hand, both Seary and Pederick have claimed in recent times that a sect member, 'Abhiik', was a catalyst for the bombing.[2]

So did Abhiik Kumar mastermind the Hilton bombing? Was this man of so many names and passports the one behind it after all? His proximity to so many international acts of violence involving Margii or Proutist foot soldiers swirling around Baba's failed appeals in the late 1970s seems to suggest a compelling circumstantial case. He had the means and motive.

Holdich's report is confident about making this assertion:

> [The bombing] is consistent with other Ananda Marga attacks on Indian officials during the period and there are grounds for strongly suspecting Ananda Marga responsibility. ASIO information <u>does not</u> support the case against Alister and Dunn, and the information on Anderson is both conflicting and inconclusive. Source information and circumstantial evidence suggests that 'Ainjali' [a woman], 'Suvod', 'Kapil' and 'Dhruva' <u>were directed by 'Abhiik' to undertake the Hilton bombing</u>. There currently appears [to be] insufficient evidence to initiate prosecutions.[3]

*

It is edifying to discover some contemporary, untainted analysis about the Margiis that sees the interconnection between segments of the sect and acts of violence in the 1970s as overt. These two sources, one from a French anthropologist and one from an American religious scholar, were both published in 2008 in the esteemed journal *Novia Religio: The Journal of Alternative and Emergent Religions*. Both articles scrupulously research through distinct methodology the role of violence in the history and functioning of Ananda Marga. It is important to note that both authors, if not somewhat sympathetic to the sect, are certainly far from hostile. Raphaël Voix's paper is titled 'Denied Violence, Glorified Fighting: Spiritual Discipline and Controversy in Ananda Marga', and Helen Crovetto's 'Ananda Marga and the Use of Force'. Both authors take it as a given that violence was an intrinsic element in the hierarchy of the sect and back their claims with substantial evidence and rigour.[4]

In Western countries 'non-violence' — the usual translation of the Sanskrit term *ahimsa* — is usually represented as the core value of Indian civilisation. As Voix explains, this is inextricably tied up with Gandhi and the Indian fight for independence. Since that point in India, 'violence and non-violence are seen as mutually exclusive poles. However, in Hindu India, concepts of violence and non-violence are much more complex.' Voix then charges into a forensic linguistic analysis of the term and reveals that in fact *ahimsa* means 'the absence of any desire to kill'. Following this definition, it is the context and the author of the act, rather than the act itself, that determines it as 'violent' or 'non-violent'.

Crovetto opens her paper with a quote from Sarkar himself: 'Like materialism, spirituality based on non-violence will be of no benefit to humanity. The words of non-violence may sound noble, and quite appealing, but on the solid ground of reality have no value whatsoever.'5 Crovetto's and Voix's primary source material relies on oral accounts from sect members and ex-members that often conflict with the sect's official written versions.

Voix observes a clear:

> … distinction between the official, collective written history of Ananda Marga — in which the movement appears as the victim of conspiracy — and the orally transmitted stories in which the Ananda Marga appears as a community of powerful ascetics. Indeed, this distinction shows how violence within Ananda Marga plays a double and apparently contradictory role. On the one hand, it reinforces the 'disciples' identification with the movement. Through a collective experience of persecution and a common history of conspiracy against them, members of the Ananda Marga have developed a shared sense of belonging. On the other hand, Ananda Marga's official history is only one reality among many conveyed in the movement. Like spiritual discipline, acts of violence for which the Ananda Marga may be responsible are secret and part of an active dissimulation strategy. Only when a disciple is fully convinced of the legitimacy of

violence does he access stories different to the official history.'⁶

Both scholars, having conducted exhaustive research with Margiis themselves, argue that any action attempting to liberate their leader, no matter how extreme in the eyes of outsiders, was not necessarily regarded as violence per se and thus could be denied publicly without contradiction. Further, this was always accepted by the inner sanctum of the sect, the elite at the top of the hierarchy.

All of this ceases to matter when the mortal embodiment of Baba — Prabhat Ranjan Sarkar — comes to an end on 21 October 1990. The Ananda Marga appears to successfully dissociate itself from allegations of violence thereafter. The sect continues its good works in supporting disaster relief, setting up schools and running yoga retreats and meditation centres. By the mid-1990s the University of Maryland Consortium for the Study of Terrorism and Responses to Terrorism classes the group as 'inactive'.

Tim Anderson left the sect well before any of this and is now a lecturer at the University of Sydney. Ross Dunn appears to have retreated into the mists but Paul Alister is still a member — recently embroiled in a federal court case over who has control of the estimated $20 million of assets belonging to the Australian wing of the sect. Evan Pederick has opted for the spiritual life and is an Anglican minister in Western Australia. Richard Seary has made various complaints and undertaken litigation over the years in a quest to legitimise his claims about the sect and defend his character. In 2012 he published an ebook about the bombing on Amazon called *Smoke and Mirrors: How the Australian Public were Screwed*.

And Abhiik Kumar? Well, his last foray in front of the Australian public occurs in 2003, on the eve of the twenty-fifth anniversary of the bombing. *The Australian* newspaper publishes a series of long investigative articles that review all that has occurred (including interviews with Seary and Pederick) in the decades since the bombing.

One story, titled 'Is this man the Hilton bomber?', plainly states that 'Abhiik Kumar was the mastermind of the Hilton Hotel bombing.'[7] While this is pretty much what all the official agencies involved in the investigation of the bombing believe, what is new is that reporters Janet Fife-Yeomans and Natalie O'Brien secure an 'exclusive interview' with Kumar, 'who has broken his silence to declare his innocence'. The interview (presumably conducted over the telephone) isn't as exciting as one might hope. Much of it consists of lengthy asides recounting the case and the players involved. There is a longish section in which Kumar recounts his outrage at having his passport confiscated in 1978, but other than that there's not much to sink your teeth into. It's all rather sunny. Of the Margiis he has this to say:

> For seven years back in the '70s, I had the privilege of working with some of the most amazing people I have ever known ... The Margiis of Australia and New Zealand were dynamic, creative, intelligent, talented and thoroughly good-hearted. Whatever project they took up, they tackled with cheerful and dedicated zeal. In a very short time, this relatively small group of remarkable people managed to establish — among other things — three primary schools, two secondary schools, a pioneering land community, a nationally distributed magazine, numerous music cassettes and art exhibitions, various women's welfare projects and even a visionary movement for Australian republicanism.
>
> They also spread the progressive ideals and yoga techniques of Ananda Marga throughout Australasia. In any circumstances that arose — good or bad — the Margiis of Australia and New Zealand always made the best of it.[8]

Of his alleged involvement with the Bangkok Three and the purchase of explosives in Thailand, he says simply, 'If such a person ... actually existed, it wasn't me.' Of the Hilton, he flat out 'denies that he or the

Ananda Marga had anything to do with the bombing and says he has never been interrogated about the incident'.[9]

What is interesting is that the journalists have managed to track him down. He now has yet another new name — this one quite a mouthful. He is now known as Abhidevanda, and is a senior monk in the Ananda Marga, living in — of all places — Israel. Jon Hoffman, who first arrived in Australia in 1973, was not only an American citizen by birth but also possibly Jewish, and perhaps able to claim citizenship under Israel's Law of Return.

He's still there. Anyone can locate him with the most cursory of internet searches. I certainly have.

Epilogue:
'My heart has been broken'

My friend Anna, an intrepid and fearless filmmaker, says I should jump on a plane and confront Kumar. Perhaps storm into some serene meditation centre in Jerusalem and wave bits of paper and demand an explanation. Personally I can't see the point of this. I'm not a detective or an investigative reporter. When I made the decision to explore the Hilton bombing archive I also made a vow not to trust the living, so why start now?

For a long time I considered seeking out the daughters of William Favell and Alec Carter, to see how they had fared in the years since the bombing. The little girls Christine, Susan and Cassandra were between seven and nine, about the age my son is now, when their fathers were killed. Yet the longer I thought about it, the more I felt it would be a crass attempt to remind people of how much was damaged that night almost 40 years ago. Like going up to relatives after a plane crash and asking them how they feel.

Then an email arrives in my inbox.

Dear Dr Landers,

My name is Terry Griffiths. I was a Police Officer injured in the Sydney Hilton Bombing on 13th February, 1978. I was present when two people were killed in front of me. Literally, blown to pieces. Another Police Officer Paul Birmistriw was fatally wounded and died 9 days later.

I was conscious the whole time. Saw and heard everything and never been able to forget it. All victims were mutilated by shrapnel. I won't go into a lengthy resume of my own wounds, but just briefly mention I had part of the top of my right foot blown out. The top of my right fibula bone blown out. A wound to the right side of my right thigh. Shrapnel punctured the right side of my abdomen and perforated my large colon which was exteriorised for two months. The shrapnel is still inside my abdomen.

Due to the noise of the blast I suffer from tinnitus in both ears. These are some of the physical injuries. I suffered post-traumatic shock and agoraphobia.

All of the above are constant reminders to me why I should never stop fighting for justice and for those responsible to be apprehended and dealt with according to law.

THE LAW in this country has done its best to turn away from dealing with and resolving this matter to the shame of all decent Australians. I have spent decades doing whatever I could to find out information and evidence to achieve the right result.

I hope you might consider communicating with me. I would be prepared to co-operate with you or your representative. I look forward to hearing from you.

Sincere regards,

Terry Griffiths.

Since beginning this book I have wanted to look only at the historical record and see what could be gleaned from it, so it's a shock to get such a stark reminder of the horrific consequences of the explosion from someone who was standing in front of it. What is more disconcerting is that Terry Griffiths is also the chief advocate of the conspiracy allegations involving ASIO,

Special Branch and so on. I know these allegations well and have found nothing in any archive that supports them.

I don't know what to do plus I'm sick with the flu and can't bring my aching fingers to stretch to the keyboard to hit reply ...

Finally I run out of excuses, send an apology and give him my number.

We speak. It's not a happy conversation. I feel I need to let him know as soon as possible that I don't share his views and that I can't see any evidence to give them credence. This makes him angry and he tells me that I am an idiot and like the rest of the idiots who believe the pack of lies that have been fed to them. A pack of lies that include most, if not all, of the 400-plus boxes of material contained in the Hilton bombing records deposited in state archives in 1995 that have been put there deliberately (and incompletely) to mislead stupid and naïve people like myself.

I spend the first half hour on the phone being a self-righteous cow trying to impress him with how much I know and how thorough I have been in my research, which has stretched far beyond just the contents of the Hilton archives in New South Wales State Records. I suddenly hear myself and think how prissy and irritating this must sound to someone who has spent his life fighting for the justice he believes has been withheld. I stop talking. He tells me about how close he has been in each decade to instigating a bipartisan inquiry or royal commission into the bombing only to see these monumental efforts collapse time after time. He explains how they made a guard stand beside him when he went to look at the Hilton bombing archive after it had first been deposited. How he knows that critical documents had been excised or eradicated. He tells me what a good detective he was and is. About the emotional and physical pain he has endured, that he has had two broken marriages and lives alone. That he wakes up every single night thinking about the bombing and the lies that were told and are still being told.

'Imagine you are me,' he says. 'My heart has been broken.'

Then I think maybe he's right, maybe the conspiracy is true — maybe everything I read in the Hilton bombing archive and beyond is fabricated, maybe every word I've written is not true. I mean it's possible. Maybe Terry Griffiths is right and I am absolutely wrong.

About an hour into the conversation we start to get on — and for a man with a lot to be bitter about, he's very charming. At one juncture I tell him that when I first started researching the bombing I used to remind myself that I could only be sure of one thing and that was that I didn't put the bomb in the bin. Terry laughs and tells me that he didn't do it either. We muse about the fact that we probably want the same thing — a transparent inquiry to lay some ghosts to rest. An inquiry I doubt will ever come.

In the end we say goodbye and arrange to continue talking and to maybe meet up some time.

'We can agree to disagree,' he says.

I agree. We can.

Note on sources

I have cross-checked the Hilton bombing material contained within New South Wales State Records against extensive archival material held in the New South Wales State Library, Trove, the National Library and the Australian Archives among others. This other material includes the transcripts and findings of the various court cases and inquiries over the years, newspaper reports extending over almost four decades and, most importantly, key documents that have been declassified by ASIO or the federal government years after the bombing and not contained in the New South Wales State Records Hilton archive. It is clear that the New South Wales State Records on the Hilton bombing are not infallible. They contain mistakes, inconsistencies and possibly omissions. The documents they contain are written by hundreds (possibly thousands) of different and diverse individuals representing a myriad of state, federal and international agencies — Interpol, ASIO, the New South Wales police, Special Branch, federal Cabinet and dozens of international police forces (New York, Washington, Hong Kong, Thailand, Manila, London and so on). If I have been unable to locate multiple (and transparently verifiable) archival sources for a discovery or development in the investigation I have been clear that there is ambiguity or conflicting versions surrounding that event. I do not, however, believe (as some indeed do) that the contents of the voluminous and chaotically compiled Hilton archive is fabricated. For that to be true all the other archival holdings not just across Australia, but also from numerous international sources would be similarly artfully deceptive. In my view this seems unlikely.

Beyond these primary sources there are a number of secondary sources — memoirs, documentaries, including accounts by those involved. But while I have read these accounts, I have tried to avoid using them as references as they are drenched in their own particular agendas. My purpose here has been not to evaluate the various conspiracy theories, but to sift the original primary documents in the various archives and to show how the investigations into the bombing unfolded.

Notes

The Hilton and me
1. Fletcher, William, Coroner's Report: 'Unknown Male believed to be William Flavell'. 13/2/78. Item no. 9/8112.1. Records relating to the Hilton bombing. Cabinet Office. New South Wales State Records.
2. Parliament of New South Wales, Legislative Assembly, 'Hilton Hotel Bombing', 9/12/1991, Hansard. *See also* Parliament of Australia, 'Hilton Hotel Bombing', 10/11/1992, Hansard. *See also* Parliament of New South Wales, Legislative Assembly, 'Hilton Hotel Bombing Inquiry Proposal', 21/9/1995, Hansard.

The story we tell
1. Statement, Norman Arthur Sheather, Detective Senior Inspector, 13 May 1982. Item no. 9/8113.1. Records relating to the Hilton bombing. Cabinet Office. New South Wales State Records.
2. '20 years jail for Hilton bomber', *Canberra Times*, 16 September 1989, p. 6.
3. Hunt, CJAT, CL Studderst and Simpson JJ. *R. v. Evan Dunstan Pederick* — BC 9701982. Supreme Court of New South Wales Court of Criminal Appeal. 60137 of 1996. 17 December 1996, 21 May 1997.

The bomb and the bin
1. 'Police launch a massive hunt for the Hilton bomber', *Sydney Morning Herald*, 14 February 1978, p. 2.
2. Note: one leader will arrive the next morning. Statement, Norman Arthur Sheather, Detective Senior Inspector, 13 May 1982, op. cit.
3. 'All Australians should mourn: Wran', *Sydney Morning Herald*, 14 February 1978, p. 2.

4   'Police launch a massive hunt for the Hilton bomber', op. cit., p. 2.
5   Bilton, Michael, *Wicked Beyond Belief: The Hunt for the Yorkshire Ripper*, HarperCollins, London, 2003.
6   Morris, P, Garbage collection schedules, 1978. 13/2/78. Scene Hilton bombing Statements. Item no. 9/8112.1. Records relating to the Hilton bombing. Cabinet Office. New South Wales State Records.
7   O'Conner, WJ, Emptied Bin 10/2/78 [i.e. his Friday night shift began on 10 February; the bin was emptied at 12:30 am on the 11th]. 13/2/78. Scene Hilton bombing Statements. Item no. 9/8112.1. Records relating to the Hilton bombing. Cabinet Office. New South Wales State Records.
8   'He was the last Council employee to empty this bin prior to the explosion.' Statement, Norman Arthur Sheather, Detective Senior Inspector, 13 May 1982, op. cit., p.7.
9   There is no better place to locate a précis of this long-held conspiracy than simply going straight to the Hilton Hotel Bombing Wikipedia page. It's all there.
10 Porter, NA, Garbage collection 11/2/78. Statement, New South Wales Police, Town Hall Kent Street, 14 February 1978. Scene Hilton bombing Statements. Item no. 9/8112.1. Records relating to the Hilton bombing. Cabinet Office. New South Wales State Records.
11 'Fraser plays host to the region', *Sydney Morning Herald*, 27 January 1978, p. 7. *See also* 'Security like Fort Knox', Sydney Morning Herald, 12 February 1978, p. 3.
12 'India's lead to the Australian summit', CHOGRM Notebook, *Sydney Morning Herald*, 11 February 1978, p. 10.
13 'Security like Fort Knox', op. cit.
14 Policing of Hilton Hotel, 5/2/78. Hilton bombing Part 1. 1965–1980 (Ministry for Police and Emergency Services). Item no. 9/8055.1. Records relating to the Hilton bombing. Cabinet Office. New South Wales State Records.
15 'Tight security for our biggest summit', *Sydney Morning Herald*, 12 February 1978, p. 38.
16 Morris, P, op. cit., p. 2.

Sunday 12 February 1978
1   Stevens, LJ, Street Sweeper. Condition of Bin. 12/2/78. Scene Hilton bombing Statements. New South Wales Police. Town Hall. Kent St. 14/2/78. Item no. 9/8112.1. Records relating to the Hilton bombing. Cabinet Office. New South Wales State Records.
2   Stoupel, J, Commissionaire at Hilton. Condition of Bin. 12/2/78. Scene Hilton bombing Statements. New South Wales Police. Town Hall. Kent St. 14/2/78. Item no. 9/8112.1. Records relating to the Hilton bombing. Cabinet Office. New South Wales State Records.
3   Airport Arrivals for CHOGRM. Policing of Hilton Hotel. 5.2.78.

Hilton bombing Part 1. 1965–1980 (Ministry for Police and Emergency Services), p. 11. Item no. 9/8055.1. Records relating to the Hilton bombing. Cabinet Office. New South Wales State Records.

4   Snashall, KR, Garbage Collection. Scene Hilton bombing Statements. New South Wales Police. Town Hall. Item no. 9/8112.1. Records relating to the Hilton bombing. Cabinet Office. New South Wales State Records.

5   'A District', Policing of Hilton Hotel. 5/2/78. Hilton bombing Part 1. 1965–1980. (Ministry for Police and Emergency Services). p. 9. Item no. 9/8055.1. Records relating to the Hilton bombing. Cabinet Office. New South Wales State Records.

6   ibid., p. 8.

7   Kevin O'Meara Gleeson witness statement, referenced in Statement, Norman Arthur Sheather, Detective Senior Inspector, 13 May 1982, op. cit., p. 7.

8   Witness statement, Edward John Patching, Public Servant. New South Wales Police. 1/10/82. Item no. 9/8112.1. Records relating to the Hilton bombing. Cabinet Office. New South Wales State Records.

9   Cuthbertson, AJ, Signwriter. Scene Hilton bombing Statements. New South Wales Police. 19/2/78. Item no. 9/8112.1. Records relating to the Hilton bombing. Cabinet Office. New South Wales State Records.

10 These photographs (particularly the question of why Abhiik Kumar's head is circled) will become the basis of contention in the 1982 inquest. Detective Senior Constable Henderson identifies photographs of Jason Holman Alexander as Abhiik. Item no. 9/8112.2. Records relating to the Hilton bombing. Cabinet Office. New South Wales State Records.

Monday 13 February 1978

1   Ebb, William John. Scene Hilton bombing Statements. New South Wales Police. 13/7/89. Item no. 9/8112.1. Records relating to the Hilton bombing. Cabinet Office. New South Wales State Records.

2   Timothy Charles Vaughan witness statement, referenced in Statement, Norman Arthur Sheather, Detective Senior Inspector, 13 May 1982, op. cit., p. 4.

3   Jones, Suzanne Jeanette. Scene Hilton bombing Statements. New South Wales Police. 29/9/89. Item no. 9/8112.1. Records relating to the Hilton bombing. Cabinet Office. New South Wales State Records. *See also* Statement, Norman Arthur Sheather, Detective Senior Inspector, 13 May 1982, p. 3.

4   'Position 9'. Policing of Hilton Hotel. 5/2/78. Hilton bombing Part 1. 1965–1980. (Ministry for Police and Emergency Services). p. 7. Item no. 9/8055.1. Records relating to the Hilton bombing. Cabinet Office. New South Wales State Records.

5   Cecil Streatfield witness statement, referenced in Statement, Norman Arthur Sheather, Detective Senior Inspector, 13 May 1982, op. cit., p. 3.

Notes to pages 33–41

6   *See also* references to the witnesses cab driver Carlo Maximo Quaglia and Hilton employee Kenneth Stuart Mackenzie. Statement, Norman Arthur Sheather, Detective Senior Inspector, 13 May 1982, op. cit.
7   Pedersen, Ernest Bramwell, Medical Practitioner. Examination of the scene. 2.45 am–4.15 am. 8/3/78. Item no. 9/8113.1. Records relating to the Hilton bombing. Cabinet Office. New South Wales State Records.
8   Gries, Manfred Von. Scene Hilton bombing statements. New South Wales Police. 13/2/78. Item no. 9/8113.1. Records relating to the Hilton bombing. Cabinet Office. New South Wales State Records.
9   'The Hilton Hotel bombing: how the crisis developed', *Sydney Morning Herald*, 14 February 1978, p. 1.
10 Statement, Norman Arthur Sheather, Detective Senior Inspector, 13 May 1982, op. cit., p. 3.
11 West, John Charles. Explosion at Sydney Hilton Hotel, George St, Sydney. Scientific Investigation section. Health Commission. 30/3/78. Item no. 9/8112.1. Records relating to the Hilton bombing. Cabinet Office. New South Wales State Records.
12 Millington, Det. Sgt RD. Explosion in George Street in Vicinity of Hilton Hotel, Sydney, 13/2/78, pp. 2–3. Running Sheets 1 – 50/12. Item no. 9/8116.1. Records relating to the Hilton bombing. Cabinet Office. New South Wales State Records.
13 Jones, Margaret, 'Bloody deaths at the Hilton', *Sydney Morning Herald*, 14 February 1978, pp. 7–8.
14 Sheather, Norman, Regarding a Fatal Bomb Explosion outside the Hilton Hotel. Item no. 9/8055.1. Records relating to the Hilton bombing. Cabinet Office. New South Wales State Records.
15 'Hilton blast: the police are still in the dark', *Sydney Morning Herald*, 14 February 1978, p. 2.

Tuesday 14 February 1978

1   Cunningham, J, 'Veil of secrecy surrounds the bomb-hunters', *Sydney Morning Herald*, 14 February 1978, p. 7.
2   'PMs fly as Army guards railway', *Sydney Morning Herald*, 15 February 1978, p. 1.
3   Holdich, R, Office of the Inspector-General of Intelligence and Security, *Complaint by Mr Richard John Seary against the Australian Security Intelligence Organisation: Final Report*, Australian Security Intelligence Organisation, Canberra, 1994.
4   Police Integrity Commission, *Report to Parliament regarding the former Special Branch of the New South Wales Police Service*, June 1998, p. 7
5   ibid.
6   ibid.
7   Holdich, R, Office of the Inspector-General of Intelligence and Security, *Complaint by Mr Richard John Seary against the Australian Security Intelligence Organisation: Final Report*, op. cit.

8   ASIO briefing of potential Hilton threats. Circa 6/2/1978. Running sheets extra. Item no. 9/8132. Records relating to the Hilton bombing. Cabinet Office. New South Wales State Records.

Wednesday 15 February 1978

1. Sutton, Michael. Statement. 13/2/78. Running sheets extra. Item no. 9/8132. Records relating to the Hilton bombing. Cabinet Office. New South Wales State Records.
2. Trotter, Robert Norman. 'Sees Anderson and passenger in taxi'. 15/2/78. Item no. 9/8112.1 Scene Hilton bombing — Statements. Records relating to the Hilton bombing. Cabinet Office. New South Wales State Records.
3. 'Ananda Marga sees a Russian presence', *Sydney Morning Herald*, 14 February 1978, p. 2.
4. 'No mercy for hotel bombers', *Sydney Morning Herald*, 16 February 1978, p. 2.
5. Musgrave, Robert Barry, Ballistics Unit, Detective Senior Constable of Police. Statement. 3/3/82. Running sheets extra. Item no. 9/8112.1 Records relating to the Hilton bombing. Cabinet Office. New South Wales State Records.
6. 'Framed, say Australians on explosives charge', *Sydney Morning Herald*, 17 February 1978, p. 1.
7. Child's name is also spelled 'Childs' in some archival sources.
8. Victim was Indian embassy (Personal?) Secretary and was stabbed in chest and neck. Also, names spelled 'Steven Michael Dwyer' and 'Victoria Sheppard' in original telex. But spelled Shepherd and Sherpherd by Manila police. Telex to Sheather from Philippines Interpol Manila 9/3/1978. Running sheets extra. Item no. 9/8132. Records relating to the Hilton bombing. Cabinet Office. New South Wales State Records.
9. Helson/Watson Special Branch. Conference with the vice-consul of India, Mr Alagh, and Detective Constable First Class Helson and Constable Watson concerning Indian terrorists and information that that country may hold regarding similar acts by Ananda Marga. 17/2/78. Item no. 9/8132. Records relating to the Hilton bombing. Cabinet Office. New South Wales State Records.
10. ibid.
11. There are a few variations on the date that Sarkar's appeal was denied. I have gone with 2 February as it appears in a number of primary sources in 1978. The 3 February date appears in Wood, J, *Report of the inquiry held under section 475 of the Crimes Act, 1900 into the convictions of Timothy Edward Anderson, Paul Shaun [i.e. Shawn] Alister and Ross Anthony Dunn at Central Criminal Court, Sydney, on 1st August, 1979*, 3 Vols. NSW Govt Printer, Sydney, 1985.

Enter the Ananda Marga
1   'A Note on Anand Marg [sic]', 11/5/76. Running sheets extra. Item no. 9/8132. Records relating to the Hilton bombing. Cabinet Office. New South Wales State Records.
2   Wood, J, *Report of the inquiry held under section 475 of the Crimes Act, 1900 into the convictions of Timothy Edward Anderson, Paul Shaun [i.e. Shawn] Alister and Ross Anthony Dunn at Central Criminal Court, Sydney, on 1st August, 1979*, 3 Vols. NSW Govt Printer, Sydney, 1985, Section B, p. 74.
3   ibid., pp. 74–83.
4   'A Note on Anand Marg [sic]', op. cit., p. 3.
5   ibid., p. 4.
6   ibid., p. 5.
7   Gupte, Pranay, *Mother India: A Political Biography of Indira Gandhi*, Penguin Books, 2012.
8   ibid.

An Australian campaign of terror
1   Toms, 'Precis of Incidents Which Have Occurred in New South Wales Involving Ananda Marga'. Running sheets extra. Item no. 9/8113.4. Records relating to the Hilton bombing. Cabinet Office. New South Wales State Records.
2   ibid.
3   Wood, J, op. cit., Appendix F 'Chronology — A background to the Inquiry', p. 3.
4   ibid., p. 3.
5   Duff will be convicted on a slightly lesser charge the following year. See Wood, J, op. cit.: 'Subsequently, John William Duff, a member of the Ananda Marga, was charged with offences arising out of this incident. He was convicted on counts under the *Crimes (International Protected Persons) Act 1976*, but acquitted of charges of attempted murder, kidnapping and breaking and entering and inflicting grievous bodily harm.' (*Duff v. R.* (1979) 28 A.L.R. 663.) Duff was found 'guilty of three offences which, according to the learned trial judge's ruling and direction to the jury, were alternative counts to the first three counts in the indictment. The appellant was convicted of the offences of attack on the person of Iqbal Singh (IS), of attack on the liberty of IS and of attack on the liberty of Darshan Kaur Singh, offences which were created by s. 8(2) of the *Crimes (Internationally Protected Persons) Act 1976*. The court (Connor J.) imposed a sentence for each offence of three years imprisonment with hard labour, the sentences to be cumulative.'
6   'Ananda Marga: a sect revered, yet dreaded in its homeland', *Sydney Morning Herald*, 19 September 1977, p. 6. *See also* 'Indian envoy's nephew tells of chase by three men', *Sydney Morning Herald*, 22 September 1977, p. 2.

7 'ASIO ran agents within the Ananda Marga', Holdich, R, Office of the Inspector-General of Intelligence and Security, *Complaint by Mr Richard John Seary against the Australian Security Intelligence Organisation: Final Report*, op. cit., p. 12.
8 Toms, 'Precis of Incidents Which Have Occurred in New South Wales Involving Ananda Marga', Hilton bombing records. Running sheets extra. Item no. 9/8113.4. Records relating to the Hilton bombing. Cabinet Office. New South Wales State Records. *See also* 'Ministerial Representations from the Consul General of India, Caltex House, 167–187 Kent Street, Sydney, to the New South Wales government, Premier's Department, concerning recent incidents and malicious damage occasioned to Indian government installations' Item no. 9/8113.4. Records relating to the Hilton bombing. Cabinet Office. New South Wales State Records.
9 Wood, J, op. cit., p. 4.
10 Toms, op. cit.
11 'Ananda Marga Inquiry — Letter Demanding Money Sent to [Redacted]', Report compiled by Krawczyk/Helson. Running sheets. Item no. 9/8113.4. Records relating to the Hilton bombing. Cabinet Office. New South Wales State Records.
12 Toms, op. cit.
13 ibid.
14 'Ananda Marga Inquiry — Threatening Letter Received By [Redacted] on 4 October 1977'. Running sheets extra. Item no. 9/8113.4. Records relating to the Hilton bombing. Cabinet Office. New South Wales State Records.
15 Letter from Prime Minister Malcolm Fraser to Premier Neville Wran. Running sheets. Item no. 9/8113.4. Records relating to the Hilton bombing. Cabinet Office. New South Wales State Records.
16 ibid.
17 ibid.
18 'Ministerial Representations from the Consul General of India, Caltex House, 167–187 Kent Street, Sydney, to the New South Wales Government, Premier's Department, concerning recent incidents and malicious damage occasioned to Indian Government installations', Hilton bombing records. Running sheets extra. Item no. 9/8113.4. Records relating to the Hilton bombing. Cabinet Office. New South Wales State Records.

Abhiik Kumar
1 National Foreign Assessment Center, Central Intelligence Agency, August 1978, International Terrorism in 1977: A Research Paper. Retrieved 11/2/16 from <www.foia.cia.gov/sites/default/files/document_conversions/89801/DOC_0000689061.pdf>
2 'Ananda Marga Inquiry — Interstate Report Submitted Concerning The Identity of Jon Hoffman Now Known As Jason Holman

Alexander Aust Leader of Ananda Marga', Hilton bombing records. Running sheets marked 1(a)1–1(b)45. Item no. 9/8113.4. Records relating to the Hilton bombing. Cabinet Office. New South Wales State Records.

3   'Activities of the Ananda Marga in New South Wales'. 21/9/77. Krawczyk/Watson. Item no. 9/8113.4. Records relating to the Hilton bombing. Cabinet Office. New South Wales State Records.

4   Confidential. P. 2. Running sheets marked 1(a)1–1(b)45. Item no. 9/8113. Records relating to the Hilton bombing. Cabinet Office. New South Wales State Records.

5   (Interview with former Ananda Marga member by ASIO?), Hilton bombing records. Running sheet 1(a)/18, 15.11.77, (interview conducted 24–27.10.77). Running sheets marked 1(a)1–1(b)45. Item no. 9/8113.4. Records relating to the Hilton bombing. Cabinet Office. New South Wales State Records.

6   ibid. The italics are mine.

7   (Untitled and Undated briefing from NYC Police Intelligence Unit), Hilton bombing records. Running sheets extra. Item no. 9/8132. Records relating to the Hilton bombing. Cabinet Office. New South Wales State Records.

8   'Ananda Marga Inquiry — Information Received from ASIO re. their interview with [redacted]', sheet 1(a)/19. Running sheets marked 1(a)1–1(b)45. Item no. 9/8113.4. Records relating to the Hilton bombing. Cabinet Office. New South Wales State Records.

9   'Report on Ananda Marga' p. 1 [A12909, 1848], Submission 1848, 1978 Cabinet Records — Selected Documents, 'Legal and security issues', p. 322, National Archives of Australia.

10   ibid., p. 324.
11   ibid.
12   ibid., p. 323.
13   ibid., p. 322.
14   ibid., pp. 324–325.
15   ibid.
16   ibid., p. 325.
17   ibid., p. 326.
18   ibid., p. 327.
19   ibid., p. 328.
20   ibid., p. 327.
21   *Sydney Morning Herald*, 14 January 1978, p. 6.

It all goes quiet

1   Last reported attack of 1977: 'An Indian Diplomat was stabbed and seriously wounded on Embassy Row here last night by an assailant wielding two knives in a bizarre attack that investigators believe may have political overtones.' *See* 'Attack on Indian Tied to Politics: Diplomat knifed on Embassy Row', *Washington Post*, 29 November 1977, p. 1.

2 Holdich, R, Office of the Inspector-General of Intelligence and Security, *Complaint by Mr Richard John Seary against the Australian Security Intelligence Organisation: Final Report*, op. cit., p. 12.
3 Special Branch Report 'Ananda Marga Inquiry — Information Received From A Reliable Source Concerning Paul Maurice O'Callaghan And An Unknown Female Attending A V.S.S. Training Camp at Anandapalli', 6/1/78. Running sheets marked 1(a)1–1(b)45. Item no. 9/8113.4. Records relating to the Hilton bombing. Cabinet Office. New South Wales State Records.
4 Special Branch Report 'Ananda Marga Inquiry — Documents Taken Possession Of On Sunday The 29th January, 1978. At Crosslands, U.K.K. Camp', 31/1/78, Sheet 1(a)40, Running sheets marked 1(a)1–1(b)45. Item no. 9/8113.4.Records relating to the Hilton bombing. Cabinet Office. New South Wales State Records.
5 Special Branch Report 'Ananda Marga Inquiry — Document Obtained From U.K.K. Camp At Crosslands On Sunday 29th January 1978', 31/1/78. Sheet 1(a)45, Running sheets marked 1(a)1 –1(b)45. Item no. 9/8113.4. Records relating to the Hilton bombing. Cabinet Office. New South Wales State Records.
6 Special Branch Report 'Ananda Marga Inquiry — Documents Taken Possession Of On Sunday The 29th January, 1978. At Crosslands, U.K.K. Camp', 31/1/78, Sheet 1(a)40, Running sheets marked 1(a)1–1(b)45. Item no. 9/8113.4. Records relating to the Hilton bombing. Cabinet Office. New South Wales State Records.
7 ibid.
8 ibid.
9 Holdich, R, Office of the Inspector-General of Intelligence and Security, *Complaint by Mr Richard John Seary against the Australian Security Intelligence Organisation: Final Report*, op. cit., p. 12.
10 ibid., p. 14.
11 Tedeschi, Mark, 1989, 'Summary of the Crown Case Against Timothy Edward Anderson', p. 16. Notes supplied to the author by Mark Tedeschi. See also Office of the Inspector-General of Intelligence and Security, *Complaint by Mr Richard John Seary against the Australian Security Intelligence Organisation: Final Report*, op. cit., p. 34.
12 'DET SEN CST HENDERSON — identifies photographs of Jason Holman Alexander as Abhiik', Hilton bombing records. Circumstantial Evidence re. Anderson. Item no. 9/8112.2. Records relating to the Hilton bombing. Cabinet Papers. New South Wales State Records.
13 'Notes of Conversation between Detective Sergeant Jackson and Timothy Anderson at the Central Police Station on 30th June 1978', Statements. Item no. 9/8113.1. Records relating to the Hilton bombing. Cabinet Papers. New South Wales State Records.

'The blast that shook Australia'
1. 'Terrorism', editorial, *Sydney Morning Herald*, 14 February 1978, p. 6.
2. 'Police Chief sacking — inquiry on', *Sydney Morning Herald*, 2 February 1978, p. 6.
3. Tom Molomby is particularly good at providing a thorough introduction to this kind of thinking. See Molomby, Tom, 'Background', *Spies, Bombs and the Path of Bliss*, Potoroo Press, Sydney, 1986, pp. 1–6. *See also* 'Wran drops inquiry on ASIO charges', *Sydney Morning Herald*, 15 February 1978. p. 1 and 'Wran backs down', editorial, *Sydney Morning Herald*, 15 February 1978, p. 6.
4. A fascinating overview of the newspaper's history can be found in Amos, Jessica, 'The *National Times*: bastard of a paper', University of Wollongong Thesis Collection, University of Wollongong, 2005.
5. Kelly, P, Leitch, D, Summers, A, Clark, A, Hickie, D and Whitton, E, 'The blast that shook Australia', *National Times*, 20–25 February 1978, p. 7.
6. ibid., p. 8.
7. ibid., p. 12.
8. 'Cowardly killer that knows no innocents: Australia in Bomb Club', *Sydney Morning Herald*, 19 February 1978, p. 102.
9. 'Aid for children of bomb victims', *Sydney Morning Herald*, 18 February 1978, p. 1.
10. '"Ring Us" plea to bomb warning man', *Sydney Morning Herald*, 16 February 1978, p. 1.
11. 'Police frustrated in bomb investigations', *Sydney Morning Herald*, 18 February 1978, p. 2.
12. Marks was contracted to act as a consultant. Mr Justice Hope conducted a review of all protective security. 'Security gets a shake-up to combat terrorism', *Sydney Morning Herald*, 24 February 1978, p. 1.

Thursday 16 February 1978
1. 'Cowardly killer that knows no innocents: Australia in Bomb Club', op. cit., pp. 55, 102.
2. 'Information Received From [Redacted] Possible Suspect Slavko Puskic — Re. Hilton Hotel', Hilton bombing records, Statements, 17/2/78. Item no. 9/8132. Records relating to the Hilton bombing. Cabinet Office. New South Wales State Records.
3. 'Telex Message no. 2130 Received From [Redacted]', Hilton bombing records, Statements, 17/2/78. Hilton bombing records, Running sheets extra. Item no. 9/8132. Records relating to the Hilton bombing. Cabinet Office. New South Wales State Records.
4. 'Record of Interview Between Detective Sergeant BJ Borthwick and [Redacted] Taken At The Criminal Investigation Branch, Sydney, on the 21st February, 1978', Hilton bombing records, Statements, 21/2/78. Item no. 9/8113.1. Records relating to the Hilton bombing. Cabinet Office. New South Wales State Records.

5   'Information Received From Senior Constable Johnson Of Criminal Records Office', Hilton bombing records. Running sheets extra. Item no. 9/8132. Records relating to the Hilton bombing. Cabinet Office. New South Wales State Records.
6   'Cowardly killer that knows no innocents: Australia in Bomb Club', op. cit., p. 102.
7   'Suspicious behaviour of a male person at AAEC on 13/2/78'. CIB. 17/2/78. Hilton bombing records. Running sheets extra. Item no. 9/8132. Records relating to the Hilton bombing. Cabinet Office. New South Wales State Records.
8   Rylance, BM, 'Letter to Officer In Charge', Hilton bombing records, Statements, 21/2/78. Hilton bombing records. Running sheets extra. Item no. 9/8132. Records relating to the Hilton bombing. Cabinet Office. New South Wales State Records.

Did the Hare Krishnas do it?

1   'Statement by SEARY, Richard John', 22/2/78, Item no. 9/8113.1. Records relating to the Hilton bombing. Cabinet Office. New South Wales State Records.
2   ibid.
3   Wood, J, op. cit., Section 9, pp. 149–150.
4   'Letter to the Officer in Charge. Subject; Matter Reference. The Hilton bombing'. Received 23 May 1978. Hilton bombing records. Running sheets extra. Item no. 9/8132. Records relating to the Hilton bombing. Cabinet Papers. New South Wales State Records.
5   Wood, J, op.cit., Section 9, p. 150.
6   ibid.

The Bangkok Three

1   'Letter sent by AB', Hilton bombing records. Running sheets extra. 16/2/78. Item no. 9/8132. Records relating to the Hilton bombing. Cabinet Office. New South Wales State Records.
2   Beere Inquiry. 22/2/78. Nemesis. 'For Information of Detective Inspector Sheather.' Item no. 9/8132. Records relating to the Hilton bombing. Cabinet Office. New South Wales State Records.
3   'Framed, say Australians on explosives charge', *Sydney Morning Herald*, 17 February 1978, p. 1.
4   Helson/Watson Special Branch. Conference with the Vice Consul of India Mr Alagh and Detective Constable First Class Helson and PC Constable Watson concerning Indian terrorists and information that that country may hold regarding similar acts by Ananda Marga.17/2/78. Item no. 9/8132. Records relating to the Hilton bombing. Cabinet Office. New South Wales State Records.
5   'Summary of photocopies of passport of Jason Holman Alexander', Running Sheet 199/2–4. 16/2/79 2000 Hrs and 17/2/78 0830 Hrs. Hilton bombing records. Running sheets extra. Item no. 9/8132.

	Records relating to the Hilton bombing. Cabinet Office. New South Wales State Records.
6	Helson/Watson Special Branch, op. cit.
7	What Norm is able to discover is that at some time in the past they were travelling with long-term Australian Margii members. Caroline Lee Spark left Australia on 11 March 1974 in company of Julie Pamela Brown aka 'Kirana' and Paul Maurice O'Callaghan aka 'Narada Muni' also known as Paul Alister (arrested for the pig's head in 1977). Timothy Thomas Hilton Jones departed Australia on 29 January 1975 in the company of Constantin Pakioufakis and Beth Rosenberg aka 'Shanti'.
8	'Secret. For Cabinet. Report on the Ananda Marga.' FM Chaney, Minister for Administrative Services. 16/11/78. Cabinet Records — Selected Documents. Released 1.1.2009 NLA. Point 6.
9	Fax from CIB 'RE: YOUR NR 472/2 Dated 16/2/78', summary of interview with Mr and Mrs T Jones. Hilton bombing records. Running sheets extra. Item no. 9/8132. Records relating to the Hilton bombing. Cabinet Office. New South Wales State Records.
10	ibid.
11	Fax 'Re. your tx 161/2 this date', Hilton bombing records. Running sheets extra. Item no. 9/8132. Records relating to the Hilton bombing. Cabinet Office. New South Wales State Records.
12	'Framed, say Australians on explosives charge', op. cit., p. 1.

From Scotland Yard to Newtown

1. Telex, 'To Scotland Yard, United Kingdom' by N. Sheather, Detective Inspector Third Class, Hilton bombing records. Running sheets extra. Item no. 9/8132. Records relating to the Hilton bombing. Cabinet Office. New South Wales State Records.
2. ibid.
3. 'Inquiries carried out through the [Redacted] concerning a list of 75 names connected with the Ananda Marga sect with the view of ascertaining any [Redacted]'. 23/2/1978, Helson, Special Branch. Hilton bombing records. Running sheets extra. Item no. 9/8132. Records relating to the Hilton bombing. Cabinet Office. New South Wales State Records.

February to March 1978

1. 'Photostat information — Possible Actions, re Gaoling of Trade Unionist in Fiji, Against Fijian Prime Minister Attending CHOGRM', 21/2/78, Hilton bombing records. Running sheets extra. Item no. 9/8132. Records relating to the Hilton bombing. Cabinet Office. New South Wales State Records.
2. 'Information Relative to Malaysian and Singaporean Groups in Australia With Terrorist Potential', Hilton bombing records. Running sheets extra. Item no. 9/8132. Records relating to the Hilton bombing.

3   Cabinet Office. New South Wales State Records.
     Fax '59: Nemesis' to Detective Inspector Sheather — CIB, sheet no.
     1056, 23/2/78, Hilton bombing records. Running sheets extra. Item
     no. 9/8132. Records relating to the Hilton bombing. Cabinet Office.
     New South Wales State Records.
4   'Record of interview between [Redacted] and Nikolai Tordanov
     Daskalov at Russell Street CIB on 23/2/78 at 7.30 pm', Hilton
     bombing records. Running sheets extra. Item no. 9/8132. Records
     relating to the Hilton bombing. Cabinet Office. New South Wales
     State Records.
5   'Man unable to aid bomb inquiry', *Sydney Morning Herald*,
     10 March 1978, p. 5.
6   'Information supplied concerning Victor Sedlacek — Hilton Enquiry',
     25/2/79, Hilton bombing records. Running sheets extra. Item no.
     9/8132. Records relating to the Hilton bombing. Cabinet Office. New
     South Wales State Records.
7   Letter to 'The Officer-in-Charge, Subject: Matter Reference: The
     Hilton bombing', Hilton bombing records. Running sheets extra. Item
     no. 9/8132. Records relating to the Hilton bombing. Cabinet Office.
     New South Wales State Records.
8   Confidential telex sent to [Redacted], 1/3/78, Hilton bombing
     records. Running sheets extra. Item no. 9/8132. Records relating to
     the Hilton bombing. Cabinet Office. New South Wales State Records.
9   Text of letter to Inspector N Sheather, regarding Hilton Bombing,
     from Roma Nabaran, posted 18/2/78 and recorded 28/2/78, Hilton
     bombing records. Running sheets extra. Item no. 9/8132. Records
     relating to the Hilton bombing. Cabinet Office. New South Wales
     State Records.
10   'Record of interview between Detective Senior Constable MD Maher
     and [Redacted] at the Criminal Investigation Branch, Sydney on the
     24th February 1978', Statements. Item no. 9/8113.1. Records relating
     to the Hilton bombing. Cabinet Office. New South Wales State
     Records.
11   Statement by Fausto Parente to Leichhardt Police, 8/3/78. Statements.
     Item no. 9/8113.1. Records relating to the Hilton bombing. Cabinet
     Office. New South Wales State Records.
12   'Police seek woman over Hilton bomb', *Sydney Morning Herald*,
     4 March 1978, p. 5.
13   Brown, M, 'Hilton bomb, NZ woman's help sought', *Sydney Morning
     Herald*, 6 March 1978, p. 1.
14   'Woman cleared in Hilton bombing', *Sydney Morning Herald*,
     7 March 1978, p. 3.
15   Running sheet 1125/1, '[Redacted] Information', 14/3/78 at
     2.30 pm, Hilton bombing records. Running sheets extra. Item
     no. 9/8132. Records relating to the Hilton bombing. Cabinet Office.
     New South Wales State Records.

Notes to pages 152–157

16 'Information received from [Redacted] compiled by the general secretariat Paris — France re. terrorist', Special Branch running sheets, 23/2/1978, Hilton bombing records. Running sheets extra. Item no. 9/8132. Records relating to the Hilton bombing. Cabinet Office. New South Wales State Records.
17 Passport and passport application documents, Hilton bombing records. Running sheets extra. Item no. 9/8132. Records relating to the Hilton bombing. Cabinet Office. New South Wales State Records.
18 Letter sent to His Excellency the Ambassador of India, Hilton bombing records. Running sheets extra. Item no. 9/8132. Records relating to the Hilton bombing. Cabinet Office. New South Wales State Records.
19 'Telex received from [Redacted] Sweden, re. Ananda Marga', Special Branch running sheet 15/3/78, Hilton bombing records. Running sheets extra. Item no. 9/8132. Records relating to the Hilton bombing. Cabinet Office. New South Wales State Records.
20 Telegram, 'Tldx Los Angeles CA' to 'Police CIB, Sydney/New South Wales Police Department', received 12/3/78, Hilton bombing records. Running sheets extra. Item no. 9/8132. Records relating to the Hilton bombing. Cabinet Office. New South Wales State Records.
21 ibid.
22 Telegram 'To Nemesis' from Philippines Interpol P 3383/78, 9/3/78. Hilton bombing records. Running sheets extra. Item no. 9/8132. Records relating to the Hilton bombing. Cabinet Office. New South Wales State Records.
23 'Information relative to the Ananda Marga Inquiry', Special Branch running sheet no. 8/5/177, received 9/3/78 3.30 pm. Hilton bombing records. Running sheets extra. Item no. 9/8132. Records relating to the Hilton bombing. Cabinet Office. New South Wales State Records.
24 ibid.
25 ibid.
26 As noted earlier, there are a few variations on the date that Sarkar's appeal was denied. I have gone with 2 February as it appears in a number of primary sources in 1978. The 3 February date appears in Wood, J, op. cit.
27 'Information relative to the Ananda Marga Inquiry', op. cit.
28 ibid., p. 109.
29 Special Branch Running Sheet 1139 from Helson, 'Telex received from [redacted] regarding a plan by Ananda Marga to sabotage Indian and Republic of Korea embassies in Bangkok, Thai government premises or hijack Thai aircraft', Hilton bombing records. Running sheets extra. Item no. 9/8132. Records relating to the Hilton bombing. Cabinet Office. New South Wales State Records.

Another bomb
1. Fax/teledex sent 'To Scorpion Melbourne, Nemesis' NR714/3, 25/3/78. Could be COMPOL? Hilton bombing records. Running sheets extra. Item no. 9/8132. Records relating to the Hilton bombing. Cabinet Office. New South Wales State Records.
2. ibid.
3. ibid.
4. ibid.
5. O'Reilly, N, 'Gelignite bomb in envoy's garden', *Sydney Morning Herald*, 26 March 1978, p. 1.
6. ibid., p. 27.
7. ibid.
8. 'Ananda Marga responsible for bomb, says diplomat', *Sydney Morning Herald*, 27 March 1978, p. 2.
9. Report by Detective Sergeant Third Class MR Blaylock, 'Explosive Device Examined at Commonwealth Police Headquarters, 25/3/78', Hilton bombing records. Running sheets extra. Item no. 9/8132. Records relating to the Hilton bombing. Cabinet Office. New South Wales State Records.
10. ibid.
11. 'Bomb Incident at Indian High Commission' report, Hilton bombing records. Running sheets extra. Item no. 9/8132. Records relating to the Hilton bombing. Cabinet Office. New South Wales State Records.
12. 'Diplomat suspect in bomb scare', *The Australian*, 28 March 1978, p. 1.
13. ibid.
14. 28 March 1978, 'An employee of the Indian High Commission in Canberra, Suresh Kumar, was found hanged', Appendix F 'Chronology — A Background to the Inquiry', Wood. J, op. cit., p. 1.

Shadowlands
1. Wood, J, op. cit., Section B, p. 159.
2. ibid., p. 160.
3. ibid., p. 159.
4. ibid., p. 160.
5. ibid., p. 160.
6. ibid., pp. 155, 157, 161–162.

28 March 1978
1. Special Branch running sheet no. 1147/5, 'Photo-fit picture of possible suspect concerning bomb incident at Indian High Commission's residence, 34 Mugga Way, Canberra, on 25th March 1978', 29/3/78, Hilton bombing records. Running sheets extra. Item no. 9/8132. Records relating to the Hilton bombing. Cabinet Office. New South Wales State Records.
2. Holdich, R, Office of the Inspector-General of Intelligence and Security, *Complaint by Mr Richard John Seary against the Australian*

       Security Intelligence Organisation: Final Report, op. cit., p. 12.
3   Wood, J, op. cit., Section 9, p. 160.
4   ibid., p. 160.
5   ibid., p. 159.
6   ibid., p. 170.
7   ibid.
8   ibid.
9   ibid., p. 304.

A new wave of terror

1   Special Branch running sheet 651/6 by Helson, 'Information received from a confidential source concerning the sect Ananda Marga and the movements of Mathew Donald Meighan', Hilton bombing records. Running sheets extra. Item no. 9/8132. Records relating to the Hilton bombing. Cabinet Office. New South Wales State Records.
2   ibid.
3   Wood, J, op. cit., pp. 37 and 164.
4   ibid., Appendix F, p. 8.
5   ibid., Appendix F, p. 9.
6   Letter to N Sheather re. 'Hilton bombing — Information', 26/4/78, Hilton bombing records. Running sheets extra. Item no. 9/8132. Records relating to the Hilton bombing. Cabinet Office. New South Wales State Records.
7   ibid.
8   Special Branch running sheet 'Information Received from [Redacted] re. possible suspect for bombing', 3/4/78, 11.00 am, Hilton bombing records. Running sheets extra. Item no. 9/8132. Records relating to the Hilton bombing. Cabinet Office. New South Wales State Records.
9   Tape 4, '27.5.78', tape transcripts, interview between Richard Seary and 'J', and 'G', Tim Anderson — Papers, 1976–1992, ML MSS 6143/ Box 11, New South Wales State Library, Mitchell Library. Note: the recording was made on 27/4/78, '27.5.78' is presumably a typo.
10   ibid.
11   ibid.
12   Molomby, T, *Spies, Bombs and the Path of Bliss*, Potoroo Press, Sydney, 1986, p. 294.
13   Seary's stints in jail are detailed in Wood, J, op. cit., Section 9, pp. 105–108.
14   Tape 4, '27.5.78', tape transcripts, interview between Richard Seary and 'J', and 'G', op. cit.
15   Wood, J, op. cit., p. 294.
16   ibid., Appendix F, p. 9.
17   ibid., p. 10.
18   Tape 1, '7.5.78', Tape Transcripts, interview between Richard Seary and 'J', and 'C', Tim Anderson — Papers, 1976–1992, ML MSS 6143/ Box 11, New South Wales State Library, Mitchell Library.

19 AM newsletter, published by the public relations department of Ananda Marga Pracaraka Samgha Australasia, May 1978, Running sheets marked 1(a)1–1(b)45. Item no. 9/8113.4. Records relating to the Hilton bombing. Cabinet Office. New South Wales State Records.
20 ibid.
21 ibid.
22 ibid.
23 Kuala Lumpur, Running sheet 'Information received from [redacted] concerning an improvised explosive device placed in the tea room of Air India, Kuala Lumpur', 12.5.78, details an IED placed in the tea room on the 14th floor of the Angkasa Raya Building, Kuala Lumpur, on 15 November 1977. It was found by an office cleaner who called police and left. The bomb exploded before the bomb squad arrived, and there were no casualties. Item no. 9/8132. Records relating to the Hilton bombing. Cabinet Office. New South Wales State Records.
24 'Copies of diagram for the manufacture of an explosive device …' 10/5/78. Hilton bombing records. Running sheets extra. Item no. 9/8132. Records relating to the Hilton bombing. Cabinet Office. New South Wales State Records.
25 Tape 3, '15.5.78', Tape Transcripts, interview between Richard Seary and 'J', and 'C', Tim Anderson — Papers, 1976–1992, ML MSS 6143/ Box 11, New South Wales State Library, Mitchell Library.
26 ibid.
27 Special Branch running sheet 'Information received from [Redacted] re. Brandon alias Hoffman alias Alexander', 15/5/78, Hilton bombing records. Running sheets extra. Item no. 9/8132. Records relating to the Hilton bombing. Cabinet Office. New South Wales State Records.
28 ibid.
29 Wood, J, op. cit., Appendix F, p. 10.
30 Brown, M, 'Bomb blast rocks police HQ', *Sydney Morning Herald*, 19 May 1978, p. 1.
31 Franklin, R, 'Three months later, the Hilton inquiry looks like being a sad, lost cause', *Sydney Morning Herald*, 21 May 1978, p. 9.

'A full-scale terrorist war'
1 Record of interview, Statements. Item no. 9/8113.1. Records relating to the Hilton bombing. Cabinet Office. New South Wales State Records.
2 Wood, J, op. cit., p. 169.
3 Information concerning Ananda Marga member sect name 'Japananda', fax received 14.6.78, Hilton bombing records. Running sheets extra. Item no. 9/8132. Records relating to the Hilton bombing. Cabinet Office. New South Wales State Records.
4 Wood, J, op. cit., p. 169.
5 Transcript of interview between Seary and Krawczyk, 24/5/78,

	Statements. Item no. 9/8113.1. Records relating to the Hilton bombing. Cabinet Office. New South Wales State Records.
6	ibid.
7	ibid.
8	The archive transcript switches from C to J — it is probable that this is a reference to Krawczyk's first name, Jan.
9	Transcript of interview between Seary and Krawczyk, 24/5/78, op. cit.
10	ibid.
11	Wood, op. cit., p. 169.
12	ibid.
13	Transcript of interview between Seary and Krawczyk, 24/5/78, op. cit.
14	ibid.
15	Tape 5, '29.5.78', Tape Transcripts, Interview between Richard Seary and 'J', Tim Anderson — Papers, 1976–1992, ML MSS 6143/ Box 11, New South Wales State Library, Mitchell Library.
16	ibid.
17	ibid.
18	ibid.
19	ibid.
20	'Swiss Hindu in Manila sets fire to herself', *The Times*, 15 June 1978, p. 8.

June 1978

1	Molomby, T, op. cit, p. 310.
2	Tape 6, '10.6.78', Tape Transcripts, Interview between Richard Seary and 'J', Tim Anderson — Papers, 1976–1992, ML MSS 6143/ Box 11, New South Wales State Library, Mitchell Library.
3	ibid.
4	Wood, J, op. cit., p. 111.
5	ibid., Section 9, p. 285.
6	ibid., Appendix K, Seary Tapes, Tape 6A 10/6/78, 'Page 1/2'.
7	ibid.
8	Mellor, B, 'Security men sure they know Hilton Hotel bombers', *Sydney Morning Herald*, 11 June 1978, p. 9.
9	'Swiss Hindu in Manila sets fire to herself', op. cit.

The madness of the day

1	Tape 8, '15.6.78', Tape Transcripts, interview between Richard Seary and 'J', Tim Anderson — Papers, 1976–1992, ML MSS 6143/ Box 11, New South Wales State Library, Mitchell Library.
2	Wood, J, op. cit., Section 9, p. 171.
3	Transcript of 'Conversation between Inspector Perrin and Richard John Seary at Police Headquarters on the 15.6.78'. Hilton bombing Inquest — Police Brief, Misc correspondence. Item no. 8052.1.

      Records relating to the Hilton bombing. Cabinet Office. New South Wales State Records.
4   ibid.
5   Wood, J, op. cit., Appendix F, Chronology, p. 12. The name the One World Revolutionary Army first appears in a letter sent to *The Australian* on 7 June 1978. The letter is a reaction to a number of media appearances by Robert Cameron on 6 June, including the Channel 9 Mike Willesee current affairs program. The letter criticises the upsurge of racist forces in the country and the formation of the Australian National Alliance and the Australian National Front. The letter continued that the Australian command of the Army would like it known that 'if the laws of the land prove too weak to restrain these anti-social racist forces … the One World Revolutionary Army will act to physically suppress the racists'.
6   Transcript of 'Conversation between Inspector Perrin and Richard John Seary', op. cit.
7   ibid., p. 5.
8   ibid., p. 6.
9   *Sydney Morning Herald*, 14 February 1978.
10   Wood, J, op. cit., Appendix A, '2. Briefing Notes (a) Document One'.
11   ibid., Section 2, The Crown Case, p. 14.
12   ibid., Appendix A, '2. Briefing Notes (a) Document One'.
13   ibid.
14   ibid., Section 2, The Crown Case, p. 14.

Yagoona

1   ibid., p. 16.
2   ibid., p. 17.
3   Molomby, T, op. cit., pp. 83–86.
4   Wood, J, op. cit., Section 2, The Crown Case, p. 26.
5   ibid., p. 22.
6   ibid., Appendix A, Section 5: Petitioner's Admissions to Police, 'Anderson — Verbal Admissions', p. 3.
7   ibid., Overall Conclusion, p. 452.
8   Holdich, R, Office of the Inspector-General of Intelligence and Security, *Complaint by Mr Richard John Seary against the Australian Security Intelligence Organisation: Final Report*, op. cit.
9   *Seary v Molomby*, 1999 New South Wales SC 981. 1999 Aust. Torts Reports 81-536. New South Wales Supreme Court.
10   Molomby, T, op. cit.
11   Transcript of 'Fight Against the Demon — Narrated by Abhiik Kumara. Obtained on Friday, 16 June 1978, from VSS Headquarters, 8 Brooklyn Street, Burwood.' Item no. 9/8052.1. Records relating to the Hilton bombing. Cabinet Office. New South Wales State Records.
12   ibid.
13   Wood, J, op. cit., p. 369.

'Have you ever seen what this stuff can do?'
1 ibid. p. 370.
2 ibid.
3 ibid., extract from Seary's journal, p. 378.
4 ibid., p. 371.
5 ibid., p. 372.
6 'Record of interview conducted between Inspector Sheather and [Redacted] at Police Headquarters on the 17th July, 1978', Statements. Item no. 9/8113.1. Records relating to the Hilton bombing. Cabinet Office. New South Wales State Records.
7 ibid.
8 ibid.
9 All reasons summarised in Wood, J, op. cit., pp. 379–385.
10 ibid., p. 393.
11 ibid.
12 ibid., p. 384.
13 ibid., p. 394.
14 ibid.

July 1978
1 'Ananda Marga convictions overruled', *Sydney Morning Herald*, 5 July 1978, p. 5.
2 ibid.
3 'Application to have [bomb making components] examined by Dr Malcolm Hall … and Dr Hilton J Kobus', New South Wales Police document, 18/7/1983, p. 3. Item no. 9/8112.2. Records relating to the Hilton bombing. Cabinet Papers. New South Wales State Records.
4 Statement to New South Wales Police by Harry Harvy Lees, 30/4/1981. Item no. 9/8112.1. Records relating to the Hilton bombing. Cabinet Papers. New South Wales State Records.
5 'Resume of the Hilton bombing', 24/10/79, pp. 7–9. Item no. 9/8112.3. Records relating to the Hilton bombing. Cabinet Papers. New South Wales State Records.
6 ibid.
7 'The Federal government cancelled Mr Brandon's passport on June 13th and confiscated it when he returned to Australia on August 9' quoted from 'Sect leader granted restricted passport', *Sydney Morning Herald*, 7 December 1978, p. 11.
8 'Ananda Marga man detained', *Sydney Morning Herald*, 10 August 1978, p. 1.
9 'Secret. For Cabinet. Report on the Ananda Marga.' FM Chaney, Minister for Administrative Services, op. cit.
10 ibid., point 6.
11 Kelly, N, 'Thailand to free Ananda Marga trio — no passport for sect leader', *Sydney Morning Herald*, 11 August 1978, p. 2.
12 ibid.

13 ibid.
14 ibid.
15 ibid.
16 ibid.
17 ibid.
18 Head, M, 'Thirty years since Sydney's Hilton bombing: Unanswered Questions', *Legal History*, 2008, Vol. 12. pp 242–243.

A hardline policy
1 'Loose safety check for law makers', *Sun-Herald*, 20 August 1978, p. 6.
2 ibid.
3 ibid.
4 'Woman showers MPs with sect's leaflets', *Sydney Morning Herald*, 21 September 1978, p. 11.
5 'Secret — Cabinet Minute. Submission no. 2520 — Policy and Organisation in Relation to Counter Terrorism', 21/9/1978. Cabinet Records — Selected Documents. Released 1.1.2009 NLA. pp. 2–3.
6 ibid., p. 3.

The immolation of Lynette Phillips
1 Williams, G, 'The tragedy of Lynette Phillips', *Sydney Morning Herald*, 14 December 1978, p. 7.
2 Frykberg, I, 'Queries over Proutist girl's death', *Sydney Morning Herald*, 13 October 1978, pp. 7, 11.
3 ibid., p. 7.
4 ibid.
5 McGregor, A, 'Fire death woman was deported from Britain,' *The Times*, 3 October 1978.
6 Williams, G, 'The tragedy of Lynette Phillips', op. cit.
7 McGregor, A, 'Fire death woman was deported from Britain,' op. cit.
8 ibid.
9 ibid.
10 Balderstone, S, 'An Heiress Dies', *The Age*, 4 October 1978, p. 1.
11 Williams, G, 'The tragedy of Lynette Phillips', op. cit.
12 ibid.
13 ibid.
14 ibid.
15 ibid.
16 ibid.
17 ibid.
18 ibid.
19 ibid.
20 ibid.
21 ibid.
22 ibid.

'Campaigns of violence and intimidation'
1   'Sinclair meets sect members on death threat', *Sydney Morning Herald*, 13 October 1978, p. 2.
2   Frykberg, I, 'Peacock faces UK controversy over Aust Proutist girl', *Sydney Morning Herald*, 12 October 1978, p. 1.
3   Williams, G, 'The tragedy of Lynette Phillips', op. cit., p. 7.
4   Frykberg, I, 'Inside the Proutist HQ', *Sydney Morning Herald*, 13 October 1978, p. 7.
5   Williams, G, 'The tragedy of Lynette Phillips', op. cit.
6   ibid.
7   ibid. p. 8.
8   ibid.
9   Frykberg, I, 'Peacock faces UK controversy over Aust Proutist girl', op. cit.
10 ibid.
11 'Sinclair meets sect members on death threat', op. cit.
12 ibid.
13 ibid.
14 Frykberg, I, 'Sect's house of tranquillity', *Sydney Morning Herald*, 13 October 1978, p. 11.
15 'Confidential — for Cabinet. Submission no. 2641 — Security and Offences in Parliament House', 5/10/1978. Cabinet Records — Selected Documents. Released 1/1/2009, NLA, p. 142.
16 ibid.
17 'Burning suicide threat dropped', *Sydney Morning Herald*, 17 October 1978, p. 1.

A new phenomenon
1   'Secret — for Cabinet. Submission no. 2742 — Report on Ananda Marga', 16/10/1978. Cabinet Records — Selected Documents. Released 1.1.2009 NLA. p. 153.
2   ibid., p. 154.
3   ibid.
4   ibid., pp. 154–155.
5   ibid., p. 157.
6   ibid.
7   ibid.
8   ibid., pp. 157–158.
9   ibid., p. 158.
10 ibid.
11 ibid., p. 159.
12 ibid.
13 ibid., p. 160.
14 ibid., pp. 160–161.
15 'Sect leader granted restricted passport', *Sydney Morning Herald*, 7 December 1978, p. 11.

1979

1. 'Statement by District Detective Sergeant Bruce Donald Jackson', 12/10/84, Goulburn Police Station. Hilton bombing records. Running sheets extra. Item no. 9/8112.1. Records relating to the Hilton bombing. Cabinet Office. New South Wales State Records.
2. Fife-Yeomans, J and O'Brien, N, 'Is this man the Hilton bomber?', *Weekend Australian*, 8 February 2003, p. 21.
3. ibid.
4. 'Judge suggests jail visit by sect minister', *Sydney Morning Herald*, 13 January 1979, p. 2.
5. 'Worried warders' editorial, *Sydney Morning Herald*, 18 January 1979, p. 6.
6. ibid.
7. ibid.
8. Fife-Yeomans, J and O'Brien, N, op. cit.
9. Testimony of Allan David Henderson, Coronial Inquest Transcript 134/1/9mc 5 October 1982. AD Henderson/Mr Court. Item no. 9/8057.19, p. 321. Records relating to the Hilton bombing. Cabinet Office. New South Wales State Records.
10. 'Police know the Hilton bombers — detective', *Sydney Morning Herald*, 2 February 1979, p. 1.
11. Fife-Yeomans, J and O'Brien, N, op. cit.
12. *Notes and Criminal History of Ananda Marga*. Item no. 9/8113.4. Records relating to the Hilton bombing. Cabinet Office. New South Wales State Records.
13. ibid., p. 3.
14. ibid., p. 6.
15. *Resume of the Hilton Hotel Bombing*, Item no. 9/8112.3, Records relating to the Hilton bombing. Cabinet Office. New South Wales State Records. NB while 24/10/79 is the date at the top it is clear that this résumé was added to for at least the next two to three years.
16. ibid., p. 7.

The locker and the gelignite

1. 'Statement in the matter of: Property located at University of New South Wales on 28 April 1981. Mrs Patricia Elson. Services Clerk.' Item no. 9/8112.2. Records relating to the Hilton bombing. Cabinet Office. New South Wales State Records.
2. Holdich, R, Office of the Inspector-General of Intelligence and Security. *Complaint by Mr Richard John Seary against the Australian Security Intelligence Organisation: Final Report*, op. cit., p. 28.
3. ibid.
4. 'Statement in the matter of: Property located at University of New South Wales on 28 April 1981. Mrs Patricia Elson. Services Clerk.' Item no. 9/8112.2. Records relating to the Hilton bombing. Cabinet Office. New South Wales State Records.

5   'Statement by Detective Senior Sergeant Geoffrey Herbert Wegg', 31 July 1989. Item no. 9/8112.2. Records relating to the Hilton bombing. Cabinet Office. New South Wales State Records.
6   ibid.
7   'Resume of the Hilton Hotel Bombing', op. cit., p. 10.
8   ibid., p. 9.
9   Holdich, R, Office of the Inspector-General of Intelligence and Security. *Complaint by Mr Richard John Seary against the Australian Security Intelligence Organisation: Final Report*, op. cit., p. 29.

The inquest, 1982
1   Statement, Norman Arthur Sheather, Detective Senior Inspector, 13 May 1982, op. cit., p. 2.
2   ibid., p. 2.
3   ibid., p. 2.
4   ibid., pp. 4–6.
5   Cook, J, 'Witness tells of threat to kidnap his son', *Sydney Morning Herald*, 30 September 1982, p. 3.
6   Transcription of 1982 Inquest into the Hilton bombing, testimony by Von Gries, M., Mr Court, Mr Robinson, 132/1/4/mc 29 September 1982. Submission covering 4 topics in relation to the New South Wales Police Service and the Hilton bombing. Item no. 9/8057.19. Records relating to the Hilton bombing. Cabinet Office. New South Wales State Records.
7   Molomby, T, op. cit., p. 257.
8   Cook, J, 'Witness tells of threat to kidnap his son', op. cit.
9   'Caller said ASIO linked to bombing', *Sydney Morning Herald*, 1 October 1982, p. 12.
10 'Seary denies colouring his story for effect', *Sydney Morning Herald*, 13 October 1982, p. 2.
11 Statement by Manfred Von Gries 13/2/78. Item no. 9/8112.2. Records relating to the Hilton bombing. Cabinet Office. New South Wales State Records.
12 ibid., p. 3.
13 ibid., p. 125. *See also* Henderson Transcription of 1982 Inquest into the Hilton bombing, testimony by A. D Henderson/ Mr Adams, 134/1/9/mc 5 October 1982. Submission covering 4 topics in relation to the New South Wales Police Service and the Hilton bombing. Item no. 9/8057.19, pp. 321–329. Records relating to the Hilton bombing. Cabinet Office. New South Wales State Records.
14 'Caller said ASIO linked to bombing', *Sydney Morning Herald*, 1 October 1982, p. 12.
15 Holdich, R, op. cit., p. 30.
16 Cook, J, 'Witness tells of threat to kidnap his son', op. cit.
17 Holdich, R, op. cit.
18 ibid., pp. 29–30.

May 1983

1. Holdich, R, Office of the Inspector-General of Intelligence and Security, *Complaint by Mr Richard John Seary against the Australian Security Intelligence Organisation: Final Report*, op. cit., p. 30.
2. ibid.
3. ibid., pp. 30–31.
4. ibid., p. 31.
5. 'Application to have exhibits and other bomb making components on hand ...', CL Helson, Detective Senior Constable, Special Branch. AD Henderson, Detective Senior Constable Special Branch. Police Headquarters. 18 July 1983. Item no. 9/8112.2, p. 1. Records relating to the Hilton bombing. Cabinet Office. New South Wales State Records.
6. ibid., p. 3.
7. ibid.
8. ibid.
9. Holdich, R, op. cit., p. 31.
10. ibid.
11. 'Physical Evidence Examinations Arising From a Series of Bombings. 1978', letter from Dr Malcolm Hall, Director, Scientific Research Directorate. P. 2. 22/3/84. Statements etc. re. Explosives. Item no. 9/8112.2. Records relating to the Hilton bombing. Cabinet Office. New South Wales State Records.
12. Movement requisition and letter from Dr Malcolm Hall, 6/3/1984. Statements etc. re. Explosives. Item no. 9/8112.2. Records relating to the Hilton bombing. Cabinet Office. New South Wales State Records.
13. Letter to Dr Roger Shackleton of the Australian Bomb Data Centre, 5/4/1984. Statements etc. re. Explosives. Item no. 8112.2. Records relating to the Hilton bombing. Cabinet Office. New South Wales State Records.
14. 'Comparisons re bombing exhibits', 29/2/84, Dr Malcolm Hall, Forensic scientist, Australian Federal Police. Statements etc. re. Explosives. Item no. 9/8112.2. Records relating to the Hilton bombing. Cabinet Office. New South Wales State Records.
15. Comparisons re Bombing Exhibits, 29/2/84 and Comparison Chart of Features of Bomb/Explosives from Series of Incidents, undated. Item no. 9/8112.2. Records relating to the Hilton bombing. Cabinet Office. New South Wales State Records.
16. Dr HJ Kobus, MSc., D Phil. Chief Forensic Scientist Department of Services and Supply. Forensic Science Centre. 17 October 1984. Statements etc. re. Explosives. Item no. 8112.2. Records relating to the Hilton bombing. Cabinet Office. New South Wales State Records.
17. ibid., Sheet 5.
18. ibid., Sheets 6 and 7.
19. Ms AE Paraybyk, Department of Services and Supply. Forensic Science Centre. 17 October 1984. Statements etc. re. Explosives. Item no.

8112.2. Records relating to the Hilton bombing. Cabinet Office. New South Wales State Records.

20 RJ Lokan, Department of Services and Supply. Forensic Science Centre. 17 October 1984. Statements etc. re. Explosives. Item no. 8112.2. Records relating to the Hilton bombing. Cabinet Office. New South Wales State Records.

21 Mr GB Smith, Sheet 3 of 3. Department of Services and Supply. Forensic Science Centre. 17 October 1984. Statements etc. re. Explosives. Item no. 8112.2. Records relating to the Hilton bombing. Cabinet Office. New South Wales State Records.

22 John Goulding, Comparison Analysis on Copper Wire from Explosive Devices. Neutron Activation Analysis Section. Australian Federal Police. Statements etc. re. Explosives. Item no. 9/8112.2, p. 4. Records relating to the Hilton bombing. Cabinet Office. New South Wales State Records.

23 ibid.

24 Dr Malcolm C. Hall, Director Scientific Research Directorate. Re. Examination of Exhibits from Series of Bombings. Australian Federal Police. October 1984. Statements etc. re. Explosives. Item no. 8112.2. Records relating to the Hilton bombing. Cabinet Office. New South Wales State Records.

25 Holdich, R, op. cit., pp. 52–53.

1989 and after

1 Holdich, R, op. cit., p. 4.
2 ibid., pp. 5–6
3 ASIO 1984 paper 'Ananda Marga and the Hilton Bombing'. Quoted in Holdich, R, op. cit. p. 31. (Author's underlining, not in original.)
4 Voix, Raphaël, 'Denied Violence, Glorified Fighting: Spiritual Discipline and Controversy in Ananda Marga', in *Nova Religio: The Journal of Alternative and Emergent Religions*, Vol. 12, Issue 1, pp. 3–25. Crovetto, Helen, 'Ananda Marga and the Use of Force', *Nova Religio: The Journal of Alternative and Emergent Religions*, Vol. 12, Issue 1, pp. 26–56.
5 Sarkar, *PROUT in a Nutshell, Part IV*, 1987 quoted in Crovetto, op. cit., p. 1.
6 Voix, op. cit., p. 19.
7 Fife-Yeomans, J and O'Brien, N, op. cit., p. 21.
8 ibid.
9 ibid.

Acknowledgments

My first thanks are to the New South Wales Premier's History Awards Committee (chaired by Associate Professor Ian Jack) who generously awarded me the New South Wales History Fellowship that allowed me to embark on the research that became this book. My second is to Phillipa McGuinness of NewSouth Publishing, who approached me the night I received the fellowship and suggested that this research could in fact be a book. This was a decision that NewSouth perhaps came to regret as my deadlines receded as I juggled a plethora of work commitments. Their patience is much appreciated.

The staff of the New South Wales State Records at Kingsford are a collective national treasure and they treated me with extraordinary kindness and forbearance, retrieving box after box after box of archives over endless days. It was inspiring to be surrounded by professional and amateur historians quietly exploring the past in that wonderfully serene space. Long may it be nurtured, funded and allowed to flourish.

Patrick May, who assisted with research, fact-checking and prevented all manner of errors, is both a great friend and one of nature's gentlemen. Testimony to his rigour is how much my heroic editor Linda Funnell was impressed with his meticulous responses to her sharp-eyed queries. Linda herself requires some kind of medal for steering the prose I originally presented her with into readable form. I think she'll be pleased to know she is almost always right.

My thanks to AAP and to Peter Logue for permission to reproduce his eyewitness account of the aftermath of the bombing at the front of the book.

My family have been a huge support through the writing of the book, particularly my passionate and inspiring mother, Lizzie, an early and enthusiastic reader who has managed to maintain her rage with remarkable grace. She was always happy to talk about this tale long after I had bored everyone else senseless. I am fortunate too to have a beautiful and brilliant husband who has accompanied me through the whole voyage from inception to completion and been a muse, a critic, and a lifeline when I hit some rocky shores — I simply couldn't have done it without him. The joy of our life and best joint production, our son, needs special thanks — he has no idea what the book is about but never fails to tell me how much he loves me.

Finally I want to thank Terry Griffiths, whose good heart touched mine.

www.ingramcontent.com/pod-product-compliance
Ingram Content Group UK Ltd.
Pitfield, Milton Keynes, MK11 3LW, UK
UKHW041302180426
11947UKWH00009B/621